T0340225

PUBLIC ECONOMICS

Public Economics: A Concise Introduction provides a concise and non-technical overview of the role of government in the economy.

Using the questions 'why?', 'what for?' and 'how?', the text initially surveys the place of the public sector in a market economy. It then considers the possible reasons which could justify government involvement. Next, the book examines the aims of state economic activity, and the instruments which a government has at its disposal. Lastly, the final chapter provides an illuminating tour of economic history and history of economic thought in relation to government economic activity.

The book offers an international focus throughout, with examples taken from all over the globe. Readers are supported with a range of pedagogical features, including example boxes, chapter objectives and summaries, and end-of-chapter multiple choice and reflection questions.

Public Economics: A Concise Introduction will be a valuable text for students on courses in public economics, welfare economics, public finance, public policy and related areas.

José Luis Gómez-Barroso is a professor at the National Distance Education University (UNED—Universidad Nacional de Educación a Distancia) in Spain.

PUBLIC ECONOMICS

A Concise Introduction

José Luis Gómez-Barroso

Routledge
Taylor & Francis Group

LONDON AND NEW YORK

First published 2022
by Routledge
2 Park Square, Milton Park, Abingdon, Oxon OX14 4RN

and by Routledge
52 Vanderbilt Avenue, New York, NY 10017

Routledge is an imprint of the Taylor & Francis Group, an informa business

© 2022 José Luis Gómez-Barroso

Translation by Jorge Barriuso Aguirre.

British Library Cataloguing-in-Publication Data
A catalogue record for this book is available from the British Library

Library of Congress Cataloging-in-Publication Data
Names: Gómez Barroso, José Luis, author.
Title: Public economics : an concise introduction / José Luis
    Gómez-Barroso.
Description: First Edition. | New York : Routledge, 2021. | Includes
    bibliographical references and index.
Identifiers: LCCN 2021010666 (print) | LCCN 2021010667 (ebook)
Subjects: LCSH: Finance, Public. | Fiscal policy. | Economic policy.
Classification: LCC HJ141 .G66 2021 (print) | LCC HJ141 (ebook) |
    DDC 336—dc23 LC record available at https://lccn.loc.
    gov/2021010666LC ebook record available at https://lccn.loc.
    gov/2021010667

ISBN: 978-1-032-00344-3 (hbk)
ISBN: 978-0-367-77308-3 (pbk)
ISBN: 978-1-003-17373-1 (ebk)

DOI: 10.4324/9781003173731

Typeset in Bembo
by Apex CoVantage, LLC

A mis Leonores

CONTENTS

READINGS

FIGURES

ABOUT THE AUTHOR

José Luis Gómez-Barroso is a professor at the National Distance Education University (UNED—Universidad Nacional de Educación a Distancia) in Spain who came to economics after having studied other fields. Perhaps that is why he maintains an unconventional position on how the discipline of economics should be oriented. He is particularly interested in the digital economy and in the social transformations that come with it (and dedicates a large part of his research to these topics). But he considers that, whatever adjective is used to describe the economy or its tendencies, public action and its interaction with market mechanisms will always condition how the surrounding economy influences people's lives. Therefore, the study of the role of the state in the economy is for him the first and a fundamental part of economics. He believes, moreover, that this area has been insufficiently, and sometimes incorrectly, addressed. With this book, he intends to contribute to correcting this situation.

PREFACE

Economics is a social science. It cannot help being so, because at the base of every economic phenomenon are decisions, be they individual or collective, isolated or grouped. Being a social science does not imply any kind of dishonour; after all, other social sciences have never reconsidered their identities. This has not been the case, however, with economics, which does not seem to feel completely comfortable within the (apparent) limits of the social sciences and which, since it reached a certain maturity, has always had aspirations to become *something more*. This was not true in the past. The name political economy, which the subject was called when it became independent as a science, referred to an integration of the economy into the surrounding social reality. Already in the 19th century, this interaction was thought of as dependence and as an imperfection, and at the same time that the adjective was removed and political economy became simply economics, laws and equilibria began to be established, and a defined method proper to economic science was sought.

Thanks to this effort, fundamental progress has been made in the understanding of many economic facts. The problem has not been to try to find answers and predictions but to forget more often than would be desirable that all those answers depend on an environment. The ceteris paribus clause is necessary to model a world with too many variables, but every model is a still photo of a reality that never stops moving. And the real economy is developed in that complex reality, not in stylized models.

The criticism is not new. More than a century ago, already voices had reproved the dissociation of theory from reality. The criticism is neither foreign nor uninformed. Many of these voices, in fact the most authoritative, were and still are internal to the profession. Formalism has had its faithful (and, above all, converts), but there has always been a minority who have acted like Jiminy Cricket, pointing out its limitations and the risks that its adoption entails.

A fundamental problem is that economics de rigueur has been imposed almost entirely on manuals, particularly on the most basic ones. Constrained to orthodoxy, they usually do not reflect on the limitations of what is described in their chapters. A distinction is made between positive economics and normative economics. What is presented is the positive variant: how the economy works. That's all. Manuals seldom include nuance or contextual circumstances. Yes, they feature the normative part, but that contains only value judgements about whether to opt for one or the other alternative, but once the decision has been made, the results that it leads to will necessarily be those predicted a priori.

However, those who read economics textbooks live in a world where hundreds of examples call into question whether economic relations are governed by exact rules. Many of these examples, in fact, do not seem to fit in any way with what is explained in the manual. A broader vision of the discipline allows us to understand the limitations of the foundations learned while still valuing their importance. So, the situation being serious, it is not so much for students of degrees such as economics or business administration—as those students advance in their knowledge, they should develop, at least that is what they are supposed to do if the curriculum that they are forced to follow is reasonable, a certain critical spirit. But the situation of students of degrees where there are only a few brushstrokes of economics, maybe one or two introductory courses, is discouraging. If, trying to take advantage of their newly acquired knowledge, someone close to them requires an explanation of some economic phenomenon, what they have learned in a television talk show or in the comments to the news read on the Internet is probably, unfortunately, a more useful reference than their economics manual. The apparent disconnect between economics and economic reality makes the discipline unhelpful and unattractive, and in many cases, it is almost immediately forgotten once it has been overcome.

This situation has no immediate solution. On the contrary, the tendency is for the divergence to widen, not narrow. Market techniques explore and exploit the apparent contradictions in consumer behaviour. Many markets move no longer with expectations but with the small print of expectations. Curves do not always move as they do in models created within a vacuum. And neither the syllabi nor the textbooks change under the pretext that the fundamentals explained in them are not altered—which is true. But if they are to contribute to an interpretation of what happens in the real world, the raw foundations are useless. The solution is not to build increasingly complex models but to make them more flexible and to give them more degrees of freedom—all the more so if the explanation is intended for an introductory course. Therefore, we must deconstruct the economic laws and recover not the nuance itself, which would lead to the infinite casuistry that the models seek to overcome, but rather an awareness of the importance of nuance, which in turn means recovering an awareness of the importance of context.

The context (both general and particular to each specific situation) conditions the behaviour of the economic agents that participate in the exchanges, behaviour that is not always automatic or even rational. Of all the agents, also of the state. The social and political context is a fundamental element to understand the role that the public reserves (or assumes) in the economic game. But the study of this part of economics does not escape from submitting to an orthodoxy with blinkers either. Indeed, if one part of economics is especially in need of reconsideration, it is this one because, besides suffering the general evils of the whole discipline, it is fragmented and dispersed, which prevents its having a coherent vision of the whole.

Beginning with the second criticism, in order to have a thorough knowledge of public activity in the economy today, one must trace it in several areas. If we look at the table of contents of the manuals in use that provide an introduction to microeconomics, the role of the public is usually concentrated in one chapter, studied as an anomaly in the interaction of supply and demand. In those on an introduction to macroeconomics, the interpretations that the two prevailing schools of economic thought (in fact, prevailing decades ago) give to fiscal or monetary policy are discussed. Many of the public economics programmes mix public finance and budget theory on one hand and public expenditure on the other, which are two independent branches in other academic itineraries. Market regulation seems to be reserved for the books on industrial economics. Those on economic policy focus on particular types of policies, especially those applied to different sectors of economic activity but leave out many others and generally do not explain the role of one or the other in the overall policy. The breakdown almost becomes meaninglessness. Under the gaze of the layperson, these fragments are apparently incongruent and difficult to fit together; they tell no story even if put together.

As for the first accusation made, although formalism has reached this area only in a limited way, what it has not escaped is the imposition of an orientation, almost an ideology, that is strict and restricted. Orthodoxy, followed in a majority of manuals, says that the state does not act but rather *intervenes* in the economy. The market, which is the best mechanism for distributing resources, does not (should not) attend to collective interests, but rather it is the selfishness shown by individual actors when they seek to maximize their own interests that guarantees the best (most efficient) outcome; in this scenario, state and market are two autonomous entities whose relationship occurs (is authorized) only in the presence of one of a series of assessed causes. Assuming that there is an optimal way to decide on the distribution means not only that the state should not "intervene", but also that, in cases where the state has some responsibility, the optimal policy is that which eliminates the barriers that guarantee the performance of the market.

Given this state of affairs, this book proposes an alternative and presents an integral and heterodox vision of the role of the state in the economy. *Integral* indicates that the pieces referred to before have been rescued and put together with others, which are necessary but generally forgotten, to assemble a puzzle that comprehensively describes public action in the economy. *Heterodox* expresses a declaration of intent: the story is not followed in the usual way and an approach is adopted that tries to recover the old link (rather than the subordinate relationship) between state and economy, between economy and politics. However, the way to deal with the problem is not discordant. The current orthodoxy in economics extends to forms, which means that criticism, in order not to be considered out of place or excessive, must highlight possible inconsistencies while respecting the methodological playing field.

The conception of this book arises from a reflection on how to orient a subject included in the programme of a degree in political science. Students earning degrees in disciplines other than economics are barely provided with the tools to understand economic reality, and this is most problematic in political science studies. Economics is the backbone of political activity. The day-to-day debate is nourished by economic discussions. This is even more evident in recent times, when political alternatives do not start from defined ideologies but take shape to a large extent by stating how they propose to redirect an economy with whose results no one, for one reason or another, seems to be satisfied. And yet, faced with this reality, students of political science are being robbed of knowledge (or at best are not being presented with knowledge in a clear way) which, although probably not sufficient, is necessary for them to form their own criteria in this debate: in what circumstances is a government (state) reasonable to act, what objectives can or should it pursue and what tools does it have at its disposal to achieve these objectives?

The book, in any case, is intended for a general and much-broader audience, in that establishing the limits of the interaction between the state and the market is the first question that has to be answered by anyone determined to define their own criteria on economic matters. The economic and social situation prevailing throughout the world at the time of writing this preface, in the early days of 2021, was conducive to pondering an answer to this question.

1

STATE ACTIVITY IN THE ECONOMY

A global perspective

1 Introduction: public activity rather than public intervention

Economics textbooks usually dedicate a chapter to explaining the reasons for government *intervention* in the economy, a term that has been almost universally adopted by economists. Political discourse employs similar expressions, perhaps without fully considering what they imply. But words have meanings, and choosing "intervention" is not, of course, insignificant. This particular expression implies that the actions of one independent entity ("the economy") can be interfered with or overseen by a second entity ("the government"). In this sense, the economy appears to be separate from politics. It has its own rules and can function autonomously; only in exceptional circumstances is external interference admissible.

This is a limited, if not an outright-erroneous, point of view. Societies are organized politically and grant some bodies (representatives and governments—generically speaking, "the state") the power to order social life. The economy is not merely an annex to society but is rather a fundamental part of it, from which it can be deduced that states have the power to organize economic activity. And they can do so without restrictions. States can and do intervene in the economy, as long as they act within the values that society agrees on. When a government blocks the development of a mining operation in an area that has scenic value, it isn't invoking any of the textbook reasons that allow public intervention. Its decision is not based on efficiency (perhaps it is cheaper to extract minerals there rather than from some nearby site) or fairness (that district may have the highest unemployment rate in the country), but instead, it is defending a certain value (the protection of certain areas) because society approves of it. In addition, beyond specific cases, the economy doesn't really have the ability to self-organize. Its rules do not always arise

DOI: 10.4324/9781003173731-1

spontaneously; an authority that has coercive power to dictate at least some of the rules of the game and enforce them is needed.

The conclusion is that the state does not *intervene* in the economy, but rather, it carries out (more or less profound) activity in economic life, as part of the foundations on which its existence is based. This does not in any way impede a government from deciding to limit its own activity within the economy to specific circumstances. But conceptually, the situation is different: governments can limit their actions, but a priori, they have no reason to do so.

Even in cases in which a state decides to limit itself, the functions assumed by the state in the economy are much more important than suggested by a simple *intervention*. The government organizes and even decides on many aspects of the economy; it also supplies, buys or provides incentives. However, this is all perfectly compatible with the fact that the interaction between supply and demand (i.e., the market) is the primary mechanism to decide what is produced and how what is produced is distributed. This compatibility can be seen in practice: in the first quarter of the 21st century, the majority of the almost two hundred nations on the planet can be classified as *mixed economies*, which means that although they have organized their economies on the basis of a market model, the public sector maintains a significant role in that organization.

The market therefore remains the starting point to study state *activity*, rather than *intervention*, in the economy. However, such activity is usually analysed through a piecemeal approach, one that should be altered. A rigorous study of state activity in a modern economy must start with studying what causes the state to occasionally arrogate the power to supplant or complement the market, which is followed by an analysis of the specific functions that it assumes in those cases and which culminates in an examination of the instruments that it employs to carry out those functions. Why, what for and how are the three basic questions that must always be answered. The key to obtaining a truly comprehensive understanding of state activity in the economy is to find a coherent link between those steps and to broadly analyse each, but with the depth that economics requires.

READING 1.1   AND SUDDENLY, THE PANDEMIC! THE *INTERVENTION* THAT NOBODY COULD HAVE EXPECTED

If any state decision in the economy really deserves to be called an *intervention*, it is undoubtedly that of paralysing (or seriously restricting) a country's economic activity. If any state decision were to be thought of as unjustifiable, and therefore implausible, it would be precisely that one.

When, on 30 December 2019, health officials in the Chinese city of Wuhan reported that they were treating cases of pneumonia of unknown cause, no one expected events (in the economic field) to take the course that they did in the following weeks. Even on 26 January 2020, when China imposed the first restrictions on economic activity, it was not reasonable to venture that within a mere two months, the states of practically the whole world were going to take measures that would bring about the greatest global economic standstill on record.

A team from Oxford University,[1] with the help of hundreds of contributors from all over the world, updated on a daily basis the list of countries where decisions had been taken to close workplaces. A visual presentation of the results (on the world map) was published on the Our World in Data website.[2] Figure 1.1 shows the world scenario as of 1 April 2020. Although the image amplifies the real situation at that time, in which conditions were not always uniform within countries (*a country is coded as "required closures" if at least some subnational regions have required closures*), it is impressive nonetheless.

The economic shutdown was not inevitable. In fact, not everyone agreed that the closure of industries and many of the services that could no longer be offered at a distance was the best response to stop the spread of the disease, and despite the picture given in Figure 1.1, not all governments shared this idea or at least not all took equally strict measures; we will return to this debate in Reading 3.2. The conclusion, then, is that in the many places where economic activity was reduced to a minimum, this was the result of a decision that forced the economy into the background. Pandemics, of course, are not mentioned in textbooks among the reasons that are usually invoked to justify public *intervention*. Even at the height of the health crisis, a large majority of

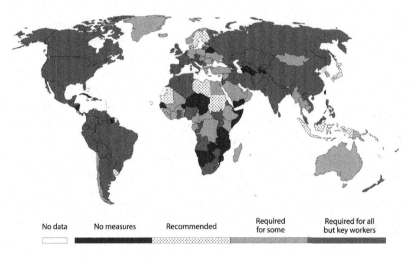

| No data | No measures | Recommended | Required for some | Required for all but key workers |

FIGURE 1.1   Workplace closures declared in the wake of the COVID-19 pandemic—as of 1 April 2020

markets could have continued to function (and probably would have wished to continue), but at least in some cases, many people believe that the economy should be subordinated to the protection of other values that society prioritizes.

1   Hale, T., Angrist, N., Cameron-Blake, E., Hallas, L., Kira, B., Majumdar, S., Petherick, A., Phillips, T., Tatlow, H., and Webster, S. (2020). *Oxford COVID-19 Government Response Tracker*. Blavatnik School of Government, Oxford University: https://www.bsg.ox.ac.uk/research/research-projects/coronavirus-government-response-tracker.
2   https://ourworldindata.org/grapher/workplace-closures-covid.

2 The market economy as a common system to organize economies

The market is a place (physical or not) in which exchanges take place. Someone offers certain goods that someone else is interested in. If they reach an agreement in which the former transfers the goods to the latter in exchange for other goods or services or in exchange for something with symbolic value (any type of money) and if this action is not sporadic but repeated frequently (regardless of whether the same actors are involved or of whether the same conditions are agreed on), then a market has been created. This act has been recurring ever since human societies evolved beyond self-sufficient communities of hunter–gatherers: exchanges, ergo markets, are the basis of economic activity, and this activity is at the heart of all social development.

This interweaving of economy and society is bidirectional: the way a society is organized is conditioned by the surrounding economic context, while the economy is mediated by the existing social (political) order. Ultimately, this means that the economy is not merely a set of spontaneously emerging markets but rather a complex system that has norms that protect, condition, control or orient those markets. Simple economic activities can be regulated. Gathering firewood or mushrooms in the woods or molluscs in the ocean might require a licence or be prohibited except on specific dates; their sale might require passing a health inspection, obtaining a permit or be restricted to a specific place. These are not modern requirements; although their content has evolved, some have existed for centuries.

Such supervision or control is carried out because, obviously, society decides that it should be so. Whoever has the authority to represent society in taking such decisions depends on the place and historical moment. If we generically refer to the person or institution who exercises that authority as the state,[1] we can conclude that the state plays a decisive role in the economy. Except for extreme situations in

---

1 In the rest of the book, *state* will be used as a generic term to refer to any expression of government, regardless of its function or territorial reach. In addition, the terms *government*, *public sector* and *public administration*, although not precise synonyms, will be used interchangeably.

which the state represses private initiative, the characteristics of any economy are shaped by the interaction between agents who act in the markets and the public sector.

Even so, the markets remain the machinery of the economy. Without the mediation of public action, *the market* (understood as all particular markets grouped together) would be the only mechanism to resolve basic questions about the economy: how a society's resources are organized, what they are used for and how the goods and services produced with them are distributed. The procedure is simple. A set of prices emerges from the exchanges that take place. Some goods and services are more expensive (more valued) than others, and those who possess them can exchange them for larger quantities of others. Because they are valuable, more people become interested in producing those goods or services or investing resources in them. Quantities and distributions emerge from this interplay that adjusts dynamically. When considered on the whole, public actions do not radically change that outcome, and so the market remains the basic mechanism that organizes economic activity. Therefore, the majority of economies, even if they are *mixed*, are *market economies*.

This is a globally valid statement today. However, in certain cases, the state heavily alters the results generated by the market. In fact, these constituted the norm in many eras in the past in which the economy was at the service of a sovereign. In more-recent times, governments of command or planned economies totally replace the markets in decisions on how to use resources and who receives the goods that are produced. This situation represents one of the poles in a state–market axis. The other pole, in which zero public activity occurs, is exceedingly implausible because at the very least, the state has to ensure that the obligations assumed in the exchanges are fulfilled. Between these two extremes, any situation is imaginable. Although we frequently use models or even ideologies to group countries, in reality there are no two states in which public activity in the economy is identical, or to put it another way, no two states have the same conviction on the suitability of leaving the market to achieve certain objectives on its own, be it a common objective or one specific to a certain economic sector or segment of the population.

In conclusion, despite all the nuances and clarifications that can be introduced, *the market* is always the starting point for any theoretical or applied study of the economy and also for the study of state activity in the economy.

READING 1.2   THE INDEX OF ECONOMIC FREEDOM

Grouping countries according to which *type of economy* they fit into is not easy. We have no established categories but rather different situations in which either the market or public activity is prevalent. Some governments leave certain sectors completely in the hands of private enterprise while maintaining strict control over others. In other countries, the situation may be inverted, or they can adopt intermediate positions. Even in countries that manifestly declare an ideological position (specifically, they claim to follow a socialist model), the real situation does not entirely comply (or does not comply at all) with that declaration.

One possible way to classify economies is provided by the Index of Economic Freedom.[1] This is a synthetic or compound index based on 12 variables, each given the same weight. As in any indicator of this kind, the way the data is aggregated affects the final result. The way factors are defined (some of them, such as "government integrity" or "business freedom", are complicated and thus difficult to measure) can also have an impact. Even more caution should be exercised when the stated "mission" of the association that prepares the index, the Heritage Foundation (although in collaboration with *The Wall Street Journal* until 2016), is "to formulate and promote conservative public policies based on the principles of free enterprise, limited government, individual freedom, traditional American values, and a strong national defense".

Even with these caveats, the classification is interesting because it is almost the only one available to rank countries by their degree of, say, confidence in the market. In the 2020 ranking, the top ten were Singapore, Hong Kong, New Zealand, Australia, Switzerland, Ireland, the United Kingdom, Denmark, Canada and Estonia. At the bottom of the list was North Korea, preceded in order by Venezuela, Cuba, Eritrea, the Republic of the Congo, Bolivia, Zimbabwe, Sudan, Kiribati and West Timor.[2]

A different and much-more-controversial issue is how the categories are established (with subjective cut-offs at certain scores). Given that the presentation for 2016 stated that "perhaps the most critical lesson for today's

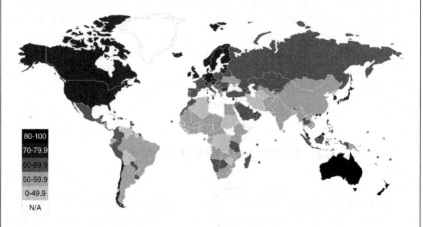

FIGURE 1.2 Index of Economic Freedom (2020)

tumultuous times is that the proven superiority of the free market system and the value of economic liberty must be steadfastly reiterated", the bar is, unsurprisingly, so high that only the first six countries enter in the *free* group; the following 31 countries are considered *mostly free*, another 62 countries are *moderately free*, 62 are *mostly unfree* and 19 have *repressed* economies. As can be seen in Figure 1.2, the majority of European countries are classified as *mostly free* or *moderately free*, a category that few African and non–Pacific Asian countries reach. South America is the region that has the greatest disparities between its countries.

1 https://www.heritage.org/index/.
2 The ranking does not include some countries that would probably be candidates for the final positions (Iraq, Libya, Somalia, Syria and Yemen).

3 The (observed) functions of the state in the economy

Before moving on to a systematic examination of public activity in the economy, from causes to objectives to instruments, we first take a purely descriptive approach to the subject. Introductory economics textbooks consider the public sector to be one of the three agents, along with consumers and businesses, that participate in the exchanges that build an economy. The usual simplified diagram represents these actors as the vertices of a triangle each of whose sides is formed by four kinds of parallel flows: two flows of goods and services (one in each direction), and another two monetary flows, as compensation or payment for the previous movements. This means that the state provides (or sells) goods and services and receives money for them, but it also receives (or purchases) and pays for them; this occurs in its relationship with individuals and in its relationship with businesses. When limited to this paradigm, the state has two functions:

1   The supplier state

Governments offer, using different methods, goods and services. Individuals and businesses can use, for example, the services of a public mail company, of public water or energy distribution companies or of a public airport management company. Although publicly produced goods are less common than services, the governments of some countries sell minerals, weapons or even food.
There is no single fixed catalogue of public supplies; it varies from country to country and, sometimes, across regions or even municipalities. In the same way, the range of prices and conditions under which the services or goods are provided also varies.

2   The client state

Public administrations need all kinds of goods and services for their daily operations. A public hospital will buy vegetables if it has its own kitchen, or it can contract a catering service. Among many other things, a school needs pencils, a cleaning service and Internet connection. Governments contract construction companies to build highways. The volume of public purchases or contracts depends on the size of the public sector, but it is usually significant in every country.

This simple perspective, which places the state at the same level as the other two agents, businesses and consumers, implicitly assumes that exchanges (i.e., the market) are the only thing that matter to the economy. But it says nothing about the specific rules that govern these exchanges or whether they are produced in a situation that conditions them. In this more-comprehensive perspective, the state ceases to be an agent on par with the others, and its broad scope of activity in the economy becomes evident. It has three other functions:

3   The organizer state

The organization of exchanges, and of all economic activity in general, is not spontaneous. It is produced in accordance to rules that involve rights and obligations. Governments dictate these rules on the basis of their power to enforce compliance with them. The rules of the game can be general, as is the case of clauses that are admissible in a commercial contract, or as specific as a list of ingredients that are banned in making bread.

Associated with this work—or, to be more precise, part of it—are the functions of supervision and monitoring. State-appointed judges and the police, both needed for protecting rights and enforcing contracts, can be included in the figure of the organizer state.

4   The decision-maker state

The decision-making authority is free to establish the rules (of which we spoke in the previous function) it wishes. The fact that certain ones are chosen or favoured over others can (in fact, does) imply that the exchanges are guided towards a specific result. On some occasions, the expected results are not merely suggested but rather explicitly established: governments set objectives and drive the economy, with varying degrees of determination, towards attaining those objectives.

For instance, governments can force banks to comply with certain conditions to concede mortgage loans (with the goal of providing incentives for or restricting buying homes), or they can set the exact price for gasoline, the currency exchange rate or the inflation rate that they desire.

5   The incentive state

States do not only impose or require. Sometimes, more subtlety, they establish conditions aimed at promoting or restraining certain activities, without restricting the freedom of businesses or consumers to act in another way.

A government can cede public land to someone who wants to establish an industry in a certain region or place. It can also provide aid or a loan to people who renovate their homes to conform with certain parameters of energy efficiency. Or, if it wants to discourage diesel fuel, it can implement aid schemes for the purchase of cars, on the condition that the vehicle does not have a diesel engine.

The previous analysis offers a succinct explanation of public activity in the economy. However, it does not provide the complete picture. A different approach is needed. Merely confirming that these five functions exist does not indicate the relative importance of each or how compatible they are with each other; the circumstances in which one or the other is employed; or the objective that they are intended to serve in each case.

4 *Why?* Reasons for the state's becoming involved in the economy

The beginning of this chapter stated that today the market economy is almost universally accepted as the primary option to organize economic activity. But the previous section showed that state functions in the economy are varied and apparently significant. If the explanation were restricted to referring to the state's action in the economy as *intervention*, reconciling these two positions would be difficult. This apparent paradox can be resolved by accepting the fact that states, as already mentioned, are not subordinate to the market, and although they accept its work, they have the power to modify it if they so decide. That said, every decision has to be justified, and when the state substitutes or complements the market, it must (should) be convinced that the result will be better than what the market would produce if left to act on its own. As a social (and therefore not exact) science, economics cannot offer certainties, and the criteria depend on an interpretation of how the events following the decision in question will evolve. But whatever those criteria are, reflection is (should be) unavoidable.

The conclusion is that, although states *could* theoretically act on the economy in any circumstance, they *should* do so only when they have a good reason. So, to determine the state's involvement in the economy, we must ask why. The answer should always be related to the shortcomings and limitations of *the market* (understood as the sum of all particular markets) or of certain specific markets. The market can have one or two kinds of shortcomings: not obtaining an efficient outcome or not adequately considering social values.

4.1 *The shortcomings of* the market

In an economic sense, efficiency refers to obtaining a certain outcome by using the minimum resources or by achieving the maximum outcome from given resources. Given that resources are limited (in textbooks, referred to as *scarce*), efficiency is a worthy objective in all economic activity. When speaking of resources, or *factors of production*, classic economics divides them into land, labour and capital (physical capital such as buildings or machines); later, human capital and technology were added to the list. Without needing to enter into a detailed description of the factors involved, if we improve the process of producing shoes in such a way that we obtain the same number of pairs (and with exactly the same quality) while saving a portion of the factors previously employed (ergo, we are more efficient), those resources will be available to use in some other activity, which is beneficial for society as a whole.

Economics shows us that, under certain conditions (*perfect* competition), the market is a mechanism that leads to an efficient outcome. The interaction between supply and demand determines the price of any product and, consequently, the prices of factors of production. Prices are signals that the market uses to know where and how resources should be allocated for their most productive (efficient) use. If we start with a set of resources and leave the market to its own devices, maximum production will be achieved. No other procedure can improve on the market in this task.

That said, four objections can be made about the market mechanism. The first is that how the product obtained will be distributed is not considered at all. Because resources are limited, so too are the products that are obtained from them. If we set a rule on how to employ the factors, we could also search for a rule on how to distribute the product. The market rewards *whoever is deserving*, but this merit is conditioned by the initial possession of factors and *attributes*. If society wants to introduce more-equitable distribution, something or someone must *force* the outcome of the free market.

The second objection refers to another concern ignored in the description of the market's efficiency: the process employed to achieve an efficient outcome. If arriving at that result requires highly polluting processes or exhausting nonrenewable resources, or if a factor is poorly compensated (e.g. offering poor wages), the market will behave in the same way. The theoretical model that demonstrates its efficiency is static (it does not include future prospects), and it does not use variables that adjust it in any way. Efficiency, specifically present efficiency, does not take anything else into consideration.

The third objection is related to the historical evolution of market economies, which is replete with instability and crises. If we put aside aspects related to welfare or quality of life, every capitalist economy has suffered from the inefficiencies generated by squandered resources (notably in long periods of unemployment) at some point in its history. Although no country's authority has ever left the economy completely in the hands of the market, so governments must take their share of responsibility for the crises that have arisen, we can still reasonably ask whether the market, when operating in real conditions, is actually capable of reaching the result that the theoretical model predicts.

These three arguments cast doubt on the virtues of a completely self-governed market and open the door to at least evaluating what would happen with an active state presence in the economy. To these we can add a fourth, nontechnical objection to the market mechanism: even the most diehard defenders of the free market assign minimum roles to the state (yet essential to the efficient operation of the market): to defend property rights and ensure that contracts are fulfilled.

Conceptually, the third and fourth arguments are explicitly related to compliance with the conditions needed for the market to obtain an efficient outcome. They would be considered market *failures*, as would the second argument in the part that refers to sustainability. The first argument and the part of the second related to the social acceptability of certain actions can be placed under the general category of arguments unrelated to efficiency.

4.2. The shortcomings of specific markets

The second paragraph of the previous section stated that the market is a mechanism that achieves an efficient outcome under certain conditions, referred to as *perfect* competition. The problem is that perfect competition does not exist. Economics has, in its quest to explain different kinds of markets, designed streamlined models that ignore the highly diverse situations that arise in real markets (necessarily, or we would end up having to do case-by-case analyses). The extreme model of competition, perfect competition, requires four conditions: a homogeneous product (identical—not differentiated in any way by any producer); perfect information (for producers and consumers); a lack of obstacles to enter the industry; and many buyers and sellers (so that neither has the weight to alter market dynamics with their decisions).

In real conditions, at least one of these requisites is always lacking, meaning that the competition is not perfect, so efficiency, at least in theory, cannot be reached. Two points must be noted. The first is that we should evaluate how far from the ideal situation we are in order to assess how significant the impact of the *imperfection* will be. A company's having some influence in a sector is not the same as a company's enjoying manifest market power and using it to hinder competition from rivals. The second note is that this situation affects *some* specific markets and not *the* market as a generic mechanism. The market is composed of the sum of all the particular markets, and if the imperfection was manifest in only a few, that should not significantly alter its global efficiency. However, this apparent irrelevance should not prevent the state from introducing some remedy in those particular markets.

Other circumstances present in certain markets also impede their efficient functioning. That is, we are in the presence of other *failures* of those markets. For example, the market could be incomplete, which means that the supply may not cover all the potential demand (e.g., no shoe store in an entire region). Or perhaps nobody is interested in offering a certain product or service, because no one can charge for it (how could you charge to see a hot air balloon exhibition?). An activity can also affect (positively or negatively) third parties not involved with the production or exchange in question. For instance, the noise from an outdoor café is not a monetary cost that has to be borne by its owner, but it does affect how well people who live in flats exposed to the noise rest (and therefore their ability to carry out tasks the next day).

In addition to these efficiency-related causes are others that occur in certain markets that would also lead to state action. There are goods and services that the government, in response to social demand, would want to promote beyond the levels provided by the market (perhaps even efficiently) and others that it would want to protect (even if it is inefficient to do so).

READING 1.3   THE WEIGHT OF THE PUBLIC SECTOR

The most graphic way of demonstrating that the role of the public sector in the economy is absolutely transcendental is to consider the weight of pub-lic spending in the country's gross domestic product (GDP). The concept of GDP will be examined in more detail in Chapter 3. That chapter also exam-ines how the approach used to measure public spending can condition the result obtained, especially when comparing data that are many years apart, as national statistics have been improved over time (or directly created) and defi-nitions and methods have been refined. Even so, comparing the ratio between public spending and GDP in different countries or its variation over time in the same country allows us to come to a preliminary conclusion regarding the weight of the public sector.

Figure 1.3 presents how this ratio has evolved globally over a century, from 1911 to 2011, in which snapshots were taken every 25 years. It is based on information on the "History of Public Expenditure" from the Our World in Data website,[1] which in turn uses similar data from the International Monetary Fund (IMF), supplemented by the series on interest payments on public debt, also published by the same body. The figure shows that the number of coun-tries for which information exists has been growing, and not until recently have the grey areas (no data) almost disappeared from the map. Despite all these possible inaccuracies, the image speaks volumes: it shows a sustained tendency for increased overall spending by the various state administrations.

In 2011, the final year that these data exist for the majority of nations, the ranking of states with the largest percentage of GDP dedicated to public expenditure is headed by European Union countries and the small countries of Oceania, with few exceptions among them. To be more precise, the first ten were Tuvalu (104.36%), Kiribati (90.62%), Ireland (69.96%), Denmark (60.35%), France (59.07%), Lesotho (58.33%), Solomon Islands (56.77%), Finland (56.50%), Belgium (56.42%) and Greece (56.05%). At the other extreme, the ten countries in which the state had the least weight in economic activity, at least in percentage of GDP, were Singapore (14.43%), Madagascar

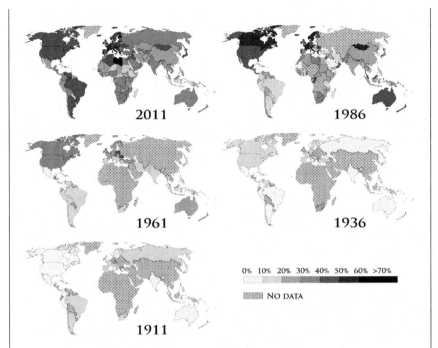

FIGURE 1.3 Evolution of government expenditure as a percentage of national GDP

(14.64%), Bangladesh (16.72%), Hong Kong (17.32%), Dominican Republic (18.00%), Cameroon (18.85%), Ethiopia (19.04%), Myanmar (19.43%), Central African Republic (19.58%) and Nepal (19.61%).

1 Ortiz-Ospina, E. (2016). *History of government spending*. https://ourworldindata. org/government-spending#history-of-government-spending.

5 *What for?* The objectives of state involvement in the economy

In each of the circumstances presented thus far, the market's activity is susceptible to improvement or correction. The state is responsible for attempting to do so, but first, it must determine whether it indeed should act. As mentioned earlier, this depends on the criteria that it employs and its evaluation of what would happen if it chose to take action. What is clear is that it's under no obligation to do so. The failure of (or in) the market may not be considered serious enough for action to be taken; the state could conclude that it does not have the means to resolve the issue or that the ends do not justify the means; or, most importantly from an ideological perspective, decision makers might determine that public action would actually make the situation worse.

But when the state does take action, it should have a clear purpose. In other words, what for is the second question that must be answered. The immediate objectives are often merely instrumental. For example, acting in a certain market to increase competition is not an end in and of itself but rather a means by which to lower prices and benefit consumers directly or indirectly (via the influence of those prices on the prices of other products). Increasing the well-being of consumers is the true or final aim. The way that increase is measured is the next problem. We attempt to resolve it through setting derived objectives.

5.1 Ultimate objectives

• Increase the general well-being of society: growth and job creation

Seeking conditions in which its citizens *live better* seems like an objective that any government should pursue. Growth and job creation are considered ways to directly achieve this—so much so that they have substituted well-being as an aspiration and are now themselves thought of as final objectives. In fact, all governments establish them as priority end goals.

Designating economic growth as the primary objective is based on a simple rationale: the greater the amount of goods and services produced in an economy, the greater the quantity available to be distributed. Growth must be stable and sustainable. Stability refers to a production model that does not suffer from imbalances that end up slowing or reversing growth. Sustainability refers to the rational use of resources over time so that production activities, and ultimately the economic model itself, are never put at risk. Both factors are related in the long term: if growth is unsustainable in the long term, it cannot be stable.

The second objective in a *healthy economy* is for anybody who wishes and can work (some might have resources to live without working and some might be unable to work) to be able do so. Work is the basic way of receiving income with which to buy goods and services, but it also has a function of social inclusion in society. From the point of view of economic theory, unemployment is a waste of productive resources.

Although economic growth and job creation appropriate the concept of welfare, they are not the only ways to increase the well-being of a society. Improving the quality of goods or services (although not increasing the quantity to distribute) and modifying an industrial process in a way that produces the same amount but with less pollution are examples of increasing well-being without growth. Job quality, not just quantity, is also a basic parameter of well-being.

• Allocation/redistribution

As already stated, the market is indifferent about the distribution of goods and services. An economy can be efficient even if it concentrates what is produced in the hands of a few, generally because the resources used for production are also unequally distributed. However, at least in modern times, societies usually want distribution to meet certain conditions; in particular, they often want all citizens to have access to a basic basket of goods. Therefore, altering the allocation of resources or redistributing what is produced are frequent objectives in every country.

• Defending social values

Obviously, any other economic objective that society decides to set is valid if the decision was made in a legitimate way. The goal is not to increase growth or achieve greater equity when culture is subsidized (e.g. a local music group or a clearly unprofitable museum) or when a marshland is protected.

5.2 Derived objectives

Measurable variables must be used to evaluate how close a certain objective is to being attained (or how effective the measures that were taken to achieve it are). Macroeconomic indicators that describe the situation and evolution of economies are used for this purpose, especially in the case of growth and job creation objectives; a subgroup of these indicators also allows the stability of the growth to be checked. As mentioned earlier, the concepts of growth and welfare have become so closely interconnected that the indicators selected to calculate growth are also used to measure welfare; however, various initiatives seek to construct more-accurate indicators. As regards distribution, no measurement is as popular as those used to measure the state of the economy, although the Gini coefficient is broadly accepted. The defence of other social values is generally impossible to measure.

The following are more-detailed descriptions of specific indicators commonly used to set objectives:

• Gross domestic product (GDP)

An economy's growth is measured through the variation of its gross domestic product (GDP). The GDP measures everything that is produced in a country during a year. The objective of governments is for the GDP to increase year after year. GDP is divided by the number of inhabitants of the country to obtain GDP per capita (or per capita income), which often serves as the main indicator of welfare.

• The unemployment rate

The unemployment rate is the percentage of unemployment in the active population. The unemployment objective set by governments is never zero. Even the most buoyant economies have always a group of people who are unemployed for different reasons, some of them circumstantial. This is what is referred to by the unfortunate term *natural rate of unemployment*.

• Stability measurements: inflation, government budget balance and balance of trade

As mentioned earlier, growth must be stable and sustainable. Certain macroeconomic indicators are related to stability:

- The inflation rate measures changes in prices. The objective is usually to have moderate inflation (though no agreement has been reached on what should be considered "moderate") rather than zero inflation.
- The government budget balance reflects the difference between government revenues and spending. The annual objective depends on the economic cycle; a balanced budget is the objective when factoring in periods of several years (so that the budget surplus of some fiscal years compensates for the deficit of others). Related to the government budget objective is that of maintaining a sustainable level of national debt.
- The balance of trade measures the difference between a nation's exports and its imports. Maintaining a trade surplus is the desired situation.

Although advances have been made in defining indicators to measure sustainability, none have become sufficiently widespread to be considered generally useful.

- The Gini coefficient

The Gini coefficient or index measures the divergence of the distribution of income from perfect equality (in which any percentage of the population has the same income; for example, 50% of the population would possess 50% of the income). This measurement is used more to describe a situation than to guide actions, because it does not set any specific value as the desired result.

5.3 Immediate objectives

If the daily actions of governments were documented, the terms *welfare*, *growth*, *inflation* and *trade balance* would not appear in the majority of them. However, beyond immediate objectives, almost all specific actions are intended to achieve one or various of those higher-level goals. The number of cases is endless (each measure has a goal associated with the situation that it is trying to modify), and therefore, the immediate objectives can't be listed.

Furthermore, not every immediate objective has a direct reflection on an ultimate objective. In fact, objectives are usually links in a sometimes-long process whose impact on the final aim may not be apparent until the end result. Setting a goal of increasing the number of people with a certain education or training is only the first milestone on the way to helping achieve a longer-term goal: companies would take advantage of that human capital to improve their position in international markets; that is, they would be able to sell more, thereby generating greater revenues and new jobs, all of which would ultimately improve the general well-being of society.

6 *How?* The instruments used by the state to act in the economy

The final step in the analysis of state activity in the economy, once the causes that support public activity have been established and the objectives have been defined, is to examine the instruments used to formalize the actions needed to reach those objectives. State activity can take many forms or, in other words, can employ diverse instruments. Some of these actions (even all) can be coordinated to fulfil a particular purpose or, stated more formally, to shape economic policies that seek to obtain a specific goal. Therefore, our analysis should now examine the *ingredients* (the instruments) and the *recipes* (the policies).

6.1 Ingredients

• Direct provision of goods and services

States can decide that the public sector, rather than the private sector, will provide certain goods or services. This does not mean that they will be provided for free; different forms of payment can be established that entirely or partially cover the cost, or taxes can be imposed either on citizens who meet certain conditions, regardless of whether they use the service or not, or on only those who actually use it.

For example, the fee charged for using a municipal sports facility can be set so that the facility will not require any other revenue, but the fee for refuse collection, if it exists, will probably not be enough to cover the total cost of the service. All workers may be required to pay a medical insurance premium, regardless of whether or not they visit the doctor; on the other hand, the registration fees for a course given at a public university should be paid by only those who register for that course.

• Regulation

On the basis of the government's primary function of defining and enforcing the legal system, it dictates regulations in which all kinds of requisites can be set. For example, opening a stationary store should require complying with only a few general rules that any retail business would have to follow. On the contrary, establishing a paper mill should probably first require authorization and then comply with a long list of environmental regulations. In both cases, shop and industry must obey labour laws.

Regulation is ex ante if the conditions required must be demonstrated in order to initiate the activity; it is ex post if the activity is not conditioned at the start but is subject to certain limits. The paper mill could be subject to prior controls (ex ante) to ensure that it will not pollute the water or could instead incur fines (ex post) if reports demonstrate that it is in fact polluting the water.

- Direct intervention in markets

On occasions, instead of just setting the rules under which markets operate, the government may also modify the basic results that arise from the activity of any market: the quantity of product exchanged and the price. Exact quantities or prices can be set, or margins or maximum or minimum limits can be established.

For instance, oil-producing countries have formed an association that fixes production quotas and, indirectly, price. Similarly, fishing for a certain species of fish may be limited to a specific number of tons. The price of certain medicines or of a cubic metre of water could be set (or limited) by the public administration.

- Taxes

Taxes are amounts of money that the state demands of every (natural or legal) person that carries out an action considered to be a *taxable event*. In one way or another, the action has to have an economic quantification in order to create a *taxable amount* on which a *tax rate* can be applied that determines (after possibly applying different reductions, surcharges or deductions) the amount to be paid.

The taxable event can be possessing something or carrying out a specific action. Examples of the former include personal income taxes and taxes for owning a vehicle. Examples of the latter are taxes applied to purchasing a can of tomatoes or a home or to importing a motorcycle.

- Grants and subsidies

In the same way that the government has the power to apply taxes, it can also grant money to individuals or businesses with or without a predetermined purpose, as nonrepayable funds or with an obligation for repayment.

People who receive unemployment benefits or a grant for large families are not required to use the money in a specific way. However, a subsidy to install an elevator or a grant to reconvert the dairy sector does require whoever receives the funds to use them for the purpose for which they were granted. In these last two examples, instead of an amount of money that does not have to be repaid, the state could grant a loan at a highly reduced interest rate or even zero interest rate.

- Nonmonetary incentives

Not all incentives employed by the state to favour or promote (or discourage) a certain activity are carried out through regulations or cash (or financial) inducements. The panoply of alternative instruments includes awareness campaigns, promoting self-regulation or in general any specific action that encourages or discourages behaviours.

Offering a quality seal to businesses that meet certain standards is one way of encouraging compliance with those standards. Allowing taxes to be processed and even paid electronically with a digital signature helps to spread the use of such signatures. Convening a roundtable of advertising professionals to try to encourage the industry to agree on a code of practice restricting the advertisement directed at children could make specific regulation unnecessary. A public television campaign could increase the consumption of oily fish.

- Public–private partnerships

Between a totally public or totally private provision of a certain service is an endless number of ways for the two sectors to collaborate. Such collaborations can manifest in arrangements, agreements or contracts that stipulate who offers or manages the service, how the required investment is distributed and the associated responsibilities and risks. It can also be a one-time agreement or be indefinite.

When extending broadband service to less-profitable rural areas, the relevant public administration could facilitate the necessary permits or carry out the civil works or even completely deploy the network itself and then offer wholesale connectivity to telecom operators interested in offering such services to homes. In contrast, governments might commission a company to build a motorway while the government retains public ownership and operation (which can also be granted to the construction company for a limited time). A public hospital can contract a private clinic to carry out magnetic resonance imaging to handle extra work only in situations where the public service is overloaded.

READING 1.4 WHAT IS PUBLIC MONEY USED FOR?

Eurostat, the official statistical office of the European Union, has a tool that can be used to examine how public money is spent.[1] Expenditures are broken down into the ten categories ("by function") presented next; subcategories are also included in each section (whenever they represent at least 0.2% of the overall expenditure). The headings are the official ones used by the European Union. The numbers in parentheses indicate the percentage the category of expenditure represented of total government spending and of GDP (the second value is in italics) for the European Union as a whole (factoring in all its then 28 member states) in 2018. Evidently, not every category has an effect on the economy (beyond the effect of the expenditure in and of itself; for example, this is the case of expenditures on public safety or defence).

- Social protection (40.6%–*18.6%*): old age (22.0%–*10.1%*); sickness and disability (5.9%–*2.7%*); family and children (3.6%–*1.7%*); survivors

(2.9%–*1.3%*); unemployment (2.5%–*1.2%*); social exclusion not else-where specified (2.0%–*0.9%*); housing (1.0%–*0.4%*); and social protection not elsewhere classified (n.e.c.) (0.6%–*0.3%*).

- Health (15.5%–*7.1%*): hospital services (7.1%–*3.2%*); outpatient services (5.0%–*2.3%*); medical products, appliances and equipment (2.2%–*1.0%*); health n.e.c. (0.6%–*0.3%*); public health services (0.4%–*0.2%*); and health-related research and development (0.3%–*0.1%*).
- General government services (12.7%–*5.8%*): public debt transactions (4.3%–*2.2%*); executive and legislative bodies, financial and fiscal affairs and foreign affairs (4.0%–*1.9%*); general services (2.4%–*1.1%*); basic research (1.1%–*0.5%*); foreign economic aid (0.7%–*0.3%*); and general public services n.e.c. (0.2%–*0.1%*).
- Education (10.2%–*4.7%*): secondary education (3.9%–*1.8%*); pre-school and primary education (3.3%–*1.5%*); tertiary education (1.6%–*0.7%*); services auxiliary to education (0.6%–*0.3%*); education not attributable to any level (0.3%–*0.2%*); education n.e.c. (0.2%–*0.1%*); postsecondary, nontertiary education (0.2%–*0.1%*).
- Economic affairs (9.2%–*4.2%*): transport (4.3%–*2.0%*); general economic, trade and labour affairs (1.9%–*0.9%*); research and development related to economic affairs (0.9%–*0.4%*); fuel and energy (0.7%–*0.3%*); agriculture, forestry, fishing and hunting (0.5%–*0.2%*); other industries (0.4%–*0.2%*); economic affairs n.e.c. (0.2%–*0.1%*); and mining, manufacturing and construction (0.2%–*0.1%*).
- Public order and security (3.7%–*1.7%*): police services (2.0%–*0.9%*); courts of law (0.7%–*0.3%*); fire protection services (0.5%–*0.2%*); and prisons (0.3%–*0.2%*).
- Defence (2.9%–*1.3%*): military defence (2.6%–*0.2%*).
- Recreation, culture and religion (2.3%–*1.1%*): cultural services (0.9%–*0.4%*); recreational and sporting services (0.8%–*0.3%*); and radio and television services and publishing services (0.4%–*0.2%*).
- Environmental protection (1.7%–*0.8%*): waste management (0.8%–*0.4%*); waste water management (0.3%–*0.1%*); and pollution abatement (0.2%–*0.1%*).
- Housing and community services (1.3%–*0.6%*): community development (0.6%–*0.3%*); urbanization (0.4%–*0.2%*); and water supply (0.2%–*0.1%*).

Figure 1.4 presents numbers for eight countries: Germany, Bulgaria, Slovenia, Spain, Finland, France, Latvia and United Kingdom. As with the overall figures, the data are from 2018 and they are measured both in the percentage of overall expenditure and as a percentage of GDP.

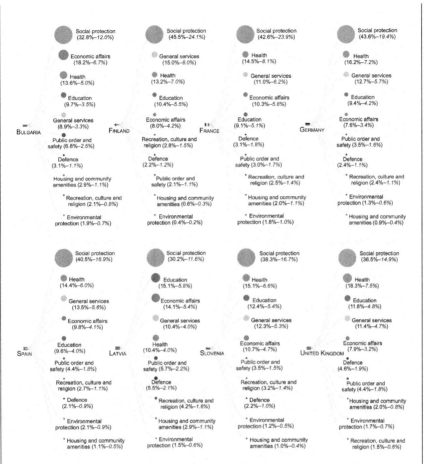

FIGURE 1.4 Government expenditure "by function" for eight EU countries as percentages of overall expenditure and percentages of GDP (2018)

Comparing countries, or comparing countries against the European average, provides striking results. In every case, social protection is by far the largest percentage; however, a country like Finland spends almost 45.5% on this category (almost five points above the European average), whereas Latvia spends barely over 30% (ten points below the average). Latvia is also one of three countries (the others are Finland and Bulgaria) in which spending on health does not follow social spending; in fact, Latvia spends much less on health than the European average (five points), just the opposite of what happens in the United Kingdom (three points above); however, it spends more than normal on education (five points), making it the country's second largest expenditure. Other significant deviations from the average are spending on general services by Bulgaria (well below); on economic affairs, Latvia and especially Bulgaria (much higher); on public order and safety, Latvia (above) and Finland (below); on defence, United Kingdom and Latvia (above); on leisure, culture and religion, Latvia and Slovenia (above); on housing and community services, Bulgaria and Latvia (above) and Finland (below); and finally, on environmental protection, Finland (below). The spending structures of Spain, France and Germany closely match the European average, showing no significant divergences in any area. A final comment can be made about the weight of each area of spending in a country's GDP. The numbers conform to the percentage of national GDP represented by total government spending. Thus, whereas in France 42.6% of total expenditure (on social protection) is 23.9% of GDP, in Germany an even higher percentage of total expenditure (43.6%) represents only 19.4% of national production, because of the lower weight of the public sector in its GDP.

1 https://ec.europa.eu/eurostat/cache/infographs/cofog/.

6.2 Recipes: economic policies

By mixing the different *ingredients* described in the previous section, the state can come up with *recipes* to meet certain objectives. The objectives are not always restricted to a single purpose, which means that the classification that follows is not strict. An obvious example is fiscal policy, which is usually catalogued as an adjustment policy, although it may also be used to pursue social objectives.

The urgency with which measures must be applied and their possible impact over time also vary. Some of the policies described next are inherently situational or structural. Many others, however, are more flexible and can be designed to deal with specific circumstances (aiming at being effective in the short term) or to generate results in the future.

- Policies organizing economic activity

General purpose, *horizontal* policies establish the basic organization and operation of markets. They affect in a general way how businesses can act and deal with other companies or individuals, both as employees and clients.

- *Property protection policies* guarantee the rights of individuals and companies to use and transmit all kinds of goods—with no limits, save those stipulated in certain controlled circumstances.
- *Competition policies* prosecute (or prevent) anticompetitive practices by companies that are sufficiently dominant in a market to be able to carry

them out. A particular aspect of the prevention work is the supervision of mergers and acquisitions by large companies.

- *Labour policies* define the possible relations in the labour market. They include norms on types of contracts, schedules, salaries and safety conditions in the workplace; they also cover other aspects of labour law, such as strikes, collective bargaining agreements and the rights and responsibilities of business and worker associations. Although they are interrelated, labour policy is different than employment policy, whose objective is to enhance the employability of workers.
- *Consumer protection policies* define the rights of customers and users of businesses that sell them goods and services. They cover a broad spectrum of issues, such as the responsibility of businesses for the products they sell; the minimum level of quality of those products; how to act in cases of unfair trade practices and misleading advertising; and the protection of personal information collected by companies.
- *Environmental policies* include all measures directed at making sure that resources are used sustainably, prohibiting or hindering activities that pollute the environment or use limited resources inadequately or, on the contrary, rewarding or encouraging alternatives that correct polluting practices.

- Policies promoting economic activity

Policies that promote economic activity are also *horizontal* policies not directed at any specific sector that seek to adapt production structures to ensure the future growth of the economy. They are, therefore, medium- or long-term policies. If the goal is to merely reactivate the economy or overcome a problematic situation, macroeconomic adjustment policies are instead used.

- *Infrastructure policies* are concerned with creating and maintaining basic infrastructures for a country, such as physical transportation and telecommunication networks, including their nodes (e.g. stations, ports, airports and repeaters), and vital supply networks, such as electricity, gas and water.
- *Training and capacity-building policies* intend to increase human capital in an economy.
- *Research and development policies* search for opportunities to progress for the economy that would have to come from the invention of new products or the improvement of manufacturing or management processes or systems.
- *Information society development policies* seek to adapt societies and economies to the change of paradigm caused by the immediate availability of all kinds of information and the existence of powerful tools to process it.
- *Development policies* are concerned with finding strategies for long-term growth. More precisely, they should be termed *strategic policies for the future*

or *strategic policies for growth* because the term *development policy* is usually reserved for policies applied by (or applied to) underdeveloped countries.

On some occasions, policies can be designed to bolster an entire economy by targeting a specific sector or economic activity. An example would be an energy policy that invests in renewable energy sources, in an attempt to provide the country with some kind of competitive advantage (related to the development, implementation or use of said energies) that is not only exploitable but also important enough to become a pillar of the country's economic activity in the future.

- Macroeconomic adjustment and stabilization policies

The main objective of such policies is to create situations that influence the tendencies of the macroeconomic indicators used to monitor economic growth and the stability of that growth. Although adjustment policies can be designed to act throughout a period of time, they are generally short-term policies that deal with problems in the present.

- *Fiscal policies* use the quantity and composition of public spending to modify the level of economic activity in order to stabilize the economic cycle; that is, they *boost* the economy during recessions and *cool it down* during peaks of activity, because continuous growth can make the economy unstable.
- *Monetary policies* set the amount of money in circulation or, contemporarily, the inflation or interest rates, in order to stabilize the economy directly (stable prices) and also to indirectly influence aggregate demand and, by extension, the level of activity.
- *Commercial policies* (also referred to as trade policies) are the measures put in place by governments to try to channel, or even control, transactions with other countries. The objective of these polices is to achieve a surplus (or at least balance) in the balance of trade, which means that the measures seek to promote exports and limit imports. *Exchange rate policies*, which seek to guide the exchange rate of the national currency with other convertible currencies, can be considered part of the trade policy.
- The objective of an *incomes policy* is to control inflation by fixing the price of certain goods and services, especially the level of wages. With this goal, maximum limits for wage increases can be established; such limits can be mandatory or merely recommended (though in this case they are usually accompanied by actions that persuade the agents involved to adopt the recommendation).

- Social policies

Social policies contribute to improving the welfare of society, in particular the well-being of individuals and groups that lack sufficient resources to reach the specific objectives that the policies seek to guarantee. Their primary purpose is therefore redistribution. It is the primary purpose, because as occurs with the majority of economic policies, they do not have a single effect, and many social policies can also serve to boost activity in the short term (e.g. through greater consumption by those that receive benefits or pensions) or the long term (through the impact of education or housing policies).

Social policies include pension and healthcare systems, employment policies (in their "active" form, providing professional training and education, and in their "passive" form, providing coverage for unemployment), territorial cohesion policy, housing policies, social aid policies for certain groups (e.g. elderly people, youths, people who have a disability and dependents) and family policies. Even cultural or sports policies can be considered social policies.

• Sectorial policies

Certain sectors of activity are habitually candidates for a specific and detailed policy. These are sectors of particular importance for the economy as a whole. The purpose of these policies is usually to combine stricter control of the sector in question (different requisites that are frequently more detailed than those needed to carry out any other activity) with creating the conditions to boost it, while often subjecting the activity of market players to a certain *guidance*.

Essential services (e.g. energy, telecommunications and water) usually have their own policies. States usually have an agriculture (and/or fishing) policy, an industrial policy, a tourism policy and a transportation policy.

READING 1.5 THE CHALLENGES OF A NEW ERA: A PUBLIC POLICY FOR ARTIFICIAL INTELLIGENCE

If a machine's performing a certain operation takes advantage of information from its past activity or from its environment to improve the way it executes the task, we can say that the machine is capable of learning, that it is *intelligent*. The term *artificial intelligence* encompasses all those situations in which the operation of an artefact or an application follows some adaptive algorithm. Such a broad definition includes a multitude of techniques and varied *degrees of intelligence*. Evidently, artificial intelligence exists in a driverless car or in a pet robot, but it is also incorporated in less-complex products such as robot vacuum cleaners, an application that offers suggestions to suit our tastes (e.g. songs, offers, advertisements and entries on social networks) or a dynamic energy-saving programme in a household appliance.

Artificial intelligence will be increasingly present in our lives. It also holds the promise of economic prosperity for those countries that specialize in *programming the guts* of smart devices. The statement can be qualified by the fact that, because artificial intelligence has a horizontal purpose (i.e. it will be incorporated into more and more sectors of activity), developers will be needed everywhere. Notwithstanding the above, the most arduous develop-ments (and possibly the most profitable because they incorporate most of the added value in expensive products) will be reserved for the leading countries in the use of these techniques. That artificial intelligence already appears in the policies that promote economic activity in many countries and will be gaining a presence in these programmes in the coming years is not in vain.

If artificial intelligence means both progress and prosperity, what should governments do other than encourage all development that includes it? With-out needing to imagine the bleak futures that some science fiction stories have shown us, the truth is that the use of artificial intelligence is not without risk. The word *use* should be emphasized. As in all technological development, some objects or services with built-in artificial intelligence will be (in fact, are) useful to a majority and others will not interest almost anyone. But what they will never be is "good" or "bad", "harmful" or "harmless". These adjectives are valid only for the use made of a technology, never for the technology itself. That said, artificial intelligence opens up possibilities for misuse or abuse that will reach an unknown dimension when it becomes ubiquitous and embed-ded in most routine activities. Moreover, artificial intelligence poses far-more-difficult challenges than any other technology. Machines will sometimes have to make decisions in dangerous, even extreme, situations. Imagine the case of a driverless car that has to decide between running over a pedestrian or going off the road and falling down a ravine to save the pedestrian.

In this scenario, some governments are seeking, as much as possible, to anticipate controversial or inadequate (even perverse) uses of artificial intel-ligence and regulate them ex ante. Others, on the other hand, are preferring to wait for events or directly attach secondary importance to these issues. Figure 1.5 shows the different positions currently held by the governments of the United States, the European Union and China on the control of the development of artificial intelligence and the possible and probable paths that these policies will follow in the future, always along a line that goes from the prevalence of the market to the centralized decision model.

The authors of the graph state that China is showing itself to be capa-ble of promoting the development of artificial intelligence with a long-term vision that is independent of the political cycle (always a determining factor in the European Union and the United States) which *builds on a different set of social values*. In their opinion, the most likely evolution of Chinese policy would be that which leads to a stage of "advanced technology" (letter D) and "opens the door to a new type of society, in which artificial intelligence is used to advance collective societal goals, even if those come at the expense of individual rights, a 'brave new world'". Other options are that technology

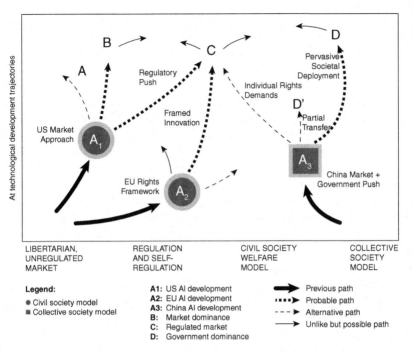

FIGURE 1.5   Artificial intelligence policy paths in the European Union, the United States and China (as of 2020)[1]

advances but that this advance is not transferred to society (letter D') or that, in a change of context, demands for the protection of individual rights are met and the specific regulation of artificial intelligence is put into place (letter C). This is, moreover, the most likely scenario in the evolution of the policy supported by the European Union and is also a likely option in the case of the United States; the other option, in the case of the United States, is one in which the technical and institutional framework continues to favour free market activity (letter B).

1 Feijóo, C., Kwon, Y., et al. (2020). "Harnessing artificial intelligence (AI) to increase wellbeing for all: The case for a new technology diplomacy". *Telecommunications Policy*, vol. 44, no. 6, art. 101988.

Summary

This chapter will serve as a presentation and preview of what is discussed in the rest of the book. It starts by making two observations. The first is that well into the 21st century, the market economy is the model by which economic activity is organized in almost every country in the world. The second is that they are *mixed market economies* in which the state can (usually) carry out a variety of functions. The state can have five functions, to be exact: to buy goods and services; to provide goods and services; to establish the framework within which economic activity takes place; to impose certain results; or simply to contribute to obtaining them.

However, merely describing state activity in the economy does not provide enough information to understand all the conceptual perspectives of such actions: the reasons, objectives, and conditions in which they take place. If the state decides to act, it does so because those who have the final say on such activity (in democratic societies, a majority of voters or constituencies) are not convinced that the desired outcome will be achieved by leaving the market to operate independently. Inefficiency, an unacceptable distribution of wealth, or defending social values could lead the state to take action. The objective of state involvement would be to correct those problems and thus improve the general welfare through stable growth and obtain a more balanced distribution of what is produced; yet sometimes its goals are based on values that are not directly related to efficiency or equity. These generic objectives, which are difficult to measure, are given practical shape by controlling certain macroeconomic variables. As the third step, states develop various economic policies (general or specific—usually to stimulate or stabilize and sometimes with social purposes but other times with merely economic ones) to achieve those objectives. These policies use some of or all the tools at the state's disposal, including passing laws, imposing taxes, directly providing goods or services or using all kinds of incentives.

Overview

This chapter included the following:

- A description of the functions carried out by the public sector in a market economy.
- An outline of state activity in the economy: *why* the state takes action, *what* it's trying to achieve, and *how* it achieves its goals.
- The motivations for public activity: failures of *the market* (understood as a system of general organization) or of *specific markets*.
- The objectives (ultimate, derived and immediate) pursued by public action.
- The instruments used to carry out these actions and the economic policies that are shaped by combining these instruments.

Self-assessment questions

The self-assessment questions are meant to evaluate how well you have understood the information presented in this chapter.

1 Countries in which the state has a strong presence in the economy are denominated by which of the following?

    a   Market economies.
    b   Planned economies.
    c   Mixed economies.
    d   Any of these models.

2 Which of the following statements is true?

    a   When there is perfect competition, the outcome generated by market activity is effective.
    b   When there is perfect competition, the outcome generated by market activity is efficient.
    c   When there is perfect competition, the outcome generated by market activity is efficient and also equitable.
    d   When there is perfect competition, the outcome generated by market activity is effective and also equitable.

3 Can a government take action that is not based on the criteria of efficiency?

    a   Yes, unconditionally, it has the authority to do so, although it should justify why it does so.
    b   Yes, but only when the decision affects the structures of the market (understood as a mechanism to organize activity) and not specific markets.
    c   Yes, but only if the decision affects only a specific market.
    d   No, it cannot.

4 The Gini coefficient is used to measure which of the following?

    a   The proportion of businesses that are concentrated in a certain sector of the economy.
    b   The distribution of income with respect to what would be an absolutely uniform distribution.
    c   The general variation in welfare observed in a natural year.
    d   The long-term sustainability of the public deficit.

5 The main objective of policies that promote economic activity/growth is which of the following?

    a   To increase the welfare of society, in particular that of groups or individuals who lack sufficient resources.
    b   To change the tendency of the macroeconomic indicators used to monitor economic growth and the stability of that growth.
    c   To establish the basic structures that organize and allow the markets to function.
    d   To adapt productive structures to ensure future economic growth.

Questions for reflection

The answers to the following questions are not in the text; they require you to search for additional information or to apply to real cases what you have learned in this chapter.

1   Is a market economy the same as a capitalist economy?
2   Think about recent activities carried out by the local government where you live. Did they follow the *why–what for–how* sequence?
3   In the actions taken by your local government, look for examples of the various *ingredients* mentioned in the text.

2
REASONS FOR STATE ECONOMIC ACTIVITY

1 Introduction

A popular way to define economics presents it as a science that studies the best way to employ scarce resources that have alternative uses. Indeed, because of this scarcity of resources, ensuring that they are used in the best way is the primary consideration when organizing economic activity. This is why the concept of economic efficiency is key: it is more efficient to use fewer resources to obtain a certain quantity of product or, alternatively, to obtain a greater amount of product by using a set number of resources.

Efficiency is so important that not only is it the primary objective of *any form of organizing* economic activity but also the factor used to *select the way to organize* economic activity. Efficiency justifies why the market economy is the preferred model, because the market, at least in theory, leads to an efficient outcome. "At least in theory" means that in practice situations arise in which the market *fails* to produce the predicted result. For many of the schools of economic thought, these market failures comprise a limited set of situations. State activity in the economy would be admissible in these situations.

More debatable is whether state activity in the economy is admissible in *only* these situations. Just because efficiency is the primary objective does not mean that it is the only objective. However, this is the position presented by the majority of textbooks. If anything, these traditional textbooks include equity, which is sometimes classified as another market failure, as a cause that justifies state *intervention* (not activity) in the economy. In reality, equity has nothing to do with efficiency, which means that it is a different (and of course legitimate) reason to justify public action. And there are other reasons. The state responds to the will of society, which transcends economic criteria. If the majority of society believes that treating certain assets or goods differently is appropriate or that certain values should be protected,

DOI: 10.4324/9781003173731-2

with no consideration for efficiency, that is argument enough for the state to obey the mandate and act accordingly.

One further clarification is necessary. The customary list of market failures describes situations that occur only in certain markets, so they should be referred to as failures of *specific markets*. On the contrary, other situations become manifest when observing *the market as a whole*, without the need to specify any particular market: these are failures of *the market*.

In addition, the *other causes* for state activity can also emerge in *the market* and in *a specific market*. We have, therefore, a dual vision of the reasons that justify public economic activity: reasons related to efficiency and others that are not, and reasons confined to a specific market and those that are general to the market model. If we maintain the traditional qualifier *failures* for cases in which efficiency is involved, we will have failures of *the market* and of *specific markets* and causes unrelated to efficiency in *the market* or in *specific markets*. These four categories are described in the following sections, although they will be preceded by the demonstration of a statement that, although essential, was simply assumed to be true: the market is a model for organizing the economy that leads, "at least in theory", to an efficient outcome. The final section of this chapter will assess these reasons that *justify* public activity.

READING 2.1   TO HELL WITH EFFICIENCY: WE JUST LIKE TO PARTY

It doesn't make much *economic sense* for a municipal government to organize (and pay for) local fiestas—at least in Spain, where scheduled activities are generally free. Concerts, dances and other celebrations attract people from nearby towns, allowing bars, restaurants and parking garages to make good money on those days. But even if we take those externalities into account, to honour the town's patron saint is still far from *profitable*. Towns and cities anywhere in Spain do it anyway. No mayoral candidate runs on the promise of eliminating the budget for fiestas. That would be the best way not to be elected.

The Gobierto website[1] has collected information on the budgets of a significant number of the municipalities in Spain. The data are official and public,[2] but the website has processed them in order to allow income and expenditure items to be ordered and to make comparisons between municipalities. Figure 2.1 presents the expenditures that were budgeted in 2020 for "traditional fiestas and festivals".

As can be seen, a fair number of municipalities exceeded 100 euros per year in spending per inhabitant on this concept (specifically 1,142 of the 4,817 that had data); at the other extreme, only 134 spent fewer than 5 euros per year per inhabitant. In absolute terms, only 25 municipalities reserved fewer

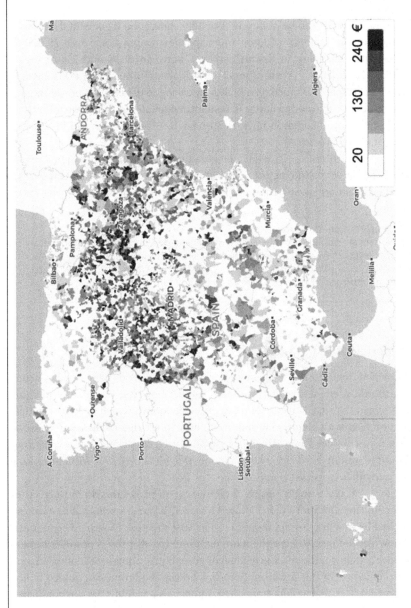

FIGURE 2.1   (Budgeted) expenditure per inhabitant by Spanish municipalities on "traditional fiestas and festivals" (in euros, 2020)

than 1,000 euros for fiestas and only 364 spent fewer than 5,000 euros; on the other side of the scale, 1,332 municipalities (almost 28%) spent 100,000 euros or more.

These numbers can be put into context by comparing them with the total budget. In the majority of large municipalities (populations over 25,000 inhabitants), spending on fiestas oscillates between 0.5% and 2% of the municipal budget. In the case of small municipalities (fewer than 1,000 inhabitants), the disparity is much greater, but, speaking in general, the percentage of the budget dedicated to fiestas is significantly greater than in large municipalities: it's not uncommon for it to surpass 10% of the total and in some cases, it is well over 20%.

A different question is, what percentage of the budgeted expenditure would be converted into actual expenditure at the end of the particular year for which data are given? The year 2020 was certainly not the best year for parties.

1 https://presupuestos.gobierto.es/.
2 The data are published by the Secretaría General de Coordinación Autonómica y Local. https://www.mptfp.gob.es/portal/politica-territorial/local/sistema_de_infor macion_local_-SIL-/informacion_local_en_organismos/administracion_general_ del_estado/sgcal.html.

2 Efficiency of the market

The provided definition of efficiency refers to a single good, which makes determining the most efficient alternative seem simple; however, doing so is anything but easy when the alternatives refer to an entire economy, which includes multiple production factors and numerous options on how to use them. The most common solution is to consider Pareto efficiency: an allocation is efficient *in the Pareto sense* if reallocating resources so as to make any one individual better off without making at least one other worse off is impossible.

The fact that not a single person can be worse off makes this dominance criterion to compare allocations demanding. However, a Pareto optimal allocation can be reached by meeting certain requisites. The first theorem of welfare economics, also known as the *invisible hand* theorem, demonstrates that this is possible. It states that under certain conditions, the general or competitive equilibrium of the market is Pareto efficient. In this situation, both individuals and businesses, guided by the same set of prices that results from their interaction, would take uncoordinated actions (i.e., exclusively in line with their own interests) that would organize the processes of production and exchange to reach the best (most efficient) allocation possible. At the point of equilibrium, any variation of price that benefits some will necessarily harm others, which is the definition of Pareto efficiency. Also take note that the efficiency reached is complete, in the sense that it affects both production and consumption: production is efficient (the largest quantity possible), and the product is distributed in the way that is most in line with individual preferences. This result leads to an immediate conclusion: if an economy needs to pursue efficiency and the market mechanism, left to operate autonomously, offers an answer (*the* answer), the free market is the best system to organize the economy.

Under these circumstances, the role of the public sector would be relegated to providing the legal structure needed for the market to operate. This wouldn't apply if in addition to striving for efficient allocation, how the allocation is undertaken is also a concern—in other words, if some kind of equitable redistribution is sought. But the market also offers an answer to this second possible demand, again at least in theory. The second theorem of welfare economics demonstrates that every possible alternative for the initial allocation of resources will lead to a long-term or competitive equilibrium. The market always finds a new set of equilibrium prices for which the supply satisfies all the demand and with which Pareto efficiency is achieved for both production and consumption. Interpreting the second theorem in the opposite sense means that the market is *agnostic* regarding the final distribution of goods and allows for any allocation; only the initial endowment that leads to the desired result needs to be found.

If the market provides an efficient and even equitable outcome by itself, why would the state be needed to correct its performance? Here we return to the first theorem of welfare economics: it states "under certain conditions", conditions that were never clarified. We now do so. A competitive market equilibrium requires the following conditions:

- All the *specific markets* that make up *the market* must be perfectly competitive, which, in addition to the particular requisites in each market, has two implications at the aggregate level: both consumers and companies act as *price takers* (without being able to influence prices), and they also have perfect information, which was obtained at no cost.
- The set of markets must be complete, in that it covers every economic activity or demand and any future contingency that the economy could present.
- There must be a complete system of individual property rights: every imaginable asset has an owner who can exclude others from using it.
- The behaviour of all actors must be perfectly rational, which means that the exclusive objective of companies is to maximize profit and that of consumers to maximize utility. In the latter case, individuals must be satiated at a certain point when obtaining greater quantities of a good; in other words, their preferences must be well established and must not present irregularities; in mathematical terms, the indifference curves are convex to the origin.
- The production functions must present a diminishing (or at least constant) relationship between cost and output. In mathematical terms, what is required is a convex form (to the origin) of the isoquant curves.
- The various activities must have no influence on third parties not involved in said activity (no externalities, see more later on in Section 5.1.2).

Can all these requisites be met simultaneously? The answer is no. This means that the market cannot guarantee the results that the welfare theorems predict. Or, put another way, in practice, the price system is not a Pareto-efficient mechanism for allocating resources, nor can it ensure that its results are equitable to any degree.

The following sections examine the reasons behind this statement. As mentioned in the introduction, these market failures are divided into failures of *the market* and of *specific markets*. In addition, other reasons for public activity have nothing to do with efficiency.

3 Reasons related to efficiency in *the market*: failures of *the market*

In any economy, *the market* is composed of the sum of the individual markets of the different goods and services that are exchanged in that economy. As a consequence, everything that occurs in the market originates in those *specific markets*. That said, the image of the market as a whole provides arguments to evaluate the efficiency of the market (now understood as a form of organizing economic activity) that are different from the arguments that can be found in specific markets.

Furthermore, not only are these arguments conceptually different, but they are different in scope. The presence of failures in some specific markets would seem at first to justify action only in those markets. But given that some actions (economic policies) deal with the economy as a whole, as we shall see in Chapter 4, the reasons for those policies should be based on the situation of the economy as a whole. These are the reasons that will be studied in this section and the next.

The first subset of arguments refers to the efficiency of the market. The first two arguments that will be presented next clearly fit in this section. The last two also deal with efficiency but introduce the time factor, which is not considered in the theorems of welfare economics. In fact, the actors in a market at a specific moment in time do not have to be interested in anything other than immediate outcomes. Even so, examining these two additional reasons in the section dealing with causes that are tied to efficiency seems more appropriate than dealing with them in the next, which examines causes that are unrelated to efficiency.

3.1 Guaranteeing rights and obligations

As mentioned several times, the market is formed by the union of various specific markets, but it is also made up of the structures that provide a framework for economic activity. One part of these structures guarantees that contracts are fulfilled and that exchanges are carried out without conflicts or alterations to the conditions that were agreed on. If parties lacked an entity that has the authority to perform this function, everything would be at the mercy of the good faith of the parties involved.

One failure of *the market* is, therefore, that it cannot supervise itself. Acknowledging this failure is not generally controversial. As we shall see later in greater detail, the (minimum) *organizing* function of the state is acknowledged even by the most recalcitrant defenders of the free market.

3.2 Inefficient outcome

Potential market efficiency has been analysed by applying theoretical economic reasoning. However, if we put aside theory for a moment and simply observe the results generated by the market system, the conclusion is clear: the market does not seem capable of reaching economic efficiency by itself.

Even countries that have left the largest portions of their economy in the hands of competition have not escaped various kinds of economic crises and imbalances. Off-kilter macroeconomic indicators would indicate that the market is not functioning correctly; that is, it is not obtaining an efficient outcome. Much more specifically, if an economy has a high rate of unemployment, then, logically, that economy could achieve a better (more efficient) outcome if it employed at least part of those "wasted resources".

Another interesting practical issue is to determine the competition model that the market tends towards when left to act autonomously. For instance, when competition has been introduced into industries that traditionally operated under monopolies (basic utilities such as telecommunications or electricity), over time, when the supervision of the market was relaxed, the companies regrouped into oligopolies or even into new monopolies. The tendency observed in many Internet or software markets is far from the perfect competition required for efficiency. These are just examples, but what interests us here is not what happened exactly in those markets but rather the situation that they may be indicating: the market as an organizational mechanism does not autonomously generate (or at least does not always generate) the competition needed to obtain results that could be considered efficient.

The criticism of the market's supposed practical inefficiency is simple: the conclusion is invalid because it speaks of "countries that have left the largest portions of their economy in the hands of competition"; the truth is that in no country and at no historical moment has the market truly been left to act by itself. In fact, the opposite is frequently argued: the imbalances are produced precisely because of a *lack of free market*, and so the solution is not for more public activity (*intervention*) but rather for *more free market*.

READING 2.2   CRISIS? WHAT CRISIS?

Many crises can be referred to here to respond to this question. Not all of them are equal. There are crises of the *real economy* and crises of the *financial economy*. Financial crises are often at the root (or at least they act as the starting point) of the majority of real crises; for example, whatever shakes up the stock markets ends up causing production to contract and destroy jobs. In fact, the most memorable crises in history were tied to financial upheaval.

The company HistoryShots InfoArt, in partnership with Princeton University Press, sells a poster that maps the history of financial crises that occurred over two centuries, between 1810 and 2010 (*Cycles of financial crises: 1810–2010*[1]). It is based on the book *This time is different: Eight centuries of financial folly*, written by Carmen M. Reinhart and Kenneth S. Rogoff, published by Princeton University Press. Figure 2.2 presents the same information but has various modifications in format. The ordinate axis measures the percentage of world GDP affected by the crisis in question (i.e., the percentage of world GDP represented by the sum of the GDPs of the countries affected). The abscissa axis marks the passage of time. The four symbols represent the following:

- Sovereign default: when a government fails to meet payments on its debt obligations.
- Banking crash: at least one of the major banks of the country closes or is bailed out by the government or by other national or international financial institutions.
- Currency crash: when the currency depreciates at a rate of 15% or more a year.
- Hyperinflation: when the inflation rate is 20% or more a year.

The graphic highlights, somewhat arbitrarily, nine crises. The idea is not to enter into the details of each episode but rather to look at the overall picture. The peaks of the wave best capture our attention: they tell us that there have been and continue to be cycles in financial health (and, by extension, economic health). The second noteworthy characteristic is that the first 100 years examined seem quieter (at least the crises were less severe) than the second 100 years. Since the beginning of World War I, there has always been some kind of crisis, all the way to the period just before the one in 2008–2009. As can be seen in the graphic, the 20th century seems to have been a century of crises. The third note has to do with the crisis of 2008–2009: its diffusion surpassed that of all the crises that occurred in the preceding 70 years, with an added peculiarity in that it happened suddenly after having reached for the first time in decades what seemed like complete global tranquillity.

With the panorama revealed by Figure 2.2, we could change the question to an exclamation: "Crisis! What crisis!" In the face of such incessant instability, the right question at all times seems to be, when is the next one coming?

1 https://www.historyshots.com/products/visual-history-of-financial-crises.

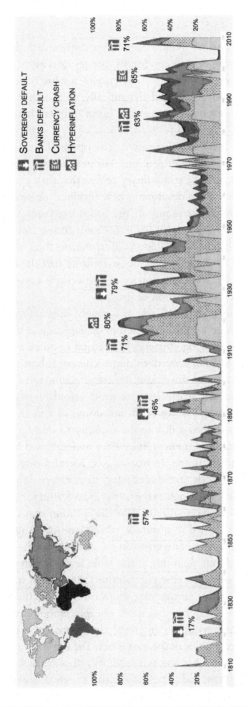

FIGURE 2.2 Financial crises in the period 1810–2010

3.3 Short-sightedness regarding the future: innovation and sustainability

The fundamental theorems of welfare economics do not include the variable of time. They state that given certain conditions, the result is assured, but nothing is said of the following period. Therefore, they employ a static concept of efficiency. However, efficiency could be defined dynamically, in which case the objective would be to obtain the best outcome not in a given moment but rather in a series of consecutive years.

Static efficiency and dynamic efficiency can be opposed. Static efficiency seeks maximum competition (perfect competition), but in situations of perfect competition, companies do not obtain extraordinary profits that they can use to invest in improving their current supply, developing new products or promoting research, all of which could drive the economy in the following years. Could the digital economy have developed in the way it has if the competition had been perfect and none of the companies had been capable of differentiating their offer? Expressed in stricter terms, reaching Pareto efficiency doesn't ensure that the limit of potential production has shifted. In fact, even a series of consecutive periods with efficient outcomes may not generate innovation or growth.

Even more important is that the lack of foresight implicit in static efficiency does not take into consideration the destruction or depletion of resources. In pursuit of reducing costs (improving efficiency), a natural resource might be depleted or a certain habitat might be destroyed: fishing is cheaper if bottom trawling techniques are used intensively, but this might put the medium-term survival of some marine life in danger; beach apartments are more affordable when it is allowed to build them freely along the entire coast, but doing so will also destroy natural habitats, and future generations will lose the capacity to decide what to do with that territory; surface mining produces more than underground mining but it also leaves behind a shattered landscape. In many cases, harmful or polluting activities affect third parties; this is what economics refers to as externalities, which will be described in later sections. Although externalities are a reason for public action, we shall see that they can be "internalized". But the solution that the market could provide for externalities does not guarantee taking care of resources: a polluting company may offer monetary compensation to all those in the region who are affected, in order to continue polluting at the same level (which could constitute, in a strictly economic sense, an efficient solution). Moreover, in other cases, no third parties are directly affected: catching more fish benefits the fishing industry and *current* consumers who can buy fish more cheaply; nobody can be considered adversely affected (in their economic interests) if no population lives on the coast where the apartments are built or in the spot where the mine is operated. The conclusion is that the market mechanism, where all its actors are seeking to realize the greatest profit in the present, lacks the self-control to ensure its own survival. Or if this conclusion is too unequivocal, it can at least be said that it lacks compassion for future generations.

READING 2.3   THE DESTRUCTION OF HABITATS: THE CULTIVATION OF OIL PALM

The African oil palm is native to the Gulf of Guinea. Although it has been exploited for centuries, in the past 30 years, demand for palm oil has exploded because of its use in the food and cosmetics industries and because of its use in the production of biofuel; it has become the most demanded source of fat, before soybean or colza oil. Exports of palm oil from Southeast Asia, where most of its production was concentrated at the start of the 1980s, has increased 25 times greater since then. Indonesia and Malaysia still account for around 85% of world production, but plantations have proliferated in other countries in Asia, South and Central America and Africa.[1]

The consumption of palm oil is associated with possible health risks (due to its high levels of saturated fat). What interests us here, however, is that the cultivation of oil palm is one of the factors contributing to the deforestation of tropical areas. The total deforestation of these areas can be seen in Figure 2.3. The greyed out sections of the graphic represent areas in which "the loss of canopy density has been greater than 30%" from 2001 to 2019.[2]

How much palm cultivation contributes to this deforestation is somewhat controversial. The source for the figure warns that the causes for deforestation are varied and, moreover, are not the same everywhere. Logic dictates that in an image like the one presented, which shows the evolution over a period of time, cultivating palms would have more to do with the disappearance of the forest in places where its cultivation was not recently introduced. Various academic articles corroborate this. One of them,[3] using satellite images, confirms that the palm is the main cause for deforestation in the island of Borneo (which, in addition to the small sultanate of Brunei, is split between Indonesia and Malaysia, the two largest producers of palm oil). According to data, between 1973 and 2015, 18 million hectares of primary forest were lost on the island; of them, seven million became plantations (the majority palm

FIGURE 2.3   Tropical areas that have lost 30% or more canopy density between 2001 and 2019

plantations, though approximately 15% of the total are trees destined to be used for paper pulp); in turn, on around 4.5 million hectares, plantations were established within five years of the disappearance of the forest. If we consider that the island of Borneo has 74.3 million hectares, the numbers are highly significant. In Figure 2.4, which is part of Figure 2.3 at a higher resolution, the substantial loss of canopy density in Borneo (and in other territories of Malaysia and Indonesia) is clear.

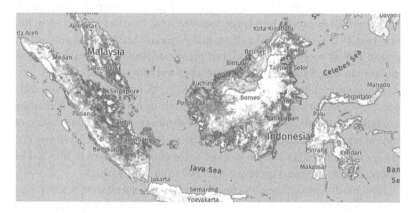

FIGURE 2.4   Greater than 30% loss of canopy density between 2001 and 2019, in Malaysia and Indonesia

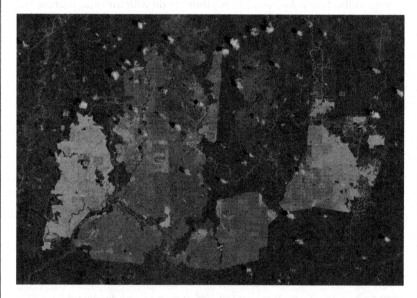

FIGURE 2.5   View from space of the oil palm plantation area in the middle of the jungle in the eastern part of the island of Borneo (East Kalimantan, Indonesia)[5]

In addition to the loss of forest (with all that the transformation in habitat implies for human populations and fauna), palm monoculture destroys the soil (after around 20 years of production, the plantations are ruined and the land is unusable for up to 25 or 30 years later), pollutes the water because of the intensive use of pesticides and fertilizers, changes hydric cycles and reduces the absorption of carbon dioxide (when it doesn't increase emissions: setting the forest on fire is a common way to gain new land for agriculture).[4]

The palm can be grown in a sustainable way, and especially after the poor image of palm oil that has been spread by some media, many producers are signing up to the *Roundtable on Sustainable Palm Oil*. However, many news pieces and reports indicate that in many cases businesses have done nothing more than merely sign the commitment.

1 https://palmoilalliance.eu/palm-oil-production/.
2 This was obtained by using the interactive tool at www.globalforestwatch.org/ map which in turn uses data from http://earthenginepartners.appspot.com/ science-2013-global-forest.
3 Gaveau, D.L.A., Sheil, D., Husnayaen, Salim, M.A., Arjasakusuma, S., Ancrenaz, M., Pacheco, P., & Meijaard, E. (2016). "Rapid conversions and avoided deforestation: examining four decades of industrial plantation expansion in Borneo". *Scientific Reports*, vol. 6, article 32017. It can also be found at https://www.nature.com/ articles/srep32017.
4 United Nations Environment Programme (2011). *Oil palm plantations: Threats and opportunities for tropical ecosystems*. Available at https://wedocs.unep.org/ handle/20.500.11822/32263.
5 Photograph *Palm oil plantations* from the European Space Agency (processed with data taken in February 2019 by the Copernicus Sentinel-2 mission). https:// www.esa.int/var/esa/storage/images/esa_multimedia/images/2019/07/palm_oil_ plantations/19484718-1-eng-GB/Palm_oil_plantations.jpg.

3.4 Unequal distribution of wealth

Situations in which the distribution of wealth is highly unequal can also be con-sidered failures of *the market*, without having to appeal to any criteria regarding equity. The first argument is that people with little purchasing power can barely "communicate" their needs to the market, because the only preferences that reach the market are of those who can pay the prices of goods and services offered by companies. A much more forceful argument adopts the same temporal perspective used in the previous section: if efficiency in the present is achieved at the cost of accepting that a significant part of society (of the market) is left out of the distribu-tion of what is (efficiently) produced, future efficiency is not guaranteed. Even if exploiting labour, including child labour, could be efficient, history has demon-strated that such a situation likely cannot remain stable indefinitely. In the long run, low productivity, absenteeism and social conflict can undermine the equilibrium that had once been achieved. In an extreme situation, widespread misery can pro-voke social movements that alter market structures or even destroy them entirely.

4 Reasons unrelated to efficiency in *the market*

The pursuit of equity is one of the arguments usually cited to support state activity in the economy. Surprisingly, amorality is not. Of course, the market is not tasked with determining what is *equitable*, what is *fair* or what is *right*. However, societies do have moral standards and thresholds for what is *permissible*. No matter what those social values may be, they must be incorporated into economic activity. Indeed, excluding economic exchanges from social conventions makes no sense. Following this reasoning, the corrective action of the state is also supported by reasons unrelated to efficiency.

4.1 Equity

The second theorem of welfare economics seems to reconcile efficiency with equity, but a problem arises with the expression "find the initial allocation that leads to the desired result". If a certain final allocation is pursued, *somebody* (other than the market) has to be in charge of organizing the initial distribution that leads to it.

In conclusion, even if the theorems of welfare economics were fulfilled, there would still be a basis for public activity. However, we have seen that they are not, which means that the field of public action must be broadened: to achieve a certain income distribution, corrective action cannot be circumscribed to adjudicating the initial allocation; in all likelihood, it should also (or alternatively) modify the outcome produced by the market.

READING 2.4   VACCINE FOR EVERYONE? DEPENDS ON YOUR PASSPORT

On 10 January 2020, only three days after the identification of the coronavirus, whose rapid spread would make the disease it causes a pandemic, its genome sequence was made public. Within weeks, several projects were underway to develop a vaccine to prevent COVID-19. In an unprecedented scientific effort, and thanks to unparalleled public and private economic resources, just one year later, there were already 42 countries where a vaccination plan had been initiated.

In that list of 42 countries, 36 of them unsurprisingly belong to the group of those considered developed economies. The richest countries had been the first to negotiate bilaterally with pharmaceutical companies, even though for the most part (with the exceptions of the United States and Russia), they were part of the alliance called COVAX (for the acronym of the COVID-19 Global Access Vaccine Fund). This partnership was launched in April 2020, its goal to bring vaccines to all countries. The plan was to sign agreements with companies that were developing vaccines in order to support them in their research and also in production if the effort was successful, in exchange for a preferential purchasing option. Countries that were able to finance the project maintained privileges on the number of vaccines that they could buy within COVAX but committed not to exceed certain limits until 20% of each country's population (also from poor countries that needed funding) had been vaccinated. In a way, COVAX represented a step forward to address a global problem with a global equity criterion, something that had not happened in the past (access to AIDS medication, which took years to reach poor countries, where the disease was more widespread, is a great example).

However, the step forward was not very big. Even without being able to say that COVAX was a failure, the figures of the first distribution of vaccines hardly present an image of equity. By the end of 2020, the partnership was only going to have 16% of the more than 8.5 billion doses purchased in firm because the "high-income" countries had decided *to go it alone*, taking together almost 50% of the doses, and the rest had been secured by middle-income countries. Thus, although Canada at that time had made contracts to buy enough doses to vaccinate its population five times (although not all the vaccines purchased had been authorized by health authorities at the time, and some might not be), there was no evidence of any direct contract between a pharmaceutical company and a poor country, countries that would depend entirely on the direction that COVAX took.[1]

The summary is that, at the moment of truth, the richer nations had finally decided that *equity begins with oneself*. In contrast, the intra-border situation was a good example of equity. In almost all, if not all, the countries where the process had begun, the states were exclusively responsible for vaccination, which was done free of charge and according to a protocol that prioritized certain particularly vulnerable sectors of the population. Vaccines could not be individually purchased, at least in that first stage,[2] so even the wealthiest person in each country would have to wait patiently for their turn (at least in words, since some were being able to game the system).

What about the market? Did it contribute in any way to making the vaccine available to everyone? By the end of 2020, the company AstraZeneca had announced that the price of its vaccine during 2021 would be just enough to cover costs and that it was making a firm commitment to make it reach any developing country at a price below USD3. Most likely, the company's policy would have been different if the research had not been conducted jointly with Oxford University.[3] The rest of the companies (Pfizer–BioNTech and Moderna, the first two in the race, and others with which agreements had already been established even though they had not reached the goal, such as Johnson & Johnson, Sanofi–Glaxo Smith Klein or CureVac) had not established a single price but were negotiating directly with each country, including in the contract a confidentiality clause regarding the price. Microeconomics textbooks posit that price discrimination (establishing different prices according to the customer), something that can be done only by those companies that have market power, is a strategy to maximize profits. And the fact is that healthcare, don't forget, is a business, also in times of pandemics—a business whose shareholders cheer any announcement, scientifically endorsed or not, that makes the price of shares rise; a business whose executives who take advantage of this rise in the stock market might be tempted to sell part of their share portfolio and make a profit that would make the reward (at least the financial reward) that the scientists, the true architects of the company's success, would have received ridiculous in comparison. But that, my friend Moustache, that's another story.

1 All the data in the paragraph come from the *Launch&Scale Speedometer* page of Duke Global Health Innovation Center of Duke University (https://launchand-scalefaster.org/COVID-19) and when consulted were referring to the date of 29 December 2020.
2 By the end of 2020, some countries, such as India, Australia and Mexico, had already opened the door to purchasing vaccines privately. However, all the vaccines available then and in the immediate future were completely taken over by public purchases.
3 When interviewed by France-Presse on 23 November 2020, Olivier Nataf, the head of AstraZeneca in France, stated that "the price is around 2.50 euros (USD3) per dose; this is the main subject of our agreement with Oxford". https://www.france24.com/en/live-news/20201123-astrazeneca-promises-virus-vaccine-at-cost-price-worldwide.

4.2 Amorality

When we discussed equity, we said that the market is *indifferent* to the distribution of wealth; this is also true regarding methods and behaviours. Economic criteria have nothing to do with moral criteria. For economic theory, if a business sets an objective not related to profit, it is behaving irrationally. The same occurs if something other than self-interest is included when calculating individual utility: compassion, altruism and philanthropy are not rational behaviours in economic terms.

However, on many occasions, efficient results are often obtained with uses or practices that at least part of society would consider reprehensible. Substituting sugar with an artificial sweetener is cheaper (more efficient), and the food industry would probably do so even in the face of studies that put in doubt the sweetener's effect on health. Producing toys that are not tested for safety is cheaper, and production countries that do not have such controls probably see the controls imposed by other countries as excessive (and some manufacturers might even falsify certification marks that indicate conformity with the norms). Making clothing in countries that pay low wages is cheaper, and almost all clothes are made in these places, even if they permit child labour or extremely harsh working conditions.

Polluting is cheaper than investing in modifying a manufacturing facility to reduce discharges. Requiring that a woman return to work immediately after giving birth is probably more efficient than having her company hire a substitute that is less familiar with the job.

5 Reasons related to efficiency in an individual market: failures of *specific markets*

Orthodox economic literature features reasonable agreement that market failures have five causes. All of them affect specific goods or markets, so they can be considered failures of *specific markets*. These causes are not mutually exclusive or even independent. They can be classified into two blocks:

- Those related to characteristics of the good or to the activity itself: public goods and externalities.
- Those related to the market situation: imperfect competition, from which information failures can be decoupled, and incomplete markets.

5.1 Intrinsic characteristics of the good or activity

5.1.1 Public goods

Two characteristics define public goods: they must be both nonexcludable and nonrivalrous. The first condition means that individuals cannot be excluded from enjoying the good, and the second means that consumption by one individual does not exhaust it or even affect the utility that others can extract from its consumption. Typical examples of public goods cited in the literature are national defence and lighthouses.

Few "pure" public goods rigorously meet these two conditions. Many goods that are considered public have these attributes only under certain conditions and could even be treated as private in different contexts. When the literature cites the example of lighthouses, a footnote usually explains that for several centuries in England, they were financed and run by ship owners and private entrepreneurs. Moreover, the situations in which we can talk about public goods are sometimes circumstantial. Use of an open wireless Internet connection is indeed nonrivalrous while there is no congestion on the network, but if there are an excessive number of simultaneous connections, one person's "consumption" of the good diminishes its utility to others, who become "rivals" for the resources. Goods with problems of congestion are usually referred to as impure public goods.

In some cases, although the underlying structure *naturally* functions as a public good, uses can be developed that break up the public space into private spheres where access is restricted. If a beach is fenced, a toll is established on a highway or a television broadcast is scrambled, exclusion is possible. In these situations, they are referred to as *club goods*.

In the case of public goods, inefficient results come from the market's not being interested in offering these goods, because in a situation where people cannot be excluded, income would depend on the willingness of whoever is using the good to pay for it: how can you charge for the "right to see" a fireworks display? Moreover, opting for exclusion would generate inefficiencies: when a good is non-rivalrous, zero marginal cost is incurred by an additional individual to enjoy it. A second cause that may lead to inefficiency is the overexploitation of goods that would otherwise be public. Excessive use would not only make its consumption rival but could also lead, in an extreme case, to the disappearance or exhaustion of common-pool resources, such as forests or aquifers.

In search of efficiency in the provision of public goods, some theoretical works have assessed how they should be financed: each person who uses them should pay according to their marginal benefit (the Lindahl tax), thereby creating a market (with a single public offeror) that would yield a Pareto-efficient result. In practice, given that this benefit is not observable and therefore impossible to determine (take the example of the fireworks), individuals would have to voluntarily reveal the marginal benefit that they obtain from using the public good. Opportunistic attitudes (the existence of free riders) make such a procedure unfeasible: the one who wasn't willing to pay a single cent to illuminate a church altarpiece runs to see it when someone else introduces a coin and the lamps turn on.

Contemporarily, the concept of public goods has been extrapolated from the local to the global scale with the introduction of the concept of *global* public goods. Widespread peace, international economic stability and the eradication of epidemics would be global public goods because once obtained nobody would be excluded from their benefits and because they would be available all over the world. The truth is that some of these concepts, such as peace, are more desirable political objectives than goods that can be provided by the market.

READING 2.5   ARE THERE GLOBAL PUBLIC *BADS*? ASK KIRIBATI

If the water of a river is no longer suitable for bathing, the misfortune affects equally all those who used the river for that purpose, and the misfortune that this produces in a particular person should not make others happier or unhappier. If noises occur at night, all the inhabitants of the area where these noises are heard will suffer equally, and the insomnia of their neighbours will not comfort those who cannot sleep. In these examples, nobody is excluded from adversity and the disutility of one individual does not affect the disutility experienced by others (in that sense, "there is no rivalry" between the disutilities). Given these characteristics, can an analogy be drawn and say that there are public *bads*? Some texts do include this concept. However, it is not included often. In the preceding examples, the evil will have a cause, and that cause will be linked to an economic activity. That activity is therefore generating negative externalities, and this is the concept that seems most appropriate to use. If the cause is not an activity but a habit (the noise comes from many in the neighbourhood, who are vacuuming or playing the trombone in the early morning), we would enter again into the concept of externalities or perhaps of demerit goods (acts).

Having said that, we can take the liberty of talking about global public *bads*. If biodiversity on the planet is a global public good because its benefits are universal and also extend to future generations, global warming would be a global public *bad*, because its damages are equally universal and timeless.

A change in the planet's climate caused by human activity was announced by some scientists decades ago, although it has been absolutely evident since the 1980s. In the 50-year period from the first Earth Day in 1970 to 2020, the UN has calculated that the planet's average temperature increased by 0.86 degrees Celsius (33.5 Fahrenheit).[1] The consequences of this shift in climate patterns are manifold. One of the most obvious is the rise in the level of the oceans because of the melting of the ice sheets and the fracture of glaciers. The increase in temperature since 1970 has meant, again according to the UN, an average rise in the seas of 112 mm. The European Environment Agency has collected data from various studies and models to provide estimates of the rise in the oceans at the end of this century: it would be in the range of 0.29–0.59 m for a low emissions scenario and 0.61–1.10 m for a high emissions scenario.[2]

A few centimetres may seem insignificant, but in this case, those centimetres would have devastating consequences. Without precise data on the location of the world's population, another estimate gives the figure of 230 million people who would be living no more than 1 m above the high tide line.[3] The same paper says that, even taking a conservative scenario for future projections, sea levels in 2050 would leave households of between 140 million and 170 million people permanently below the high tide threshold. A large proportion of those affected would be living in Asian developing countries. However, if the relative population (percentage of the total country) were taken instead of the size of the affected population, many Pacific island countries would be at the top of these bleak forecasts. One of them, Kiribati, has the dubious honour of being considered the first country that would disappear under water if ocean flooding is not stopped.

Kiribati is made up of 33 atolls scattered along the line between Australia and Hawaii (only 21 of which are inhabited). The highest altitude of all the islands is just 80 m (262 ft), but on most of them, the maximum altitude is no more than 2 m (6 ft). For a country with this geography, a rising sea is its worst nightmare. That the threat is serious is shown by the fact that the two flattest islands of all (Tebua Tarawa and Abanuea, both uninhabited) were already swallowed up by the sea in 1999. The threat is also clear when a storm turns the sea rough: on those occasions, the waves increasingly penetrate inland, contaminating fresh water tanks, washing away crops and flooding homes.

The country's government is obviously the first to be aware of this threat, and apart from seeking temporary solutions (e.g. mangrove plantations and displacing villages along the coastline), in 2014 it bought a piece of land in the neighbouring country ("neighbouring" given the distances in the region) of Fiji. The purpose of the purchase is, for the time being, to develop crops there in a more secure manner but also, and above all, to have a place to evacuate the population if the situation becomes unsustainable (although this would require the agreement of the Fijian authorities because owning a piece of land does not mean having sovereignty over it).

We suspect that the Kiribati people are not interested in knowing whether every tonne of carbon dioxide emitted into the atmosphere should be considered a public *bad* or a case of negative externality. What they should really be concerned about is whether the international commitments to adopt a change in the production model will really pay off before they become neighbours of the god Neptune.

FIGURE 2.6 Sign in South Tarawa, capital of Kiribati[4]

1 United Nations (22 April 2020). *Fall in COVID-linked carbon emissions won't halt climate change—UN weather agency chief.* https://news.un.org/en/story/2020/04/1062332.

2 European Environment Agency (11 December 2020). *Global and European sea level rise*. https://www.eea.europa.eu/data-and-maps/indicators/sea-level-rise-7/ assessment.

3 Kulp, S.A., and Strauss, B.H. (2019). "New elevation data triple estimates of global vulnerability to sea-level rise and coastal flooding". *Nature Communications*, vol. 10, art. 4844.

4 Photograph by Erin Magee/DFAT (Department of Foreign Affairs and Trade. Australian Government) taken in 2011 and titled *As an extremely low-lying country, surrounded by vast oceans, Kiribati is at risk from the negative effects of climate change, such as sea-level rise and storm surges*. Downloaded from https://www.flickr.com/photos/dfataustralianaid/12426392094/.

5.1.2 Externalities

An externality exists when a specific activity affects other activities or individuals who do not directly participate in the first activity. Externalities can be positive, if the effect is beneficial, or negative, if they are harmful in some way. The most typical examples found in the literature are, respectively, the (somewhat-convoluted) case of the fruit tree plantation whose flowers are pollinated by the bees of a nearby beekeeper (although at the same time the bees extract nectar from flowers to feed on, which means the positive externality goes in both directions) and that of contaminating a river. Positive and negative externalities can coexist in some cases, and even affect the same subject: people living next to a tourist attraction may benefit from better maintained roads while also having problems finding parking; they would have access to a much-broader range of restaurants, but at higher prices than if it was not a tourist area.

In addition to the internal cost reflected on a company's ledger, the presence of externalities leads to a *social cost*. For example, opening various cocktail bars in a neighbourhood may favour certain businesses in the area (e.g. parking garages and takeout food shops), but it can negatively affect the people who live nearby. Ignoring the social cost of a good (whether positive or negative) will lead to its being produced either more than or less than is socially desirable, generating a deficient allocation of resources—that is, an inefficient situation. This could be resolved if the parties involved negotiated (thereby "internalizing" the externalities), as the Coase theorem proposes. But even if all the potential beneficiaries or injured parties could be identified, reaching agreements would be difficult, and if they were achieved, the transaction costs could exceed the benefits generated by eliminating the undesired external effects.

Today, network externalities, which are associated with the growth of the number of people who use a service, are gaining importance. There are direct and indirect network effects. Direct effects arise from the fact that each new user benefits from access to the set of pre-existing users but at the same time supposes a new possibility of (real or potential) contact for the base of users who are already subscribed. This is clearly the case for the telephone and social networks. The indirect effects result from an increase in the quality or quantity of the service or associated services; the increase is greater the more users there are to allow the novelty or improvement to be capitalized. This is the case also for applications and programs that are developed to run on popular operating systems (and not on others) and for the frequency of service on heavily used bus routes.

READING 2.6 A TEXTBOOK CASE OF AN (IMMORAL, NOT AMORAL) EXTERNALITY

In 1996, approximate 3,500 residents of the US city of Anniston filed a class-action lawsuit against the Monsanto Company and its subsidiary Solutia, Inc. They argued that for decades the company had contaminated the city's environment with polychlorinated biphenyls (PCBs) and fully knew of the problems that it was causing and would cause but did not inform the community of the dangers.

Because of its low flammability, compounds with PCBs had been used as insulating fluids in transformers, circuit breakers, capacitors and thermostats; in the composition of oils used in the petrochemical industry; and in other activities that posed fire hazards. Since 1935, when it bought the company that had started selling them in 1927, Monsanto had a near monopoly over the commercial production of PCBs until 1977, when they were banned. Throughout those decades, the plant released close to 50,000 tons of PCBs a year into a nearby river and buried or released into the atmosphere around a million tons of toxic waste.

The lawyers of the plaintiffs carried out various analyses of the air, soil and even the dust in homes, finding levels 1,000 to 2,000 times over safety thresholds, despite the fact that the plant had closed 20 years earlier. Equally astronomical levels of PCBs were found in blood samples taken from residents. Residents of the areas surrounding Anniston were diagnosed with tumours and other illnesses far above national averages. In the past, PCBs had been included on the lists of the most harmful chemical compounds. At the time of the lawsuit, their use had already been banned for years almost everywhere in the world.

In the end, the trial did not reach a verdict, because the company settled out of court for $700 million ($600 million in cash, and the rest to cover the costs of various clean-up, prescription drug, and other programmes) in order "to concentrate our efforts on our agricultural business, while removing an area of great uncertainty for our shareowners and employees related to our contingent liabilities".

During the trial, many of the company's internal documents were declassified and came to light, some marked as "confidential: read and destroy", advice which, fortunately for the plaintiffs and anybody who wants to know the truth, was not always followed. The record of events hidden by the company that was revealed in those documents is horrifying. When it bought the plant, it already knew that the product "cannot be considered non-toxic". Shortly after, around 1937, a Harvard study found that prolonged exposure could cause liver damage and rashes; Monsanto then hired the scientist who led the study as a consultant, and the issue was swept away. The number of times the company was warned of possible or real problems continued to grow, without its taking any actions (but making comments like "there is no point in going to expensive extremes in limiting discharges") or even providing information about the hazards; in one case, it warned its clients of some of the dangers, but not the community. Of all these episodes, two stand out. One is the story of a resident of Anniston who decades later continued to wonder why one day a man from the Monsanto plant had offered to buy his pigs (for ten dollars apiece, plus a bottle of whiskey), those pigs whose mouths had turned green for some unknown reason. The second, truly shocking, happened when the company itself hired a biologist to conduct some studies around its Anniston plant. The biologist arrived with tanks full of fish, which he submerged at various points along nearby creeks in which Monsanto dumped its waste: they immediately went belly up, looking like "they had been dunked in battery acid".

Just a few years later, at the end of the 1960s, when concern regarding the effects of PCBs was a hot topic in the national media (traces of PCBs had been found all over the country, throughout the food chain, in pine needles, in wild animals and even in some children's hair), Monsanto began to prepare for a media war but also to control its production since "it only seems a matter of time before the regulatory agencies will be looking down our throats". Its idea, declared in internal documents, was to maintain one of its most profitable businesses as long as possible while taking care to "reduce our exposure in terms of liability".

When it stopped producing PCBs, the company would surely have liked to have closed the door on the issue and never open it again, but in this case, it was forced to do so almost 20 years later. This is not usually the case. In many similar cases, the door of impunity is closed, and no key can open it.[1]

1 Many news items and reports were read to prepare this reading. The three major sources are an article from the *New York Times*, written for the *Associated Press* and published on 21 August 2003 ("$700 million settlement in Alabama PCB lawsuit"—which can be found at https://www.nytimes.com/2003/08/21/business/700-million-settlement-in-alabama-pcb-lawsuit.html); a *Washington Post* article written by Michael Grunwald and published on 1 January 2002 ("Monsanto hid decades of pollution"— which can be found at https://www.commondreams.org/headlines02/0101-02.htm); and a third article, by the *Nation*, written by Nancy Beiles and published on 11 May 2000 ("What Monsanto knew"—which can be found at https://www.thenation.com/article/what-monsanto-knew/).

5.2 Market situation

5.2.1 Imperfect competition

Perfect competition is necessary to generate efficient results. The problem is that markets with perfect competition are fictitious, in that the conditions needed to achieve it are impossible to meet in practice. In the real world, various kinds of obstacles to developing competition violate each of these conditions: differentiated (non-uniform) products, imperfect information, large producers influential enough to hinder the actions of their rivals or a need for previous investments. The prevailing situation in real markets is that of businesses' trying to gain customer loyalty by offering products that are not identical to others that have a similar function (products that are differentiated even more by publicity, which complicates objective comparison) and using every advantage that they can as a barrier to entry for potential competitors. In practice, therefore, almost all markets have imperfect competition. Or, seen another way, almost all markets are subject to market failure.

Because the range of possibilities is enormous, spanning every situation between perfect competition and monopoly, the problem lies in deciding when the failure in competition is significant enough to generate inefficiency. In addition, markets are dynamic, and circumstances change. In this sense, we must interpret how long (how "reasonable") the waiting period should be until we assess whether the obstacles to developing "sufficient" competition are disappearing.

Natural monopolies enter into the category of imperfect competition, although they are occasionally cited as independent market failures. Natural monopolies are often identified with large industries in which elevated fixed costs must be incurred in order to produce at relatively small marginal costs, which causes average total costs to continuously decline. Most agree that the sewage system or railroad network cannot be duplicated, but many disagree on whether the same is true for some Internet services (or whether it will be true as their fixed costs grow). But also, natural monopolies manifest in geographically restricted activities that supposedly lack space, because of the demand and costs, for two companies. How would two cafés survive in a town of 200 people? The competition would end up forcing one, or perhaps both, to close.

The market structure *per se* does not generate a market failure. The failure may lie in the result to which such a structure could lead: one single bicycle rental shop's existing on an island is not a problem; it would be a problem, however, if the shop owner took advantage of the fact that it was the only source of bicycles to set exorbitant prices or abusive conditions.

5.2.2 Incomplete markets

In this case, the problem is not that the market structure is far from perfect competition. It is merely that nobody provides the service to certain potential users. Speaking strictly in terms of efficiency, incomplete markets exist only when the cost of satisfying this unmet demand is less than what those requesting the product are willing to pay. A grocery store may be perfectly viable in remote villages that contain ageing populations, but it may not exist, simply because nobody wants to run a business in that setting.

5.2.3 Information failures

Strictly speaking, information failures are another of the causes leading to imperfect competition. The reason why it is considered an independent market failure comes from its special importance and because it also affects the demand side, in contrast to the other "imperfections" associated with the supply side.

If information is incomplete or scarce, the producer might not use the most appropriate factors or not reach all those demanding the product, and thus, consumers cannot choose the product or provider best suited to their needs. Choosing between products is especially difficult when the information is convoluted (as is the case with many financial products), when it is difficult to compare (packaged offers that include various telecommunication or television services) or when its acquisition is quite costly (customers must spend a great deal of time until they *understand* the differences between washing machines). A particular case is that of "goods that must be tried", which require previous experience in order to completely appreciate their value: consumer unawareness could reduce potential demand.

When information is asymmetrical, the parties have different knowledge on a specific fact and the better-informed party can use it to its advantage. An unscrupulous taxi driver may overcharge a person who has just arrived in the country and doesn't have a way to estimate the approximate cost of the trip. Information asymmetries can lead to various inefficient situations. Two of them have been formalized as specific categories:

- *Adverse selection* describes a situation in which a market is captured by goods/ clients/producers that the other party would not have chosen if they had had all the information. This occurs because one of the parties, who is unable to discern the quality of the goods (or the "quality of the clients"), is willing to pay (accept) an average price. This average price is low for the high-quality product, which "escapes" from the market, but high for the bad product, which "is attracted" by that price. Alternatively, the price is expensive for the type of client desired by the business but attractive to a client who could be considered problematic. The examples always cited by textbooks include, first, a health insurance policy that would mostly bought by those with the greatest probability of needing it and, second, a used goods market, in which many of the goods on offer have hidden defects (the market for "lemons"). Other examples include offering judges (or other high-level public servants) a salary in accordance with their category as a way of avoiding that the position is occupied mainly by lawyers (or politicians) who, regardless of their desire to serve society, do not believe that they are capable of obtaining a higher salary in private business.

• *Moral hazard* can occur when someone bears the costs of an action of another, an action that is not observable to the first person. People might take on more risks, or even be tempted to commit fraud, when they do not have to assume the possible negative consequences of their actions. An individual might drive more recklessly in a rented vehicle if covered by full risk insurance; some might even simulate an accident if the policy includes compensation. A bank might demand fewer guarantees from clients for a mortgage if the bank trusts that the central bank will bail it out if its debts mount and its position becomes untenable.

READING 2.7   INTERNET PLATFORMS: AN OBSTACLE TO COMPETITION?

When the dematerialization of economic exchanges was at its earlier stages, it was said that it would contribute to increased competition. In markets without geographical barriers, any buyer could contact any seller free of charge and vice versa. However, when that gleaming future became reality, the image turned out to be different. In most digital markets, one or a limited set of intermediary platforms clearly dominates the market. These platforms have grown so much that they have almost taken over the top positions in the global list of companies with the largest capitalization; the best known among them obtain annual revenues similar to the GDP of a medium-size country.

How have they reached this size? Let us take the United Kingdom as an example: before the COVID-19 pandemic, UK Internet users were spending an average of three hours and 24 minutes each day online; in April 2020, while most people were confined to their homes, the time increased by 32 minutes a day, to nearly four hours. Of their total online time, 83% was spent on the top 1,000 properties, although 50% of total time was spent browsing on the top ten properties, and just the first two account for 37% of the time (24% on Google sites and 13% on Facebook sites); a simple calculation tells us that Google (its branded services, plus YouTube) attracted the attention of every UK Internet user for an average of almost an hour a day.[1]

Given this situation, these platforms seem to be in a position to interfere with the development of competition in the digital markets. Is this really the case? If the answer is yes, should their activity be controlled, and if so, how?

Not all online platforms have similar features, nor do they adopt the same business model. They share, however, many peculiarities that potentially

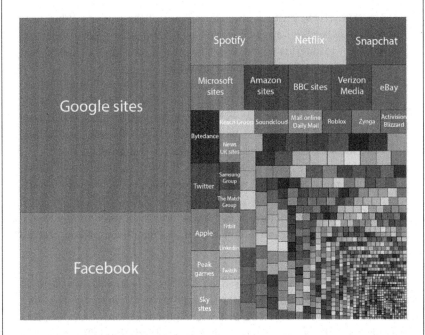

FIGURE 2.7 The distribution of time spent by UK Internet consumers on the top 1,000 online properties (February 2020)[2]

invalidate the way competition is currently assessed. At least five of these characteristics are transcendent:

1   The first of these lies in the role of these platforms as intermediaries. Looking for a *real-world* analogy, they have managed to become the owners of the main street that absolutely everyone walks down, so any company that wants visibility is obliged to rent a window on that street. Consequently, their market power is exercised on what in economic jargon is called "both sides of the market"—that is, both with consumers and with the companies that wish to contact those consumers.

2   The second is that many of the services offered to end users are free. This makes using the methods employed by the competition authorities on the basis of hypotheses of what would happen if the price were raised by a certain percentage impossible. But they have a price, even if it is not monetary. As the saying goes, if you are not paying for the product, you are the product. And in fact, personal data are the most valuable asset for many of these companies, because they can be used to personalize services and for many marketing activities, specifically to target the advertising that is served to users (see Reading 4.1).

3   The third characteristic is the diffuse limits of the markets. What does a social network or a search engine sell? If they really compete for our attention to offer us advertising, then in the context of a competition analysis, do they belong to the same market ?

4   The fourth, linked to the previous one, is that, because of their nature, cost structure and present dominant position (enjoying the trust of the users and, don't forget, having their data), extending the scope of their business by offering consumers new products that in some way complement the original ones is relatively easy for the platforms.

5   The fifth and last is the speed with which digital markets evolve. Given the time required to enact legal and regulatory procedures, the law frequently lags behind social reality. But in these rapidly changing markets, a much greater risk looms in that by the time legal solutions are found, the problems have ceased to exist or their effects have already become impossible to reverse.

Accepting the challenges posed by all these constraints, competition authorities have continuously put these platforms in the crosshairs. The European Commission has adopted a belligerent attitude towards them for years; in Reading 4.2, the fines imposed on Big Tech are listed. The United States had not shown the same degree of concern, but at the end of July 2020, the leaders of Amazon, Apple, Facebook and Google were asked to testify before the US House's top antitrust committee in a process that aimed to decide whether they were abusing their market power. It was followed by a Congressional Committee report, published in October, which gave a positive answer to this question, describing several anticompetitive practices; the end of the process, however, still seemed a long way off. Even in China, somewhat unexpectedly, an investigation into the giant Alibaba for suspicious monopoly practices was opened on Christmas 2020.

These actions are far from being unanimously supported. Many believe that digital markets would not be so extraordinarily innovative if the activities of these companies that are today Internet giants had been controlled when they were startups. They argue that the dynamics of the market itself will eventually bring down the current leaders and replace them with others, as has happened in the past. This scenario is possible, but the truth is that markets have now reached a degree of maturity never seen in the past, and these companies now have the *financial muscle* to quickly absorb any company that presents even a hint of future competition. At the very least, we should ask ourselves, where is the perfect competition that the markets should tend to generate on their own?

The possible regulation of online platforms is a long-standing issue. With increasingly digital economies and societies, their influence is growing all the time. Two news items related to Facebook, the scandal regarding the use of data by Cambridge Analytica and the proposed creation of its cryptocurrency diem (formerly libra) are excellent examples of why the role of the state in the control of online platforms might not be limited to the analysis of competition.

1 UK Competition and Markets Authority. *Online platforms and digital advertising— Market study final report.* July 2020. https;//www.gov.uk/cma-cases/online-plat forms-and-digital-advertising-market-study#final-report. The data are taken from the *Comscore MMX Multiplatform survey. Total Digital Population, desktop aged 6+, mobile aged 13+* conducted in February 2020 by Comscore.
2 The figure, taken from the report cited earlier, is from Comscore.

6 Reasons unrelated to efficiency in *specific markets*

The previous section examined situations that called into question the market mechanism's ability to generate efficient results in specific markets. However, another reason would still justify public economic activity, even if the market did lead to efficiency: the existence of socially desirable goods that society tries to support or encourage (merit goods) or protect (protected goods).

6.1 Merit goods

A merit good is a commodity or service that the state deems "positive" and, therefore, tries to promote. Some examples are education, attending artistic events or children's consuming fruits and vegetables. On many occasions, the consumption of a certain good is not the final objective, but rather, the good is a "necessary tool" to enjoy other goods or to achieve different objectives. In the case of vegetables, what is pursued is improved health among children and, by extension, achieving savings on future health services. Other examples include promoting Internet access for everyone (which is only a way of providing access to the public good that is information or, more broadly speaking, knowledge) or the mandatory use of seat belts in cars. The opposite of merit goods are demerit goods, whose consumption must be discouraged or even prohibited. This is the case of drugs or, recently in some countries, sugar-sweetened beverages.

Some authors believe that these are cases of "consumer myopia", in which consumers are unable to adequately assess their own interest; in this sense, merit goods would be exceptions to the premise that individuals themselves are in the best position to maximize their own welfare in accordance with their present income. The consumption of certain demerit goods can even be considered irrational behaviour. For example, despite being perfectly informed regarding the possible adverse health effects of smoking tobacco, many individuals continue to do so. In any case, it is more adequate to think that in merit (or demerit) goods, public judgement differs from private judgement: an interest can be attributed to the community as a whole that doesn't result from merely adding individual interests.

Merit goods are placed in a different category among the possible justifications for public action because the argument presented in the previous paragraph has nothing to do with the market's capacity or incapacity to provide these goods efficiently. In spite of this, it is not unusual to find merit goods in the category of market failures, because some consider them to merely be a case in which externalities are present; however, this requires defining externalities in such a broad and loose way (*social* externalities?) that they would not meet the rigorous economic definition provided earlier.

6.2 Protected goods

Some goods are not provided by the market, because it is not efficient to do so. A documentary on an historical episode of a country, an auteur movie and a movie filmed in an ethnic minority language will not earn at the box office enough to recover the cost of making them. These movies are not public goods (anyone who does not pay for a ticket is excluded), and they do not generate externalities (again considered in a strictly economic sense). Their creation has nothing to do with equity. Neither are they merit goods, because the public interest is not served by its massive consumption, but rather, value lies in the very existence of these works: in fact, the state could subsidize only its production and not a plan to encourage its viewing.

Conversely, other goods would be destroyed by the market. Leaving two centenary trees standing on a plot of land where a building is to be constructed or to restore the façade of an old building that is still standing is not efficient. Just as in the example in the previous paragraph, none of the reasons that would support public activity described thus far is applicable in these cases, but even so, the state could intervene and obligate companies to respect such goods. Moreover, in some cases, it could do this even at the expense of or over other arguments that suggest the opposite. Whaling may be efficient (if the whales are not hunted, the meat, blubber and skin of the whale are "idle resources") and be supported in terms of equity (the whale hunters would be unemployed and have few opportunities to find new work in the possibly depressed areas in which they live), but even so, a country may prohibit whaling simply for the *uneconomic* reason of protecting an endangered species.

7 Reasons to act versus need to act

For the majority of schools of thought in modern economics, and for most governments, efficiency is the primary objective of an economy. The market could be the means by which this objective is reached, but only under certain conditions, which in practice cannot exist. If it doesn't meet the required conditions, the result of an *imperfect* market's activity could be inferior (in terms of efficiency) to what is achieved in other kinds of *imperfect* markets and even to what is attained by organizing the economy in a different way. Recent historical experiences with alternatives to the market have ended up failing, which is why the market continues to almost universally be the primary mechanism to allocate resources and products. So we must decide what kind of imperfect market is preferable, and given that we have no theoretical criteria to help us make this decision, the door is open to corrective public activity that seeks to improve results that are sure to be inefficient.

As we have seen, public action is theoretically justified by market failures (i.e., failures of *the market* or of *specific markets*), criteria based on morals and equity and the consideration that some goods are socially desirable. That said, we have no criteria for sorting these causes, and finding a remedy that fits each case is even less likely. In fact, we cannot even affirm that acting is necessary: *finding justification* for action does not imply an *obligation* to act. Economic theory is fairly unanimous in admitting the existence of market failures (at least some of the ones described here), but agreement disappears when deciding on what kind of corrective action should be taken by the public sector. However, whatever action is taken cannot be inconsistent with the conclusions reached from analysing the situation of the market (of specific markets). The timeliness and magnitude of public activity should be in line with the intensity with which the motives appear and which of them is predominant. Ultimately, this means that, regardless of political or ideological ideas on the role of the state in the economy, every coherent opinion put forth in the debate on whether public action is justified and of the characteristics of any action taken should be preceded by an examination and appraisal of the reasons that back it, the reasons of the *why* behind the (possible) action. This said, in real markets, the assessment that was just demanded can be (in fact is) more complex than what is posited by strictly theoretical models. The analysis carried out is based on a series of axioms and conditions that should be analysed in greater detail:

- First, markets with perfect competition have been assumed to produce the most efficient results. Beyond the near impossibility of finding this market model in real situations, the comparison between the outcome obtained by different forms of market is based on the supposition that in every case the same production technique is used, when in reality large monopolistic or oligopolistic companies can have access to more resources or different technologies and be more efficient (at least on the production side) than a group of small companies can be.
- The second remark affects the definition of efficiency itself. The condition of efficiency in the Pareto sense is too strict (a reallocation that goes beyond an exchange in which nobody is adversely affected is difficult to imagine), which makes it unwieldy. Welfare economics has developed different compensation criteria or tests to choose between two alternative states. The most used is the Kaldor–Hicks (or Scitovsky) criterion based on "potential compensation": an outcome is considered more efficient if those who are made better off could compensate those who are made worse off and even so still be beneficial for them (Kaldor criterion) or if those that are made worse off cannot "bribe"

those who are better off so that the latter do not make the change (Hicks criterion). The problem is knowing beforehand (with no real negotiation) what compensation would be accepted. Therefore, applying this criterion in practice is not a simple task.

- Finally, the theoretical formulations of the various concepts used are much simpler (and elegant) than their practical formulations. For instance, externalities are difficult to assess (sometimes extraordinarily so) and establishing what are socially desirable merit goods is also problematic. Even after organizing a national consultation, deducing a formula that allows for knowing the exact level of redistribution that is desirable or what specific practices are rejected by society would not be straightforward. A final example of the practical constraints is that, as mentioned, no rule stipulates *how imperfect* competition must be in order to be considered a problem.

The final conclusion is that establishing *why* public action should be taken is much easier than deciding *how* and on the basis of what *justification*. Put another way, there is far more agreement that the state could act than on how it actually should act and, if it does, what the scope of its action should be and what tools should be employed. How this controversy is reflected in political thought is crucial. Because the market economy is almost universally accepted to be the only option to organize economic life, the level of state action ("the public weight") is what differentiates some ideologies (or perhaps better talk of political orientations) from others.

Summary

This chapter examines the reasons why the state assumes (or at least could assume) certain functions in the development of economic activity. As a starting point, the results generated by the market are evaluated. The two fundamental theorems of welfare economics demonstrate, first, that under certain conditions the market achieves an efficient outcome and, second, that the final distribution of resources can be whatever is considered optimal. However, in practice, the conditions required for these theorems to come true never occur, which provides theoretical support for government action. Support can also be found in reasons other than efficiency, as society might demand certain values to be defended or certain situations to be corrected, regardless of whether such actions will lead to an economically efficient position.

If the real activity of *the market* (understood as a black box containing all *specific markets*) is evaluated, the conclusion is that the results are not generally efficient, given that some resources are wasted and historically there have always been periods of instability and crisis. Moreover, the market model needs rules to be enforced for it to function properly, and in the long term, the model can be unsustainable because efficiency does not imply that resources will be conserved. Beyond efficiency, the market does not respect the moral criteria that society may agree on, and how it distributes wealth is usually far from any standard of equity.

If the activity of *specific markets* is evaluated, sometimes circumstances arise in them that suggest that its result is (could be) more efficient. This includes the impossibility, or at least difficulty, in actually creating the market (public goods), the impact the activity has on third parties (externalities), the existence of companies with the power to manipulate prices (competition failures), the lack of supply in certain places (incomplete markets) and problems in the flow of information. Another reason for public action, this time not related to efficiency, is the existence of goods and services that are socially desirable, either because their consumption generates greater social well-being than the sum of individual utilities (merit goods) or because society wants them to be preserved (protected goods).

Finally, it needs to be stressed that just because states have a *catalogue* of reasons that theoretically justify public activity in the economy does not mean that they will always feel obligated to act.

Overview

The objectives of this chapter were as follows:

- To help the reader understand the fundamental theorems of welfare economics.
- To describe and analyse reasons for which market activity is censurable.
- To examine failures of *the market* (understood as a model for organizing economic activity), such as a lack of autonomy to make sure obligations are met, inefficient and unsustainable results.
- To classify and analyse failures of *specific markets*, such as public goods, externalities, imperfect competition, incomplete markets and information failures.
- To analyse the reasons for public action not related to efficiency, such as equity, amorality and socially desirable goods.

Self-assessment questions

The self-assessment questions are meant to evaluate how well you have understood the information presented in this chapter.

1   The second theorem of welfare economics demonstrates which of the following?

    a   Any competitive equilibrium in the market is Pareto efficient.

    b   Any competitive equilibrium in the market always leads to a fixed final distribution of resources.

    c   Each possible initial allocation of resources leads to a competitive equilibrium.

    d   Each possible initial allocation of resources leads to the preferred final distribution of resources.

2 Which one of the following answers is correct?

    a   If static efficiency exists, dynamic efficiency must also exist.
    b   If dynamic efficiency exists, static efficiency must also exist.
    c   If static efficiency exists, dynamic efficiency cannot exist.
    d   Static and dynamic efficiency could be mutually exclusive.

3 Public goods are _____

    a   Owned by the state.
    b   Those whose owner is unknown or nonexistent.
    c   Those in which exclusion is impossible and consumption is nonrivalrous.
    d   All the above.

4 In a nightclub that is not properly soundproofed, a negative externality is suffered by whom?

    a   Clients of the bar.
    b   Employees of the bar.
    c   Neighbours living in the apartments located above the bar in the same building.
    d   All the above.

5 Situations in which a market is captured by goods/clients/producers that the other part would not have chosen if they had had all available information are referred to as what?

    a   Induced risk.
    b   Adverse selection.
    c   Risk of ignorance.
    d   Imperfect competition.

Questions for reflection

The answers to the following questions are not in the text; they require you to search for additional information or to apply to real cases what you have learned in this chapter.

1 Do you agree that improving equity is a reason for government action in the economy? If you answer yes, how far should redistribution go?
2 Some digital economy markets contain companies who have a monopoly (or near monopoly). Is this best for consumers? Is action necessary, or at least advisable, to be taken in those markets in order to remedy the situation and try to increase competition?
3 Find examples of externalities that affect your daily life in some way.

3

OBJECTIVES OF STATE ECONOMIC ACTIVITY

1 Introduction: types of objectives

At the end of the fiscal year, the ministers of economy of every country present their government's objectives for the following year. These objectives are specified in *macroeconomic forecasts* of the economy. The indicators on which these forecasts are based make the headlines every month or trimester, whenever the statistics offices publish data about their actual evolution during that period. In this state of affairs, everyone runs the risk of being convinced of *how important it is for the country* for the GDP to grow or to contain inflation.

But it is not. What is important for a society is (or should be) the welfare of its members (all of them) and maintaining the values that sustain the existence of the society itself. These aims cannot be achieved separately from the economy, because the economy is an integral part of social life. Therefore, these are also (or should be) the main or ultimate objectives of public activity in the economy.

However, these objectives are hard to get a handle on, because they are vague. "Welfare" or "values" are concepts that are difficult to define and impossible to measure, so they must be clarified by using other variables. This is where all the indicators elaborated by national statistics offices come into play. Such indicators are quantitative, so their evolution can be studied and compared to that of other countries' indicators. These are derived objectives.

These derived objectives do not appear, however, on the list of goals prepared by those in charge of monitoring or correcting specific areas of economic activity. Their job is not to achieve GDP growth but rather, for example, to ensure that the rights of financial services clients are respected. These third level objectives are referred to as immediate objectives. These *day-to-day* actions lay the foundation to obtaining the higher objectives.

DOI: 10.4324/9781003173731-3

2 Ultimate objectives

2.1 Improving well-being: growth and employment

Oxford dictionary defines *well-being* as "the state of being comfortable, healthy or happy". That the state is concerned with making sure that its citizens are "comfortable, healthy or happy" seems like not only a legitimate objective for its activity but an essential one. The obvious problem is to determine what it exactly means *to be comfortable, healthy or happy*. Therefore, a much more precise definition of *well-being* is needed to make this objective obtainable.

Economics has provided some possible answers, with roots in philosophy. The orthodox or dominant approach at the moment ties the concept of well-being or welfare to that of utility. Individuals are better off the more utility they obtain from their activities, especially the utility obtained from consuming goods and services. Utility corresponds to the pleasure or happiness felt in that particular situation. This concept cannot be measured, but it can be ordered. Given the choice between two situations, individuals are able to select the one that provides them the greatest utility, which allows them to create a ranking if they have more than two options. The goodness of each situation depends exclusively on the utility that it offers, putting aside considerations unrelated to the sphere of their self-interest (ethical or altruistic motives). In this sense, all subjects are *Homo economicus* (they behave rationally and are selfish).

Defining the well-being of individuals is already a complicated first step. The second step is even more complex: defining the welfare of a society and determining what situation is preferable when selecting between two options that put different individuals in different situations. We must choose when neither of the situations is better than the other, in the Pareto sense (i.e. in neither situation are all individuals *at least* equal to how they are in the other; if it were true in one of them, the choice would be evident). Various solutions have been provided, and the following are the most common:

- According to the Rawlsian approach (named in honour of John Rawls, who posited that social welfare is determined by the well-being of the person who is worst off), an action that improves the welfare of everyone except for the poorest person would leave the function of social welfare unaltered. That is why the function that formalizes this postulate is based on the maximin principle (maximizes the situation of the minimum).
- Utilitarianism or Benthamism (in honour of Jeremy Bentham, one of the architects of utilitarianism) follows the rule of *the best for the majority*. This means that the function used for selection is based on the sum of all the individual utilities. Because it is merely addition, all individuals are equal. Therefore, the social situation reached is the same when either the wealthiest individual or the poorest individual in the society has an identical increase in their utility.

By focusing completely or not at all on the specific situation of the individual who is worst off, these two concepts represent the extremes of all possible combinations that can be formed by assigning different values to the situations of individuals.

Yet, despite being fundamental to developing any theory, particularly in welfare economics, that any social welfare function imaginable could serve as a policy objective is doubtful, precisely because social welfare functions are based on the concept of utility. Utility depends on the circumstances of each subject, and increasing or maximizing utility is an exceedingly vague criterion.

This is why welfare is not named as the final objective. Instead, it's been substituted by economic growth. When the economy grows, it has more goods and services than it had before. In principle, this means an increase in the utility of those individuals who enjoy them and, by extension, of society as a whole. We added "in principle" because growth does not necessarily mean that all the old goods are maintained and new ones are added; it might be the case that the quantity of some diminishes, although in this case, the quantities of others must increase enough for the final tally to be positive. If the composition of goods varies, the utilities also vary, but not necessarily proportionally, as the marginal utility is a decreasing function. The first automobile owned provides much more utility than the second, which in turn provides more than the third and so on, until a point is reached in which one more unit almost does not increase utility at all (except in the case of a collector, nobody who has six cars increases their well-being much if they purchase a seventh). Inversely, utility does not vary in the same way if an automobile is "taken away" from someone who has three as it would if it was taken away by someone who has only one. If we take away an individual's only car and give two to someone who has already three, it may be that the loss of utility to the first person is in absolute terms greater, even much greater, than the utility gained by the second. Using any welfare function that adds utilities, social welfare would have diminished even with growth (an extra car is now in the economy).

Despite this important caveat and bearing in mind the unmanageability of the concept of utility, when economic growth occurs, it is taken as a given that social welfare improves. In this way, economic growth is the final (and often priority) objective that states pursue in their economic activity.

That said, and although most governments seem to be satisfied as long as the growth indicator increases year after year, the causes and consequences of growth are extraordinarily important factors. The type of activities on which growth is based, the conditions in which those activities are carried out and the impact that they generate can create radically different scenarios for the same increase in the economy. *Stable* (in the sense of permanent but also balanced) and *sustainable* are two adjectives that must be added to growth.

Complementary to the objective of growth is job creation. Although again quibbles could be made and situations could easily be imagined in which the following is not so, growth usually implies an increase in jobs. However, like growth, increasing employment should not be an unconditional objective. The characteristics of the employment count, and quite a lot, not only for the strictly economic function of employment but also for its social functions.

READING 3.1 IS GDP PER CAPITA A GOOD WAY TO MEASURE WELFARE?

The website Our World in Data gives us an answer by creating a graphic that shows GDP per capita and a measurement of life satisfaction[1] (with data from 2015). Figure 3.1 reproduces this graphic. The data on GDP per capita, taken from the World Bank, are in US dollars, normalized using purchasing power parity as a conversion factor and taking 2011 as reference. Satisfaction data was taken from a Gallup world poll that researched how satisfied those surveyed were with their lives, on a scale from 0 to 10 (10 being the highest possible life satisfaction) with just one question: "Please imagine a ladder with steps numbered from 0 at the bottom to 10 at the top. Suppose we say that the top of the ladder represents the best possible life for you, and the bottom of the ladder represents the worst possible life for you. On which step of the ladder would you say you personally feel you stand at this time?" Obviously, this is not the best way of measuring welfare, but if we had a variable that made measuring it easy, we wouldn't be interested in knowing if we could replace it with GDP per capita.

The shape of the cloud of dots indicates a correlation between the two variables, allowing us to give a preliminary answer: yes, generally speaking, the higher the GDP per capita, the happier people are. But many factors can condition this conclusion:

- The first is suggested by the extremes of the graphic: below $5,000, not even a 5 in satisfaction is reached; on the other end, no country above $30,000 is below a 5. Therefore, when there are no resources to lead a dignified life, it's impossible to be happy; when you have more than enough, you're at least moderately satisfied with your life.
- The second is that this apparent correlation hides a disparity. At nearly equal income, a Tajik is more satisfied with their life than a Tanzanian; a Guatemalan seems much happier than a Ukrainian or a Georgian; a Panamanian is more satisfied than a Croat or a Portuguese person; and a Fin reports greater satisfaction than someone in Britain or France.
- The third factor is that the correlation simply doesn't exist in many cases: a Moldavian or a Nicaraguan is much happier than many people in countries whose GDP per capita is up to five or six times greater; with a third of the money, a Costa Rican is just as happy as a Belgian; an inhabitant of Sierra Leone, living well below the minimum income level, feels just as satisfied as a Bulgarian who has 12 times the first's income.
- The fourth is the existence of sharp interregional differences: Latin American countries seem to always be happier than others with the same income (Central Americans even more so than South Americans); on the

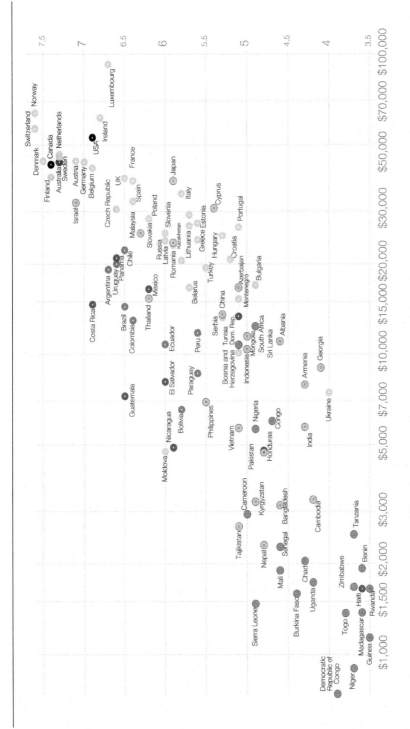

FIGURE 3.1 GDP per capita vs self-reported life satisfaction (2015)

other extreme, Asians have a worse impression about their lives, not only than people from the Americas but also than Europeans; finally, in Africa, there are not enough observations above minimum subsistence to talk about optimism or pessimism.
- The fifth and final factor points to the also notable intraregional differences: with similar low economic resources, Dominicans are much less happy than Colombians, Brazilians or Costa Ricans; in Europe, the Portuguese are less satisfied with their lives than the entire group of countries with a similar GDP, a group headed by Czech Republic, which is nearly 1.5 points higher than Portugal on the satisfaction scale.

All this makes defending, without reservations, GDP per capita untenable as a measure of welfare. Instead, a pragmatic stance should be taken: lacking a better indicator, it's a reasonable substitute.

An additional problem, which cannot be seen in the figure but which is studied in the chapter, is the limitations involved in the construction and interpretation of GDP. As an example, in the right corner, Ireland appears among the richest countries (but not among the happiest). Reading 3.3 explains why this shouldn't be its position.

1 https://ourworldindata.org/happiness-and-life-satisfaction.

2.2 Allocation/redistribution

The definition adopted for social welfare is not neutral in regard to how *social justice* is interpreted. This is evident in how the least fortunate are treated in the Rawlsian function. But except for in that function (or similar ones that can be imagined), social welfare functions aggregate the well-being of every individual, thus hiding individual situations. If we think of a function that adds individual utilities (even with different weights), we could reach the same final result with different combinations. Therefore, some criterion must order these options. This leads us to the fundamental question of whether an optimal composition of different individual welfares exists—that is, if a certain criterion of equity allows us to decide between unequal distributions of the goods and services available in the economy. The question that immediately follows is whether some redistribution process should be undertaken if the situation isn't optimal. The answer to these two questions cannot be provided by economic theory; it can be provided only by the political process by which a society decides what should be done.

Despite this, as in the case of welfare, a *manageable* approach is necessary to understand what equity involves and, therefore, what redistribution involves. The concept is further clarified when equity is depicted in terms of horizontal and vertical equity. Horizontal equity is *treating equals equally*: those who are in the same situation (e.g. training, motivation and effort) should receive the same. The principle is clear despite the difficulty involved in identifying who are *equals*. On the other hand, applying vertical equity allows those who are not equals to be treated unequally. The door to redistribution is opened by allowing different categories to be treated differently. Almost without exception, modern states accept both equity criteria: two people who have the same income (obtained in similar fashions) pay the same income tax, but the rate applied usually increases as income increases.

A different focus assesses the equity of the process rather than the equity of the results. If the rules of the economy are fair, the results that it generates must be accepted regardless of what they are. This rule has been used frequently, dating back to the work of Robert Nozick, to justify the *minimal state*. But the rule itself is not incompatible with the active role of the state, although when trying to introduce social justice criteria, the state should not act a posteriori (redistribution) but rather a priori (on the allocation).

A further step in specifying redistribution/allocation as a goal for state economic action is to determine if not the degree of inequality that is admissible then the limit of inequality that should not be surpassed. Again, there have been various contributions in this area. According to John Rawls, equality refers to *primary social goods*: "the things that every rational man desires". This interpretation, which focuses on the result and not on the process, is related to the definition of fundamental rights. Amartya Sen's definition of *equity* focuses on allocation, in that it talks about the equality of "core capacities", a notion that isn't concerned with capabilities as an end in themselves but rather with their *impact* on the individual. Within this meaning, equity consists not in guaranteeing that every individual reaches a specific social or economic level but rather in ensuring the effective possibility or real opportunity for an individual to attain it. Although it may seem more flexible than the concept of primary social goods, Sen himself acknowledges that it is difficult to apply because it is also tied to cultural conventions.

These criteria can be used as a conceptual rule for action. But the specification problem persists: of course they are not valid to establish objectives, but even if this were possible, measuring how near or far we are from achieving them would not be yet feasible. Let us leave aside all theoretical discussion here; in practice, a simple procedure has been sought to determine how equitable a society is. This is income distribution: the more uniformly income is distributed, the more equitable the society. Or interpreted another way, if income is less unequally distributed than it was the previous year, the objective of redistribution is considered to be advanced.

2.3 Defence of social values

Growth and redistribution are not the only objectives of a society. In general, every collective is concerned with preserving the territories, traditions, symbols and cultural and even religious expressions ("values") that make up its identity. This preservation often interferes with economic activity. Or seen from another angle, one of the objectives of public activity in the economy is to protect those values.

Otherwise, what is the sense of declaring holidays to commemorate a transcendent event for that society? Why prohibit gambling in one region even though that it is the main source of income for a neighbouring region? Why spend public money on contracting the best coach to manage the national team in an upcoming competition for a popular sport in the country?

When deciding what values are worth defending, conceptually we encounter the same problem already encountered when trying to order possible distributions of income among individuals. We could create "baskets" with different compositions of social values, analyse the utility that they produce for each individual and later add those individual utilities. The practical impossibility of such a procedure makes the collective's decision-making process the only mechanism that can determine what values are worthy of protection and what exact protection they are given.

READING 3.2   ECONOMY OR HEALTH: A NEW DEBATE?

On 11 March 2020, the World Health Organization classified the spread of the disease known as COVID-19 caused by the coronavirus SARS-CoV-2 as a pandemic. All the countries of the world had to decide (they are still having to decide at the time of writing) what measures to take to combat its spread. Many of these measures have had obvious (and profound) effects on the economy. Is protecting people's health the "moral" or the "right" thing to do, and must it override any economic arguments? Not everyone would answer yes or at least not without nuance. The best proof of this is the debate that arose over whether nations should opt for health or the economy. In the face of those for whom "health comes first", others had doubts or even an openly contrary opinion that could well be summarized in the phrase from the then president of the United States, Donald Trump: "we can't let the cure be worse than the problem itself".

Is this a real debate? Can and should the choice really be made between saving lives and keeping the economy afloat? This does not seem to be the case in the long term, as a runaway epidemic would undermine the productive structure and, crucially, the confidence of businesses and consumers, which would probably end up leading to an economic scenario not much different from that caused by a forced halt in activity. But this does not seem to be the case in the short term either, as shown, despite the precautions that must be taken with regard to how the number of deaths from COVID-19 is counted, by the table on the website Our World in Data. Figure 3.2 shows that the countries which were suffering the greatest recessions in the second quarter of 2020 (presumably as a result of more severe restrictions on mobility and

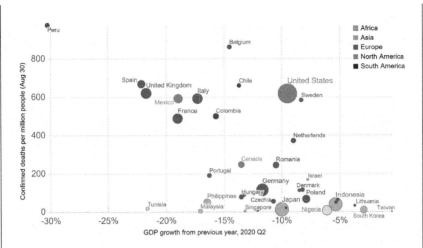

FIGURE 3.2   Economic decline in the second quarter of 2020 vs rate of confirmed
              deaths due to COVID-19[1]

trade) did not necessarily have lower mortality rates; conversely, those who
were better off economically were not always worse off in terms of the severity
of the pandemic. It is not a good idea to turn complex problems into a mere
trade-off, leaving out many other factors that influence the equation.

On the other hand, is this a new debate? The answer is no. Perhaps never
before has it reached such a dimension (nor had it garnered so much public
opinion), but other examples of this alleged dilemma can be found. The most
obvious is that of tobacco. Mechanization and mass marketing towards the
end of the 19th century popularized the cigarette habit, *causing a global epidemic of lung cancer*.[2] Not until the middle of the last century, however, were
cigarettes shown to be primarily responsible for the disease. Manufacturers
denied this evidence and began an aggressive (and successful) propaganda
campaign. Although years later, there was no longer any doubt about the
harmful effects of smoking, the tobacco industry lobby continued to suc-
ceed in stopping (or delaying for decades) measures for curbing smoking,
which seemed inexcusable at a time when the impact of tobacco had already
been well established (measured not only in human lives but also in health
costs and in loss of productivity due to workers' sick leave). Moreover, aid to
domestic tobacco producers was not suspended in many cases until well into
the 21st century (2010 in the European Union, 2014 in the United States).

In the second decade of this century, many countries have enacted antismoking laws that prohibit smoking in certain public spaces and/or require
explicit messages about its health risks to appear on cigarette packets; their
price has also been raised through taxation, and advertising restrictions are
sometimes imposed. Even so, the World Health Organization claimed that in

2020, the world had 1.3 billion smokers; more strikingly, that tobacco continues to kill more than 8.0 million people each year (approximately 1.2 million are the result of nonsmokers' being exposed to second-hand smoke); and that tobacco kills no fewer than half of its users.[3] Although, according to the same source, over 80% of the world's tobacco users live in low- and middle-income countries, in a country like the United States, its administration estimates that cigarette smoking causes about one of every five deaths (more than 480,000 deaths annually), with the life expectancy for smokers at least ten years fewer than that for nonsmokers.[4]

In contrast to these figures, consider that it took COVID-19 nine months to reach the first million deaths worldwide, at which time about 32 million had been infected. Clearly, comparisons between the two pandemics are not valid, as they differ considerably in many aspects. One important difference is that the cost to the economy of eliminating tobacco would be much lower than that associated with many of the plans orchestrated to stop the novel coronavirus. Another difference, linked to the previous one, is that coronaviruses do not have an industry behind them that supports their interests and spends $8.4 billion annually in the United States alone on advertising and promotion.[5]

1 https://ourworldindata.org/covid-health-economy. Data from European Centre for Disease Prevention and Control, Eurostat, OECD and individual national statistics agencies. This does not include data from China as in Q2 of 2020 it already showed a growth of 3.2% (compared to a fall of 6.8% in Q1). The page is signed by Joe Hasell.
2 Proctor, R.N. (2012). "The history of the discovery of the cigarette–lung cancer link: evidentiary traditions, corporate denial, global toll". *Tobacco Control*, vol. 21, n° 2, pp. 87–91.
3 https://www.who.int/news-room/fact-sheets/detail/tobacco.
4 Office on Smoking and Health, National Center for Chronic Disease Prevention and Health Promotion. https://www.cdc.gov/tobacco/data_statistics/fact_sheets/health_effects/tobacco_related_mortality/index.htm.
5 U.S. Federal Trade Commission (FTC). *Cigarette Report for 2018*. Washington: FTC, 2019.

3 Derived objectives

Derived objectives quantitatively "interpret" the basic or ultimate objectives. There follows the study of GDP as an indicator of growth (complemented by inflation, public deficit and external deficit to assess the stability of that growth), of the unemployment rate and finally of the Gini coefficient (which measures income distribution). We have no commonly used indicators that measure the sustainability of growth or (unfeasible in this case) the level of respect for social values.

3.1 Measuring growth: gross domestic product

The gross domestic product (GDP) is the most common indicator to determine the size of an economy. Its evolution over time is the quintessential measurement of growth. The annual variation rate of GDP (with quarterly advances) is used to conclude whether the economic situation of a country is improving or worsening.

The GDP is the total market value of all the final goods and services produced in the country by national or foreign businesses/individuals over a period of time (generally a year). *Market value* is the result of multiplying quantities by market prices. *Final* goods and services imply that the intermediate goods needed to produce them are not counted (if a car is sold, only the value of the car is added to GDP, not the value of its components or accessories). Finally, *produced* means that goods could have been sold or not and that transactions involving second-hand (already produced) products do not enter into the estimate.

If we analyse the final destination of all these goods and services, everything produced must be dedicated to consumption, investment, government spending or exports. Then we can calculate the GDP by adding these four categories. But if we add them without making any adjustments (using e.g. *total* household consumption and *total* investment), we would be including a part that was not produced in the country. Therefore, we must subtract imports. In this way, we obtain GDP by adding consumption, investment, public spending and net exports (exports minus imports).

The preceding approach is called the *expenditure* approach (to calculate GDP). There are alternative methods that should lead to the same result unless an error occurs. The *added-value* approach calculates the value that each company adds in the consecutive steps needed to create a product. By factoring in all goods and services, the sum would give GDP *at factor cost*; to get from factor cost to market prices, indirect taxes minus subsidies are added. The third method is the *income* approach, which estimates GDP by using the sum of incomes received by the different actors who intervene in the production process, specifically salaries and gross operating surplus (composed of interests, rents and dividends).

A necessary distinction is made between nominal and real GDP. As we have seen, GDP is the value of the goods and services produced in an economy, understood as price multiplied by quantity. Changes in GDP are, therefore, the combined effect of changes in quantities and prices. If we multiply what is produced in a specific year by the market prices of the previous year (base year), the difference between that GDP (of the year in question, calculated as indicated) and the GDP of the base year would only be due to quantities. That is why GDP calculated with the prices of the base year is known as *real* or *constant (prices)* GDP. Unadjusted GDP, on the other hand, is referred to as *nominal* or *current (prices)* GDP. We wrote earlier that the distinction between nominal GDP and real GDP is necessary because growth occurs only if the real GDP increases. If nominal GDP is greater than that of the previous year but real GDP is less, that means that fewer goods and services were produced but that their price was higher.

Other measurements of a country's product are also often used:

- Gross national product (GNP) is the market value of all the goods and services produced in one year by the citizens of a country (individuals, companies) inside or outside of the country, deducting the part of that activity that accrues to foreigners.

  If a company residing in country A does work in country B, what it is paid for the service is part of country A's GNP (because it is a national company), but not of its GDP (because the work was not done in the country). Inversely, it is part of the GDP of country B (because the work was carried out in its territory), but not of the GNP of country B (because it isn't a national company). If the service was carried out with the help of a local supply company, that quantity must be deducted from the GNP of country A, and of course, it would not alter its GDP (because the activity, with or without subcontractors, still took place outside of its borders). The GNP of country B would increase (the supply company resides there), but it would not change its GDP (because when we measure what is "domestic," the total cost of the operation is already taken into account, regardless of the nationality of who carried it out).

  For this "national" approach, the income perspective is used more often than the expenditure approach, and therefore, the term *gross national income* (GNI) is used much more frequently than *gross national product*.

- Net domestic product (NDP) equals the GDP minus depreciation on a country's capital goods. This depreciation (the "consumption of fixed capital") is calculated by using accounting conventions that determine the amortization applicable each year.
- Net national product (NNP) modifies GDP with the two corrections referred to in the two previous points. If the income and factor cost approaches are used, it is obtained by subtracting the depreciation and the taxes applied to goods and services (minus subsidies) from the income received by national actors. This provides us with what is referred to as net national income or, simply, national income. If depreciation is not discounted, it is referred to as gross national income (it would then be equal to GNI at factor cost).
- To define disposable income (or disposable personal income), line items that cannot be spent (or saved) by individuals are subtracted from the net national income. This includes direct taxes (paid by families or companies), social protection contributions, profits retained by firms and transfers without consideration received by families (in this case with the opposite sign because they increase the disposable income).

The absolute value of GDP, or of any of the alternative indicators, gives an idea of how big an economy is. To determine *how rich* the inhabitants of a country are, the GDP must be divided by the population. This is GDP *per capita*. Its evolution over time depends on the evolution of the GDP but also, evidently, on variations in the size of the population.

READING 3.3   DOMESTIC IS NOT THE SAME AS NATIONAL, AND GROSS IS NOT THE SAME AS NET: THE CASE OF IRELAND

Are the Irish (on average) among the richest citizens in Europe? The answer is, it depends. If we look at GDP per capita, the answer is "yes, not only in Europe but in the entire world". If we look at the "national" indicator (GNI), the answer is "well, not so much". If we look at net terms and measure national income or, better yet, disposable income, the answer becomes no.

Figure 3.3 displays the difference between nominal GDP and GNI in every country in the European Union in 2016 as a percentage of GNI.[1] In 26 of the 28 member states, this discrepancy (positive or negative) is barely over 5%. Exceptions are Luxemburg, whose GDP is 1.5 times its GNI (so its GNI is just over 70% of its GDP), and Ireland, whose GNI is only a slightly more than 80% of its GDP.

We are focusing on Ireland so we won't look at Luxemburg's numbers, although *official* explanations speak of its role as an international financial centre and of the thousands of people who cross the border each day to work there, despite living in neighbouring countries. The *official* explanation of why this happens in Ireland comes from the Irish Department of Finance. A

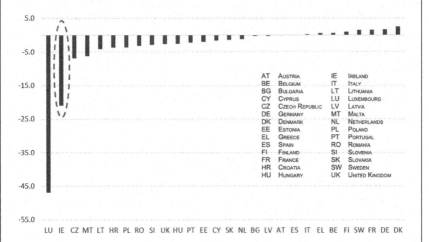

FIGURE 3.3   Differences between nominal GDP and GNI, in the European Union, percentage of GNI (2016)

not-so-official explanation is provided in Reading 5.3. The official one says the following:

> Ireland is somewhat unusual, however, in that the owners of a large part of the capital stock are, in fact, non-residents. This situation has arisen from the importance of inward foreign direct investment to the Irish economy from the 1960s onwards. As the pace of globalisation has accelerated over the past few decades, the Irish economy has become progressively more and more embedded in global supply-chains. An important consequence of this is that a significant part of the income arising from the production of goods and services in Ireland accrues to the foreign owners of capital assets based in Ireland. Hence, the GDP aggregate overstates the living standards of Irish residents.[2]

If the GDP inflates the results, it would be enough to use the GNI. However, GNI doesn't provide a perfect vision either. Ireland's GNI in 2016 includes around EUR35 billion in depreciation, of which the majority (around EUR30 billion) is accounted for by foreign-owned intellectual property assets, and almost all the rest come from the aircraft-leasing business. Given that the GNI of that year was around EUR275 billion, these amounts are significant.

Faced with this evidence, in 2017, the Central Bank of Ireland created a modified GNI that discounted this depreciation and the income from *redomiciled* firms. In 2016, the modified GNI was EUR189 billion, which elevated its discrepancy with GDP by more than 45% (inversely, the modified GNI was only 68.5% of GDP). The idea is to use this new GNI to calculate other economic variables. This includes the balance of payments or the amount of public debt (calculated as a percentage of modified GNI, it will be much higher than calculated in reference to its GDP).

1 Figure published in *GDP and 'modified GNI'—Explanatory note*. Note published in May 2018 by Ireland's Department of Finance—found at https://www.gov.ie/en/publication/498058-gdp-and-modified-gni-explanatory-note-may-2018.
2 Same document as that for footnote 1.

3.2 Measuring employment: unemployment rate

Not everyone is in a position to work. Some aren't of working age (either too young or too old), others are sick or occupied in other activities (e.g. they study or take care of children) and others don't want to. The rest, those not meeting any of these conditions, make up a country's labour force. The unemployment rate is calculated as a percentage by dividing the number of unemployed individuals by all individuals currently in the labour force.

Although this is the basic definition, economics adds various adjectives to the term unemployment:

- Not all people who leave a job start another one the next day. If a business closes, even if its workers are qualified to be hired by others, they will go through a transition period in which they search for a new job and assess offers. During this time, even if it is brief, they are unemployed. This is called *frictional unemployment*.
- In some scenarios, unemployment can exist while jobs are left unfilled. However, in this case, the situation is not quickly resolved (as is the case in frictional unemployment), because the skills of the unemployed workers in that area don't match the skills required for the jobs that are demanding labour (in the economic sense, businesses demand labour, despite the fact that in the newspapers, this demand appears under the heading of "job offers"). This is referred to as *structural unemployment*. The solution, which is unattainable in the short term, is to provide training to unemployed workers so that they learn the skills that the market requires.
- The previous two types of unemployment always exist, even in a buoyant economy. Their sum is referred to by the textbooks as the *natural rate of unemployment*. As a result of supposedly inevitable unemployment rate, the state of full employment, in which the economy is producing at its *potential output*, does not mean that there is zero unemployment but rather that there is a low level of unemployment (which cannot be precisely determined).

READING 3.4   EMPLOYMENT AND GROWTH: DIRECTLY RELATED?

The World Bank's website provides unemployment data from around the world (always as a percentage of the total labour force), using data published by the International Labour Organization.[1] Figure 3.4 shows the evolution between 1995 and 2019 of the unemployment rate in eight countries: Bahrain, Brazil, Cambodia, China, Spain, the United States, Jordan and South Africa.

During this period, total unemployment (as a percentage of the entire world population) was between 5.5% and 6.5%. However, the figure shows that the situations in each country were totally disparate. The stability of the rate observed over the years in some cases might make us think that the economic situation in those countries remained constant throughout this period or that they had reached natural employment, in which the rate, therefore, could not drop.

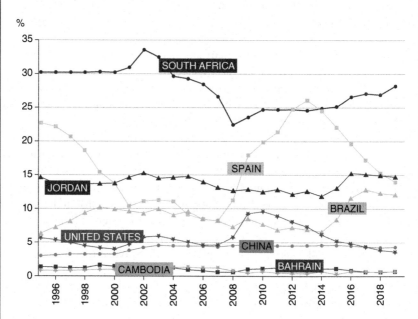

FIGURE 3.4 Evolution of the unemployment rate in eight selected countries (1995–2019)

To choose one of these explanations, we have to examine the progress of the economies of those countries during the same period. Figure 3.5 shows the annual percentage of GDP growth. This information was also obtained from the World Bank's website,[2] which uses data from the World Bank and the OECD.

Economic logic states that unemployment should follow (perhaps with a slight delay) changes in the GDP. This is not always the case. Indeed, the examples don't seem to show a relationship between how much an economy grows (or contracts) and how much unemployment declines (or increases). Periods of GDP growth have been compatible with stable employment in Brazil and even with increased unemployment in South Africa. On the contrary, in Spain, the unemployment rate does seem to be more significantly related to the GDP, although its variations are much more susceptible to changes in the economic cycle than they are in, for example, the United States, where fluctuations in employment are always much more constrained. Meanwhile, the four countries whose unemployment curves are almost flat do not have flat GDP growth curves and, moreover, their GDP growth has been almost invariably above zero.

This lends credence to the second hypothesis that was suggested earlier: perhaps there is a threshold of natural unemployment. It can be assumed in the cases of China and Bahrain. Both countries have had robust economic

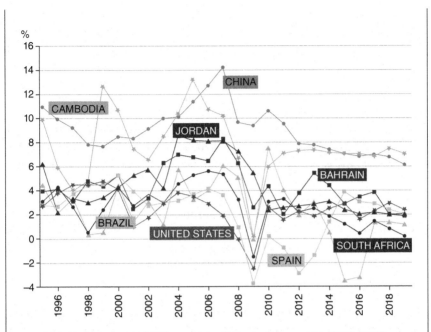

FIGURE 3.5   Annual rate of GDP growth in eight selected countries (1995–2019)

growth, and the increase in GDP should have been associated with an increase in productivity. Natural unemployment in China would then be at around 4% and in Bahrain at around 1%. But Jordan went through a period of sustained economic growth (even surpassing 6% in the period 2004–2009) and had a stable unemployment rate near 15%. Shouldn't an economy like Jordan's (which is based on tourism, producing phosphates for fertilizers and manufacturing textile products) have created jobs in these conditions? Cambodia went from a 13% GDP growth in 2005 to zero growth in 2009 and did so without affecting employment; moreover, the rate dropped a few tenths, moving even closer to full employment and has been maintained that since then. Has Cambodia found a magic formula to keep the entire population working?

Perhaps before providing conclusive answers, we should be prudent and, once again, question the reliability of the indicators that we use.

1 https://data.worldbank.org/indicator/SL.UEM.TOTL.ZS.
2 https://data.worldbank.org/indicator/NY.GDP.MKTP.KD.ZG.

3.3 Measuring stability

3.3.1 Inflation

Prices are the basic reference in a market economy. When the price level rises and the *monetary* income of consumers doesn't keep pace, consumers' purchasing power varies (their *real* income varies). Meanwhile, businesses adjust their earnings expectations upwards or downwards (in fact, their profits change if they maintain the same level of sales but prices vary). If price changes are small, the state of the economy as a whole will remain stable. But if they are large, the agents will begin to react. Businesses that can afford to do so (because they have fewer competitors and/or their products are basic necessities) transfer the rise in costs to the price of their products, provoking further rises in prices. At the same time, workers who are in a position to demand a rise in salary will do so to compensate for the new *cost of living*. All this generates instability and uncertainty. It also produces a redistribution of wealth because in these movements some agents win and others lose. The effect extends to every corner of the economy. For example, because debts are expressed in monetary terms, an increase in the general level of prices makes repaying the borrowed sum less onerous in real terms for the debtor and, inversely, less profitable for the creditor (because upon receiving repayment, the creditor can buy fewer goods than they could have bought if the prices had not risen). Sharp price changes lead to speculation, and savings shift from productive activities to safe haven assets, such as precious metals or properties.

All this would occur in a closed economy, without outside contact. If the economy is open, the internal problems are compounded by the economy's becoming less competitive in international markets. If the exchange rates are not modified, inflation has a direct influence on exports (national goods become more expensive when sold abroad) and imports (foreign goods become comparatively cheaper and more in demand in the internal market, which negatively impacts national production and employment).

For all these reasons, inflation, the sustained general increase of prices over time, is a risk to the *health of the economy* and to its growth. A *general* increase refers to a rise that affects a large number of goods and services: this does not necessarily include all of them; not all prices have to rise in the same quantity, and some prices can even fall. A *sustained* increase means that it's maintained for long periods of time and is not merely a seasonal rise (prices tend to rise during certain times of year, like summer and Christmas).

The inflation rate can be measured in two basic ways: the first is through the GDP deflator and the second, more commonly used, is through a consumer price index (CPI).

- The GDP deflator is based on the variation of the GDP over two consecutive years. As we saw earlier, the GDP varies when either quantities or prices change. By multiplying what is produced in a year by the prices of the previous year, we are eliminating the influence of prices. Stated another way, the difference between the GDP of year two with prices from year two and the GDP of year two with prices from year one is due to price changes. In economic terms, this means that the GDP deflator is obtained by dividing the nominal GDP by the real GDP (with the previous year as the base year).

- Because the price deflator procedure is precise but laborious (so at best provides only quarterly information), the CPI is often used instead. The CPI measures changes in the price level of a "basket" of basic goods that, according to household expenditure surveys, are judged to be the most widely consumed by the majority of the population. This *market basket* includes different line items (e.g. food, clothing and footwear, or transportation) that are given different weights; in turn, each line item consists of a weighted selection of goods and services (e.g. the transportation heading typically includes personal transportation and different urban or interurban transportation tickets). The list of line items and products must be updated to reflect the changing uses and tastes of societies.

The two most interesting CPI adjustments are *core inflation*, which is obtained by removing fresh food and energy products from the general index, and CPI *at constant taxes*, which removes the influence of changes in taxes on consumption.

3.3.2 Public deficit

Evidently, income and expenditures must be watched by every economic actor (i.e. individuals, households, businesses and administrations). This is particularly important if expenditures are greater than revenues (which means a deficit) and loans must be taken out—even more so if the situation is prolonged over various periods and new loans must be obtained while also repaying (with interest) the earlier loans. Given the dimension that the state's economic activity generally reaches, the general government deficit or public deficit is logically a measure of the entire economy's stability.

A government budget is a financial statement presenting the government's estimated revenues and proposed spending over a specific period (generally a year). The budget is also a political document that outlines how the government will act that year by answering questions such as what policies (and exactly what headings) are going to receive funding, who can spend and to what limit, and how the revenues will be obtained to finance the spending. The following will analyse the public spending and public revenue and the account balances that result from the difference between the two.

Government spending

Expenditures can be classified by the area to which they are assigned, the body that executes the spending or the purpose for which they are used. For the last option (the purpose), government spending is divided into current or capital expenditures.

- Current expenditures include operating expenditures for the public sector (on personnel or on goods and services consumed in its activity), financial

expenditures (in particular servicing public debt) and unrequited payments (e.g. pensions or subsidies).
- Capital expenditures include real investments and capital transfers and include expenses related to financial operations.

Government revenues

The public sector finances its expenditures through the following:

- Taxes, which are in turn of two types.

    - Direct taxes are levied on specific taxpayers. They tax income or wealth. They are imposed on natural persons or legal persons (corporations).

      Social contributions that tax work income (generally salaries) fall in this category. They are referred to in this way because the money collected is used to cover social spending (e.g. healthcare and pensions).

    - Indirect taxes are imposed on uses of income—that is, on the consumption of goods and services or the purchase of certain assets. There is no particular recipient of these taxes but rather a generic one: any person who consumes or buys taxable assets or goods.

- Fees collected in exchange for some of the services that the public sector provides or for the private use of the public domain (occupying a pavement, use of the radio spectrum).
- Dividends from invested companies, income from public properties and interest from loans granted.
- Disposal of assets, including financial assets, business shares or real estate properties.
- Noncompulsory transfers, which are the amounts received without consideration from the private sector, other administrations or even supranational bodies.
- Issuance of public debt.
- Other revenues: lotteries, or penalties and fines.

Government budget balance

Because this is an accounting document, the budget must be formally balanced; that is, the total of the spending column must always be equal to revenues. Despite this balance, from an economic point of view, the budget registers a deficit (or surplus) when certain expenditures are larger (or smaller) than certain revenues. No rule determines which expenditures or revenues need to be considered. Evidently, the result will vary depending on what operations are included or excluded but also on whether some public bodies are left out, on the exact moment at which the movements are recorded, on whether inflation adjustments are applied or not, or even on whether the circumstantial (cyclical) or structural (permanent) nature of the different revenues and expenditures is taken into account. This means that we have no one way to measure the deficit or surplus, and even if the line items used to calculate it are agreed on, the result is conditional on the decisions taken regarding the other dilemmas listed earlier. That said, the most frequent measures used are the following:

- The *primary deficit* or *surplus* is obtained by comparing total income with out-flows but excluding interest on debt. In general terms, it reflects the budget orientation for the current year, in that the debt is "inherited" from past budgets.
- If in addition to the interest on debt other financial expenses are also deducted, the result will be *net lending/net borrowing* (difference between total income and nonfinancial expenditures). Adding to this result the net variation of financial assets obtains the *borrowing capacity* or *need*, which tells us whether borrowing money is necessary to fulfil the operations of the current financial year (or, on the contrary, whether part of the existing debt can be amortized).
- If all resources in the economy are being fully used, the budget result would show a *structural deficit* (or *surplus*) that would indicate the validity of the fiscal structure: if in this situation there is already a budget imbalance, any down-turn in the economy will only exacerbate the deficit. This happens because tax revenues automatically drop during recessions while spending on subsidies such as unemployment rise (see the concept of automatic stabilizers in the next section). The impact of fluctuations in economic activity on public revenues and expenditures, along with possible extraordinary expenses (e.g. a bank bailout), is termed a *cyclical* or *temporary deficit* (or *surplus*). Returning to the *structural deficit*, this is usually divided into *trend deficit*, incurred under "normal economic circumstances", and *discretionary deficit*, linked to the government's discretionary policies.

In contrast to the primary deficit or net lending/net borrowing, which are easily calculated by simply adding or subtracting budget line items, the concepts presented in this final point are more theoretical and difficult to determine because they refer to hypothetical situations such as "full use of resources" or "normal economic circumstances".

3.3.3 External deficit

Just as the public sector's balance of revenues and expenditures is an important variable to determine economic stability, so too is the balance of international transactions. If what a country spends in its relations with other countries is repeat-edly higher than what it receives, the situation can become unsustainable. Being permanently in debt with other countries would deplete its foreign currency reserves, making either diverting resources to buy new currencies or paying loans necessary.

The economic transactions among residents of a country and the rest of the world are recorded in the balance of payments. The balance of payments has three basic subsections: the current account, the capital account and the financial account.

1   The current account is in turn divided into three accounts: the goods and services account, the income account and the transfers account.

What a country buys and sells is recorded in the goods account (if they are goods) and in the services account (if they are services, obviously). The balance of these accounts determines, respectively, the difference in value between exported and imported merchandise and the difference in value between the services that residents of the country provided abroad and vice versa. The term *balance of trade* was traditionally tied only to the exchange of goods, and it is still sometimes used with this meaning, although it makes perfect sense to identify such exchanges with the goods and services account.
As regards the income account, it reflects, in both directions (i.e. national citizens abroad and foreigners residing in the country), the compensation paid to factors of production who are not residents of the country concerned (including salaries of temporary foreign workers, dividends, interest payments and rents). Finally, the transfers account covers current transfers—that is, transfers of goods or money with nothing received in return (remittances made by emigrants, inheritances and the payment of pensions generated in another country).

2   The capital account registers transfers of capital (e.g. capital movements linked to the acquisition or disposal of fixed assets) and the sale of intangible assets (e.g. patents and copyrights).
3   The financial account includes investments (e.g. stocks, bonds and properties) and other items, such as loans, trade credits, financial derivatives or deposits. These are, of course, always operations carried out by foreigners in the country or by nationals abroad. It also includes the net movement of foreign reserves.

As occurred with the government budget, because this is an accounting document, the balance of payments is always balanced. But every account presents an independent balance that can be positive or negative. Two of these partial balances have the clearest economic sense:

•   The *commercial deficit or surplus* (from the account of the balance of trade, understood as the difference between imports and exports of goods and also services) is the most notable parameter in any analysis of an economic situation.

- The joint balance of the current account and the capital account determines the *net lending/net borrowing* of the country (not the government) in regard to the rest of the world. If the balance is negative, the income associated with the movements reflected in the two accounts is not sufficient to cover the payments resulting from those movements, thereby generating a net debt with the rest of the world that is offset, in accounting terms, by the result of the financial account. If the balance is positive, the country is a net creditor with the rest of the world as a whole (though the balance could be negative in relation to a specific country).

3.4 Measuring equity: the Gini coefficient

The most common way of assessing equity is through the distribution of income or wealth among individuals or families. The Gini coefficient or index, which refers to income or earnings (but can also refer to wealth), is almost always used.

Imagine that we wanted to rank all the inhabitants (or households) of a country by levels of income. If they all had exactly the same income level, any percentage of the population would have an equal percentage of the total income; for example, 10% of the population would have 10% of the income. If we were to represent this distribution on a coordinate plane (percentage of the population on the abscissa axis and percentage of income on the ordinate axis) the result would be a straight line with a slope of one. In reality, however, income is never uniformly distributed. In the previous example, the poorest 10% of the population obtains less than 10% of the income, whereas the richest 10% always has more than 10% of the income (and the other 90% of the population has less than 90% of the total income). The resulting representation in this case is not a straight line but rather a convex downward curve. This is known as the Lorenz curve.

In the first situation described, the absolutely uniform distribution of income, the Lorenz curve would be, as we said, a line. This "line of equality" can be understood as the hypotenuse of an isosceles triangle in which the legs are the abscissa axis and the parallel to the ordinate axis traced from the point in which the population is 100%. Because of its convex shape, any other Lorenz curve would remain within this triangle. The Gini coefficient is the ratio of the area that lies between the curve and the hypotenuse over the total area of the triangle. The Gini coefficient oscillates between zero and one. The closer the Lorenz curve is to the hypotenuse, the more equitable is the distribution of income (remember that the hypotenuse is the "line of equality" that represents absolutely uniform income) and the closer the Gini coefficient is to zero; on the contrary, the closer the Gini coefficient is to one, the more concentrated is the total income in the hands of the richest parts of the population. Sometimes the Gini coefficient is instead referred to as an index. The index is the coefficient multiplied by 100 so that the range oscillates between 0 and 100.

READING 3.5 TOWARDS GREATER INEQUALITY?

The Gini index is not an indicator published in national accounts. Therefore, there are no exact calculations but rather estimates carried out at different times by various institutions (even by research groups). The World Bank is one of these institutions.[1] Although the data in the series that it publishes date back to 1974, they are incomplete, and even the most recent years still have large gaps (the periodicity of the data is not always annual). Figure 3.6 presents the most recent information available for each country (relative to 2018 or earlier).

More interesting than a snapshot is how inequality indicators develop over time. The World Inequality Database[2] offers a collection of data, and it published a report in 2018[3] that was used to assemble Figures 3.7 and 3.8.

Figure 3.7 presents the evolution of the percentage of national income received by the richest 10% and the poorest 50% of the population of various countries and regions, from 1980 (or 1990) to 2017. The 10% richest increased their share of the pie in every case, except in countries or regions in which at the start of the series they had already controlled more than 50% of the total income. As we can see in the lower part of the figure, this increase largely came at the cost of the poorest half of the population, except in Europe, where the situation of this half recovered slightly after 1995.

Figure 3.8 presents the percentage of the national income received annually by the *ultra-rich*, the wealthiest 1% in each country, approximately from the start of the 20th century (each series starts at a different moment). There are four different graphs: English-speaking countries, Northern European countries, Central and Southern European countries and other countries. The figure shows that at the start of the 20th century the *ultra-rich* 1% commonly accounted for more than 20% of the total income. That percentage began to decline at the start of the 1920s, and by the 1980s in the best of cases, their income reached "only" around 10%. However, since around 1985 the tables have turned and it seems that every year the wealthiest accumulate a larger part of the income. The situation is less extreme in non-English-speaking Europe, particularly Northern Europe, where the accumulation of income by the wealthiest is growing, but at a moderate rate compared to what is happening in English-speaking countries (in which the curve has a clear valley shape) or in the China–India–Russia trio.

1 http://databank.worldbank.org/data/source/world-development-indicators.
2 https://wid.world/.
3 Alvaredo. F., Chancel, L., Piketty, T., Saez, E., & Zucman, G. (coordinators). *World Inequality Report 2018*. World Inequality Lab. Available at https://wir2018.wid. world/.

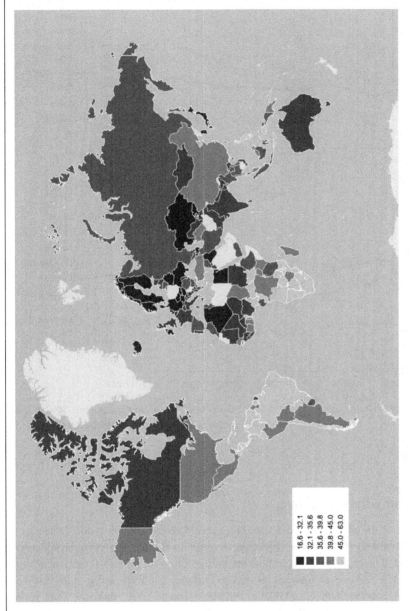

FIGURE 3.6 The Gini index (data from 2018 or earlier)

16.6 - 32.1
32.1 - 35.6
35.6 - 39.8
39.8 - 45.0
45.0 - 63.0

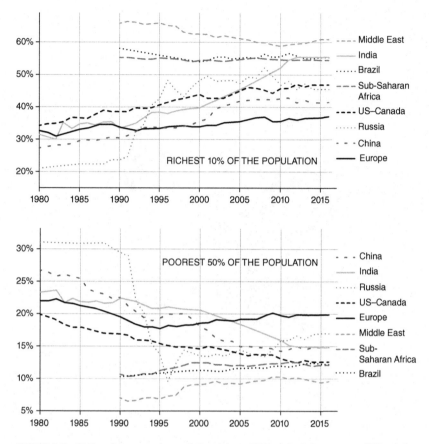

FIGURE 3.7 National income share of the richest 10% and of the poorest 50% of the population in different countries or regions over time (1980–2017)

4 Immediate objectives

Many of the reasons *why* the state takes action in the economy don't seem to be connected to the ultimate objectives or even to the derived objectives just presented. This is the case when there are failures of *specific markets*. Resolving a negative externality or a situation that features asymmetric information does not seem to be related to changes in GDP or inflation. However, we could say, more appropriately, that although such actions are not directly related to derived objectives, they are indirectly related. When united, these apparently lesser actions are what make the economy *function better* and allow it to reach higher objectives.

In fact, the purpose of the majority of daily public activities is to achieve what we can refer to as *immediate objectives*: tearing down obstacles to competition in

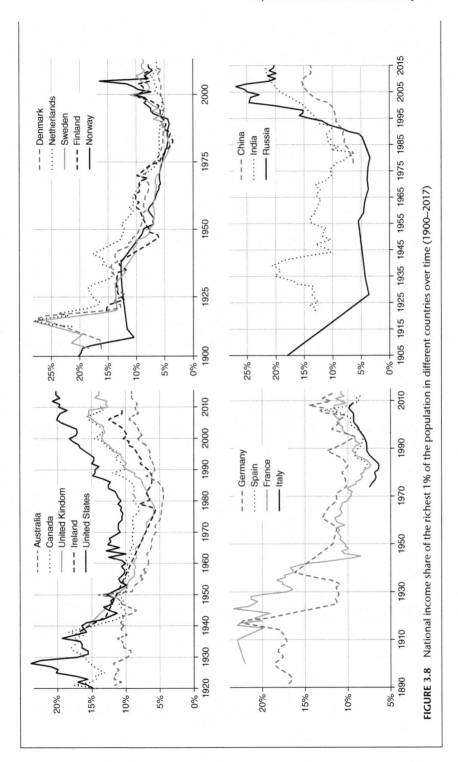

FIGURE 3.8 National income share of the richest 1% of the population in different countries over time (1900–2017)

the fuel market, supporting research on new semiconductor materials, providing incentives to use bicycles in cities, setting the maximum price for commissions on banking services, increasing the number of people studying abroad. Despite the stand-alone importance of these actions, we should never lose sight of the other objectives that *immediate* public actions are contributing to or of the reasons behind them.

5 Criticisms of the indicators used

"What we measure affects what we do. If we have the wrong metrics, we will strive for the wrong things". This was said by Joseph Stiglitz, Amartya Sen and Jean-Paul Fitoussi in a book published in 2010, the result of their work in a commission set up a few years earlier by the French presidency to evaluate the reliability of GDP as an instrument to measure social and economic progress.

Indeed, the selection of an indicator could be inadequate for two reasons: it might correspond to the desired end but have limitations, or it might be unreliable when determining what it seeks to measure. In the next subsection, the inaccuracies derived from the method of building the indicators described in the previous sections will be discussed, especially GDP and the inflation rate. In the following two subsections, the GDP's inadequacy in measuring the welfare of a society will be discussed.

5.1 The quality of the indicators

Is GDP a good measure of economic activity? Is the inflation rate a good measure of the variation of prices? The indicators described earlier have a series of limitations and in some cases even inaccuracies.

- GDP doesn't account for uncompensated activities. If a family contracts domestic service to clean their house or take care of the children, that activity is calculated as part of GDP, but it isn't included if the family itself takes care of it; in the same way, it is included if they wash their clothes at a laundromat, but not if they do it at home. Likewise, buying tomatoes at the market enters into the GDP, but not on-farm consumption. Volunteer work is also not considered a productive activity, because it isn't compensated. Moreover, for an economic activity to be accounted for, it has to be declared. If a person contracts domestic service but does not register the employee, the payment isn't included in the public accounts. The same is true for illegal activities, like drug trafficking, even though it can be the main source of income for entire regions.

A second problem, which will be examined in the following subsections, is that GDP does not distinguish between the types of production activities on which it is based. The same GDP could include different ratios between mere consumption and investments meant to increase the capacity for future growth. It also does not differentiate, for example, between industrial activities that destroy natural resources on one hand and sustainable activities on the other.

GDP also does not take into consideration the price or quality of goods and services. If two countries produce/consume the same amount, but in one the prices are lower, this second country would be considered poorer because it would have a lower GDP. Alternatively, a third country with the same prices as the first would be equally as rich even if its goods and services were of higher quality. If (and how) quality should be taken into account is a question that affects services in particular, especially public services. Services are measured by examining the inputs that they use, but not their results or quality. For example, the same expenditure on education could originate from highly disparate situations in terms of the number of students and the quality of the learning system.

Finally, we here make a few observations regarding how GDP relates to other ways of measuring the product of a country. GDP is a measurement of the growth of a country's internal production. But *domestic* production is not *national* production. If a country carries out an activity whose profits go abroad, then from the point of view of its citizens, whether the country's economy has grown to the same degree as its production is debatable. Also consider that this activity could be polluting or that it could impose terrible working conditions. Globalization is making the discrepancy between GDP and GNP ever larger. Selecting one or the other indicator is not politically neutral.

In the same way, the distinction between gross values and net values is relevant. As a "gross" indicator, GDP does not take into account the depreciation of capital goods. But if a country does reserve a part of its production to renew the provision of said goods, the part that could be dedicated to consumption is much smaller. Having said that, the influence of this qualification is more difficult to evaluate because, as mentioned, calculating the annual depreciation needed to determine NDP is based on accounting conventions, which makes calculating this indicator discretionary, to a certain degree.

• As regards inflation, even if an attempt is made to ensure that the basket of products used to measure it reflects typical consumption patterns (or precisely because it reflects typical consumption), it does not represent the change in prices that different social groups must deal with. Logic indicates that the population with the fewest resources spends a large percentage of its income on basic products (on certain kinds of foods or essential supplies), and *rich people* spend more on entertainment. Age or the characteristics of the setting in which one lives (rural/urban) also influence the type of consumption.

As occurred with GDP, the second problem of measuring inflation is assessing quality. Some believe that the inflation rate is overstated because the prices of some goods don't vary in the same measure as their quality (this is evidently the case of electronic devices or household appliances). However, taking into account the change in price of a device that may not even be manufactured anymore doesn't make sense; substituting it with the device that now satisfies the equivalent kind of demand seems more sensible. The case of services is similar but more complex. The price of medical services, for example, does not take into account how long a patient is under care or the complexity of the treatment.

- The unemployment rate says nothing about the quality of employment, average salary or working conditions. A decrease in unemployment could be due to a genuine improvement in the economy but also to a change in the labour market that allows for the creation of more low-paying, temporary jobs.
- The limitations on the way the public deficit can be measured were already revealed when it was described. As mentioned, we have no unequivocal way to determine its amount, but rather, it depends on what items are evaluated and the evaluation criteria adopted, which has at times opened the door to "creative" public accounting.
- The Gini coefficient usually refers to income, which is a general shortcoming (income isn't the same as wealth), but especially for countries in which income is not always monetary or is not always reflected in statistics (a strong *informal* or agrarian economy). Furthermore, the Gini coefficient is not unambiguous (in the sense that the same coefficient can result from two different Lorenz curves) and its value is more sensitive to variations in the central fractions than is to those that occur at the extremes.

5.2 Growth versus sustainable development

The first conceptual criticism that can be levelled at GDP is its inability to evaluate the sustainability of the economic activity that it measures. When describing its limitations, we have already seen that operations that deplete resources and degrade the environment count the same as those that are respectful of the environment; GDP knows nothing of externalities, and it is built from market prices and not from shadow prices (which would include opportunity costs).

A first step towards at least obtaining information regarding the environmental impact of economic activity is to employ *environmental accounting*. The United Nations Statistical Commission set standards (accounting concepts, definitions, classifications and rules) with which to generate internationally comparable environmental statistics. This is the System of Environmental-Economic Accounting (SEEA), which was proposed as the basis for the creation of a *satellite* account to accompany conventional national accounts. The system attempts to measure resource depletion, pollution levels and environmental degradation, and the costs of environmental protection and the recovery of degraded environments. To maintain consistency with conventional accounts, the environmental activity account must use market prices, either actual or allocated (though, on occasion, calculations are based on records that have "physical" rather than economic measurements of environmental assets).

Environmental accounting complements but does not reform the present indicators. A further step is to use these (or similar) measures to modify them. Although the creation of a *green GDP* has been discussed frequently (China even published an indicator with this name in 2006, referring to 2004, but it never repeated it), the most methodologically developed indicators are Adjusted Net Savings and the Inclusive Wealth Index:

- *Adjusted Net Savings* corrects net national savings (defined as national income minus consumption expenditure, both public and private) by taking into account investments in human capital (measured by spending on education), the use of nonrenewable natural resources and the damage caused by carbon dioxide and harmful particle emissions. A negative final result indicates that the use of natural resources and the damage caused by pollution are even greater than the physical capital and human capital that are generated; in other words, the economy in question is "dissaving".
- The *Inclusive Wealth Index* determines the "social value" of an economy's capital goods. To do so, it classifies capital goods into three categories: natural capital (made up of arable land, forests, fossil fuels, and metals and minerals), produced capital and human capital. All of them are adjusted by three factors: damage caused by pollution, fluctuations in the price of fuel and total productivity of the factors (to include the effect of technological change). More important than its absolute value is how the index and the capital goods that it includes change over time.

READING 3.6 THE *DISSAVINGS* OF THE POOREST COUNTRIES: THE DEPLETION OF RESOURCES

The World Bank estimates *adjusted net savings*. As explained in the main text, this indicator is obtained by adjusting national savings to include investment in human capital and subtracting for pollution and for the overexploitation of nonrenewable resources.

Adjusting for the use of resources is particularly interesting. Its historical series of data is presented under the heading "adjusted savings: natural resources depletion".[1] The adjustment is measured as a percentage of gross national income (GNI). It is calculated as "the sum of net forest depletion, energy depletion, and mineral depletion". Net forest depletion is calculated from the excess of roundwood harvest over natural growth; energy depletion and mineral depletion are "the ratio of the value of the stock of resources to the remaining reserve lifetime (capped at 25 years)".[2]

Figure 3.9 presents the result of this calculation for the low-income-group countries from the start of the 1980s to 2018. The required adjustment for the overexploitation of resources grew to a peak in 2003 (over 14% of gross income), falling in the latter part of the period to 8% of gross income by 2018, the last year in the series (compared to 1.3% for the world as a whole). In 2018, it surpassed 10% in Burkina Faso, Burundi, Chad and Sudan, and it was close to 20% in Eritrea, Liberia and the Democratic Republic of the Congo.

We have no equivalent time series for nonadjusted savings, as the series of gross savings used by the World Bank[3] starts in 2005 for these low-income countries. In the period 2005—2018, the values of this group as a whole were between 12% and 21% (always as a percentage of gross income). For the countries mentioned earlier, in Burkina Faso gross savings in 2018 were 23%, in Burundi 4%, in Eritrea 16%, in the Democratic Republic of the Congo 19% and in Sudan 17% but Chad had no recent data; a separate case is Liberia, where savings were already negative at no less than -74%. By comparing these numbers with the earlier ones while also taking into consideration that they refer to gross savings (thus, we must also consider depreciation), we conclude that dissavings are higher, even much higher, than savings in practically all these countries. In other words, current growth (if there is any) may occur at the cost of potential future growth.

This is confirmed by consulting the data for the *adjusted net savings, including the particulate emission damage* indicator (for which all adjustments are already considered), which the World Bank, as mentioned at the beginning, also provides.[4] For the same group of low-income countries, in the period

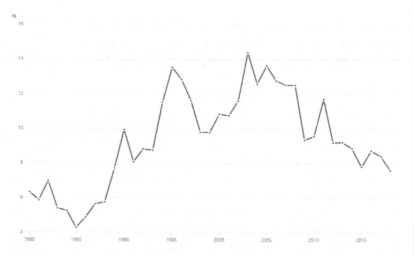

FIGURE 3.9 Dissavings caused by natural resource depletion, in percentage of GNI, for "low-income" countries (1980–2018)

2005–2018, the result was always negative until 2014, and since then, it has been positive, having values between 0.7% and 2.4%. Individually, of the 22 countries for which data were available for 2018, in 12 the indicator was negative. In the Democratic Republic of the Congo, Gambia, Malawi, Sudan and Uganda, adjusted net dissaving was between 5% and 10% of GNI; in Guinea it was just over 10%; in Burundi it was almost 17%; in Sierra Leone it was over 20%; and in Liberia it was almost 100%. Other countries, such as Syria, Somalia and Yemen, were outside the list because data were not available, but these countries were candidates to be in this group of the *biggest dissavers*.

1 https://data.worldbank.org/indicator/NY.ADJ.DRES.GN.ZS.
2 The details of the calculation can be found in Table A.2 of World Bank (2011). *The Changing Wealth of Nations: Measuring Sustainable Development in the New Millennium*. Washington, DC. This can be found at https://openknowledge.worldbank.org/handle/10986/2252.
3 https://data.worldbank.org/indicator/NY.GNS.ICTR.GN.ZS.
4 https://data.worldbank.org/indicator/NY.ADJ.SVNG.GN.ZS.

5.3 Growth versus quality of life

Despite the apparent connection between growth and welfare, greater production does not necessarily lead to greater well-being. Stiglitz, Sen and Fitoussi state in their report, cited earlier, that "one of the reasons that the majority of people feel they are worse off, although the average GDP rises, is *because they are in fact worse off* (emphasis added)".

Why is this so? First of all, let's revisit some of the arguments already presented when we revealed that GDP doesn't include the characteristics of the productive activities. Growth based on certain kinds of activities could even be undesirable. The question becomes even more complicated when we examine not only the type of activity but also the causes behind some movements in GDP. Sometimes this leads to a genuine paradox: the consumption of gasoline may increase not because the number of trips increases but rather because of the number of traffic jams; spending on fighting the negative health effects of pollution or stress contributes to economic growth; the means employed to fight a fire or an environmental disaster also increases GDP. Second, the level of equity counts: if we are discussing quality of life, how GDP is distributed must be taken into consideration.

More importantly, beyond quantitative measures, such as income, quality of life also depends on a broad set of qualitative factors that include how income is obtained (it is not the same to be a rentier as it is to be a salaried worker; it is not the same to obtain the same salary working four hours in an office as it is working 12 hours in agriculture) and many others, such as health, personal and leisure activities, the physical and social setting and the degree of physical and economic insecurity. Although all these factors are difficult to measure (and are often subjective) alternative indicators that seek to mitigate the shortcomings of GDP have been developed. Of course, all these indicators (except for the extremely limited, despite its name, Human Development Index) also consider environmental aspects, which is an essential part of any definition of quality of life; they are, however, different from the indicators presented in the previous section in that they try to measure welfare and not just sustainability. The best known among them are as follows:

- Rather than use GDP, the *Human Development Index* combines real per capita GNI (which means it is considered in terms of purchasing power parity) with other parameters: what is denominated "a long and healthy life" (although it is limited to life expectancy at birth) and an education index (mean years of schooling and expected years of schooling).
- The *Index of Sustainable Economic Welfare* is calculated by adding personal consumption, government spending (excluding defence expenditures), capital formation and the value of domestic and personal services produced for own household consumption, and subtracting the costs of environmental degradation and the depreciation of natural capital.
- The *Genuine Progress Indicator* attempts to improve on the previous indicator by incorporating certain factors (e.g. income distribution, the value of volunteer work or leisure time in relation to time spent working) and eliminating others (e.g. the costs of crime or commuting).
- The *Better Life Index* includes 11 factors: job, income, housing, community, education, work–life balance, environment, civic engagement, health, life satisfaction and safety. It has no overall classification. The 11 topics included in the index are not weighted by default; instead, users of the statistical tool set their own weights, thereby creating a customized index.

READING 3.7   GENUINE PROGRESS?

Some alternatives to GDP have been created and promoted by international organizations and even by private entities. Usually, an annual report with the results obtained by each country is published. This is not the case of the *genuine progress indicator* (GPI). The GPI is a refined version (carried out by Canadian researchers) of the *index of sustainable economic welfare* proposed in a book published in 1989 by economist Herman Daly and theologian John B. Cobb.[1] This is why no associated rankings or headlines indicate which country heads the list or how many positions individual countries rise or fall.

Some states in the United States have constructed this indicator for their territory. More interesting, however, are the conclusions of some academic studies in which the GPI was calculated and compared with other indicators. Of particular interest is the study published in 2013 by a group of researchers from different institutions.[2] We here reproduce, with a few modifications, two of the graphics that were included in that article.

Figure 3.10 compares the historical evolution of the value per capita of different indicators (GDP, the Human Development Index and another three that are not explained in the main text: *ecological footprint*, *biocapacity* and the *life satisfaction index*, which was discussed in Reading 3.1) with changes in the GPI, also per capita, that the researchers had calculated. The work presents the results for 17 countries, although here we have selected nine of them. The graphs are far from homogenous, but a situation repeats: the only indicator that has grown without interruptions during the period studied (1950–2005) has been GDP per capita; in the second half of the period, GDP growth has even accelerated while the rest of the indicators often stagnated or even declined.

Figure 3.11 compares the global estimates of GPI per capita and GDP per capita from 1950 to 2005.[3] The overwhelming conclusion is that the world, considered as a whole, has not genuinely progressed since 1978 (it has even regressed somewhat). To be more specific, the article estimates that up to the threshold of USD7,000 per capita, both indicators are highly correlated, but after that point, they no longer are (a weaker and, moreover, negative correlation); in other words, this conclusion supports the theory that up to a certain amount of money (different in each setting), economic growth implies an improvement in the quality of life, but after that point, the relation is lost (quality of life can even deteriorate because of the costs associated with continued growth).[4]

The authors point out that "GPI is not a perfect measure of overall human well-being, since it emphasizes economic welfare and leaves out other important aspects of well-being. It is, however, a far better indicator than GDP, which is not designed to measure welfare at all". Even with this caveat, and also taking into consideration that these estimates are probably not carried out with all the resources necessary, their conclusions still clearly point in a single direction: focusing all our energy on making sure that the GDP grows is myopic (erroneous).

1 Daly, H.E., & Cobb Jr., J.B. (1989). *For the common good: Redirecting the economy toward community, the environment, and a sustainable future.* Beacon Press. Boston (United States).
2 Kubiszewski, I., Costanza, R., Franco, C., Lawn, P., Talberth, J., Jackson, T., & Aylmer, C. (2013). "Beyond GDP: Measuring and achieving global genuine progress". *Ecological Economics*, vol. 93, no. 5, pp. 57–68. Figures 3.10 and 3.11 are reprinted from the article, with permission from Elsevier.
3 In USD, using 2005 as a reference and making the necessary adjustments.
4 This theory appears to be discredited by Figure 3.1 from Reading 3.1, in which the relation between GDP per capita and life satisfaction is continuous and does not seem to be broken after a certain level of income. However, the data presented there (referring, moreover, to a single year) and those used to calculate GPI are not sufficiently robust to be conclusive to support or refute a theory such as this.

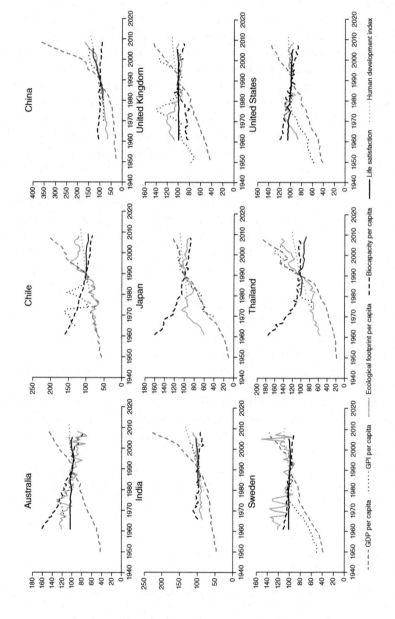

FIGURE 3.10   Changes in different indicators related to well-being in various countries (1950–2005)

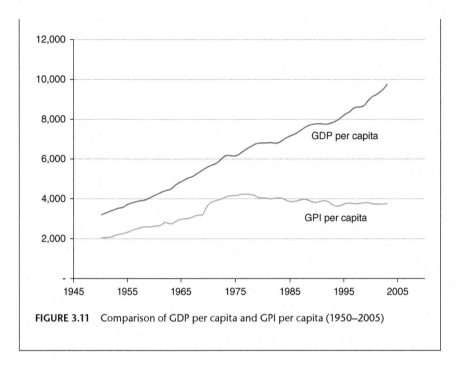

FIGURE 3.11   Comparison of GDP per capita and GPI per capita (1950–2005)

Summary

After we learned the reasons why the state might take action in the economy, we in this chapter examined the economic objectives that such actions pursue and the problems associated with controlling and measuring their effects. The first part of the chapter was dedicated to primary or ultimate objectives. These focus on ensuring the economy grows in a stable and sustainable way (and, as a consequence, that employment is available to all) and that wealth is distributed in a certain way. However, certain goals don't fit either of these categories; broadly speaking, they can be understood as defending social values.

The problem with ultimate objectives is that they're not directly measurable. They have to be represented by variables based on data that are relatively easy to compile. Changes in GDP are most commonly used to measure growth, just as the unemployment rate is used to keep track of employment. For equity, the Gini coefficient is the most widely used measurement. Other macroeconomic variables are subject to public control; they are not directly related to economic growth per se, but they can be used to measure the stability and solidity of growth: inflation, public deficit and the balance of trade. We have no commonly used measurement for sustainability.

However, changes in these indicators do not guide the majority of public actions, which simply have more-defined and more-immediate objectives. Pursing these short-term objectives still allows for progress in achieving larger goals.

An additional question that must be asked is whether the control variables selected are appropriate (or the most appropriate) to guide public activity in the economy.

Overview

The contents of this chapter included the following:

- An introduction to the objectives the state wishes to achieve with its economic activity.
- Descriptions and analyses of the macroeconomic indicators chosen to control those objectives.
- Critical analyses of the instruments habitually used to measure the objectives.

Self-evaluation questions

The self-assessment questions are meant to evaluate how well you have understood the information presented in this chapter.

1 From a *Rawlsian* perspective, the social welfare function _____

   a   Remains unchanged if the welfare of everyone except the worst-off member of society improves.

   b   Is obtained by adding the individual welfare of every member of society.

   c   Undergoes the same variation if either the richest member or the poorest member of society has had the same increase in their utility.

   d   Is unchanged if the welfare of the worst-off individual increases in the same amount as it reduces for the richest.

2 If in a given year all the prices of an economy have increased in comparison with the previous year (which is taken as the base year) but production remains the same, then _____

   a   The nominal GDP of that year would be equal to the real GDP.

   b   The real GDP of that year would be equal to that of the previous year.

   c   The nominal GDP of that year would be equal to that of the previous year.

   d   The nominal GDP of that year would be equal to the GNP.

3 Which people without jobs make up frictional unemployment?

   a   Those not qualified to occupy jobs for which there is demand.

   b   Those who have recently left a job and are searching for work and weighing offers.

   c   Those who can't find work even when the economy has reached its potential level of production.

d Those who have left their job because of disagreements ("friction") with their superiors in the company.

4 The primary deficit or surplus is obtained by which of the following?

a Comparing the revenues and spending of the central government, without counting those of regional or local governments.

b Comparing total public revenues and spending that must be paid before the end of the fiscal year.

c Comparing total public revenues and spending, excluding interest on outstanding debt.

d Comparing total public revenues and spending, excluding any that can be considered financial expenditure.

5 Why is GDP not a good measurement of economic activity?

a It measures the informal economy, even though it is not made up of legal activities.

b It doesn't distinguish between the types of activities that it comprises.

c It overestimates the value of products considered to be high quality.

d All the above.

Questions for reflection

The answers to the following questions are not in the text; they require you to search for additional information or to apply to real cases what you have learned in this chapter.

1 If you had to create a social welfare function, would you give equal weight to the welfare of every individual, or would you prioritize that of a particular group in some way? If you choose the latter, what individuals would you prioritize? How would you define the function?

2 In the economic scenario of the 21st century, do you consider the objectives of growth and redistribution to be compatible? Can a country grow while also being concerned with equity?

3 In yesterday's news, find examples of public actions that pursue an immediate objective. Think about how that objective contributes to achieving larger goals.

4

INSTRUMENTS OF STATE ECONOMIC ACTIVITY

1 Introduction

The sets of measures that states develop to pursue specific economic objectives are referred to as economic policies. We speak of "sets of measures" because the same objective can be achieved (can be pursued) through different actions or, much more commonly, through a combination of actions. The various *ingredients* used to prepare an economic policy are discussed in the first part of this chapter. They arguably represent the toolbox available to public policy managers. Depending on the objectives pursued and the specific circumstances, they can use just one or they may need to employ several. These tools are studied here in a general way, without entering into detail on how they are specifically applied in each policy.

On the other hand, as seen in the previous chapter, a wide range of objectives are pursued, which means that many economic policies are feasible. Horizontal policies affect all economic activity, whereas sectorial policies are centred on a specific area of the economy. Some policies organize economic activity, and other policies modify or correct the activity once it has been organized. Some policies focus on growth, and others focus on redistribution. In this chapter, five kinds of policies are presented. Separating the policies into different categories is useful, from a didactic perspective, but we must emphasize that economic policies can have more than one purpose. They're not hermetically sealed, and obvious connections, even overlaps, can be observed between some policies that are presented here separately. The same occurs at the level of political organization, where, more frequently than would be desirable, functions are duplicated, and there are even disagreements over who should take responsibility for directing a certain economic policy.

DOI: 10.4324/9781003173731-4

2 The ingredients of economic policies

States can use different kinds of tools to take action in the economy:

- Some involve direct action. Those examined in the following two subsections (i.e. direct provision and direct intervention) seek to ensure a precise end, replacing the market in all activity (provision) or in its capacity to set prices and the quantities exchanged.
- Many other times, the action is indirect. Some conditions are established that restrict or orient the market's activity, although it remains autonomous. This category includes establishing regulations and taxes (or, instead, granting subsidies) and creating nonmonetary incentives.
- Public–private partnerships constitute a category unto themselves because the state, which in the earlier cases exercises its power to decide, places itself at the same level of some private actors with which it negotiates an agreement to carry out an activity. The agreement in question usually takes the form of a contract.

2.1 Direct provision of goods and services

This category includes situations in which the government directly provides goods and services. We leave aside cases in which the public administration supplies a good or service to its citizens by buying the good and later distributing it. For instance, a vaccine that it offers for free (it might even be available only in a public health centre) but that was bought from private laboratories. Conceptually, as a tool for public action, this would be considered a subsidy in kind.

The public production of goods and services can be organized in various ways. Sometimes the body or institution is superimposed onto the administration itself, while in other cases, self-governing public companies are created. Between these two extremes, any intermediate option is possible.

Public provision does not imply that the product or service is provided for free. In general, performances by a public orchestra in a municipal theatre are not free, although there can be ways of putting on performances that do not require payment (e.g. free entrance until filled to capacity). The price charged can serve to cover costs or as a mechanism to select who will enjoy the product. The problem is that by selecting the demand not only people who are uninterested in the product but also people who are unable to pay the price remain outside. To avoid the price's being a barrier to entry, various prices can be established (in the previous example, reduced prices for young people, elderly people or unemployed people) or other *tools in the catalogue* can be used (in particular, assistance can be offered; grants for university students with fewer financial resources are a good example). The obligation to pay is more frequent in cases in which only a limited number of people can use a good before it becomes rivalrous. When no limit is imposed or when reaching one is difficult (as happens with parks and highways), payment is less frequent and might even be imposed only when congestion occurs (e.g. a public highway might impose a toll only between 7:00 a.m. and 9:00 a.m.). In any case, this rule is not always applied: many parks charge entry, and conversely, some services are offered for free because exclusion is considered unacceptable, even if doing so can generate congestion (free universal healthcare).

We can deduce from some of the aforementioned examples that public provision does not imply universality. Sometimes public provision is limited and offered through a selection mechanism. The price, as we have seen, is one such mechanism, but access to a good or service can also be restricted by offering it only to individuals who meet certain criteria or even by selecting beneficiaries through a competitive process. A public training programme can be reserved for unemployed people who have a certain profile, or candidates can be selected after presenting their résumé/curriculum vitae (CV).

Finally, public provision does not imply monopoly. The municipal theatre mentioned earlier could offer shows at the same time as private theatres, just as in many countries, public healthcare and education systems coexist with private options. However, when a service is considered a natural monopoly (and is also "socially important"), the likelihood that it will be offered by the public sector is greater. Water supply and rubbish collection services are often managed by a public company, and in many countries (as long as these sectors have not been opened to competition), the same occurs with other basic services, such as rail transport and air traffic control.

2.2 Direct intervention in markets

A public administration can set the conditions under which an activity is carried out. This isn't what we consider "direct intervention" (it would be regulation, as we shall see in the next section); direct intervention refers to actions that alter the result of the trade that a market generates spontaneously—that is, when prices or quantities are fixed.

A government can set a sales price or set a price floor or price ceiling for a certain product. Economic theory clarifies that these limitations are effective only when the minimum price is greater than the market price or the maximum price is lower. Establishing a single price will always have an effect unless it exactly coincides with the equilibrium price.

A maximum limit can also be placed on the quantity traded in a market (setting a minimum quantity wouldn't make sense). As in the previous case, the measure has an effect only if the quantity set is inferior to what had been otherwise traded; if no other restrictions are placed on it, the effect will raise the product's price.

Controlling prices and quantities can be done in the entire market or apply just to certain sellers, as occurs when they are imposed exclusively on an imported product. An example would be setting a cap (a limit on the number) on Japanese motorcycles that can be imported or setting a minimum price for them.

Generally, restrictions are placed on trades in a standard market (without public presence), but they can also be imposed in situations in which the state uses this tool as a buyer. In the example provided in the first paragraph of the previous section, in which the government buys vaccines (even monopolizing the demand if the vaccine can be procured only in a public health centre), it can determine a *fair price* that it will pay for each dose.

A particular and crucial type of direct intervention on price controls occurs in internal and supranational money markets. Setting the interest rates applied to certain basic operations conditions the interest rates applied to many other financial and commercial transactions. Similarly, the government's establishing a specific exchange rate between the national currency and other currencies is common.

2.3 Regulation

Under this heading are included all binding rules that in some way condition economic activity. Norms setting out economic substance requirements can have different legal ranks. For instance, some fundamental rules can be included in constitutions. On the other extreme, the most specific details or less-important aspects can be published in ordinances or low-level norms.

Like any other legal norms, spatial scope, recipients and coercive nature can be highly varied. A norm can affect the entire economy and be applied in the entire country, or it can affect only a certain economic sector, a specific geographic area or even a single subject. Regulations on acceptable means of payment are general; sectorial norms include those like establishing sanitary conditions for canning factories, which can be enforced nationwide or can vary in each region; meanwhile, an order can expropriate a tract of land from a private individual. The distribution of competences among the different levels of the public administration determines who has the responsibility (or simply the possibility) of regulating a specific activity.

When sectorial regulation is especially complex or affects particularly important sectors, specialized bodies are frequently put in charge of overseeing the regulation and ensuring that the norms are complied with, such as a stock exchange regulator or an office that monitors consumer rights. Sometimes the regulator has been "professionalized" by creating autonomous entities detached from the administration with the purpose (or excuse) of ensuring that it can act independently; if in practice its independence is illusory, it is termed *regulatory capture*.

Regulation can be applied ex ante or ex post. In the former, actors affected by the regulation must demonstrate that they are in compliance before starting the activity. In the latter, the activity is allowed without proof, but a sanction is established if noncompliance is discovered. Before being allowed to open a dental clinic, the interested party would most likely be required to provide a dental degree and other documentation; to work in a restaurant, the cook may need a licence to handle food that must be provided if an inspector visits the establishment. Ex ante regulation doesn't have to be more rigorous than ex post regulation. In fact, it could be the same. Why one is chosen over the other depends on the risk that noncompliance poses for the activity being regulated. The level of such risk can even vary over time. When the telecommunications sector was opened to competition, the former monopolies had to grant usage of their fixed networks to possible competitors, to ensure that competition developed. That meant that for a long time, these companies had to demonstrate to the sectorial regulator that they were not placing obstacles to that usage; as the market developed and infrastructures were replicated, the line rental obligations (if they still exist today) have now become analysed ex post by the generic competition authorities—or they will end up being so.

Any norm would be meaningless without a system that backed it and made sure it was complied with. Sanctions can therefore be considered another aspect of regulation. Such penalties can be economic (e.g. a fine and returning benefit overpayments); they can limit activity (e.g. inability to handle dangerous goods for a year); or, in extreme cases, they can lead to a ban from working in the activity.

2.4 Taxation

Taxes serve different purposes. Their main function is to collect funds that are used carry out public activity. But taxes can also be used as a tool to selectively influence economic activities. A high tax on buying a home stimulates the rental market. In the many countries where value-added tax (VAT) exists (an indirect tax that applies to all activities involving the production and consumption of goods and the provision of services), if movie tickets pass from the general VAT group to the reduced VAT group, it will encourage people to go to the movies. A much-reduced tax on corporations in a certain territory seeks to encourage companies to move to that territory.

A particular case of taxation with a specific aim are Pigovian taxes, which seek to correct the situation caused by a negative externality. They are used above all to control polluting activities.

2.5 Benefits and subsidies

Benefits and subsidies can be given without tying them to a specific aim, to people or to entities fulfilling certain conditions. This is the case of unemployment allowances or grants to couples who have had a child. However, the benefit is usually contingent on being used for a specific purpose as long as the receiver (the natural or legal person) can demonstrate that they meet certain requirements. Two examples are university financial aid and grants given to nongovernmental organizations (NGOs) that are required to use them for the projects presented in the subsidy application.

Assistance can be monetary or in kind (e.g. seeds given to a farmer or baby food for a poor family) and can consist of a fixed amount, can consist of a percentage of the cost of an activity or can even be tied to the contribution of the beneficiary (e.g. one euro is granted for every five euros that the business invests in research and development).

Assistance is offered in special circumstances, either for belonging to a group that arguably should be treated differently (reduced train ticket prices for people over the age of 65), because a situation must be reversed or alleviated (aid to workers in declining industrial sectors) or to encourage or stimulate an activity (grants to buy electric cars). Even economically unfeasible activities can be stimulated in this way if enough public support warrants doing so. This is the case when a national company is provided assistance during the time it needs to develop so that it can compete in the international market or when subsidies are provided for pharmaceutical research. Another particular circumstance is that of natural monopolies in which the service is offered by a private company. Without receiving a subsidy, companies would not be interested in transporting passengers to a remote area. In this case, the compensation that should be offered is not evident, as it depends on the company's costs and the knowledge that the administration has of those costs (it is a case of information asymmetry).

Finally, an issue related to benefits (at least some benefits) is how they affect what in another context would be the normal actions of the economic actors involved. To the degree possible, they should be designed in a way that doesn't distort the incentives that exist without assistance. If the monopoly from the earlier example knows that it will receive the difference between revenues and expenditures no matter what, it has no incentive to reduce costs the way any other business in the industry would. A generous and indefinite unemployment benefit could make the receiver delay looking for a new job.

2.6 Nonmonetary incentives

The state has ways to influence a part of the economy without having to dictate norms, create taxes or provide benefits. Classifying all the possibilities is difficult, so only specific examples are given:

- Awarding a protected designation-of-origin label or granting a trust mark to ecommerce websites recognizes (and therefore benefits) those who meet quality standards.
- Reducing the number of lanes in the avenues within a large city is a way of reducing the use of automobiles.
- Conversely, increasing the opening hours of a museum not only encourages visits to the museum but also seeks to attract more tourists to that place.
- If taxes can be paid online using an electronic signature, then when citizens realize its usefulness, the use of safe electronic transactions might become widespread.
- Institutional publicity campaigns attempt to convince citizens (or businesses) to adapt their behaviour to what they advocate.

- Instead of dictating a norm that imposes conditions that must be met in television advertising, advertisers and communications companies can be encouraged to sign a commitment to self-regulate their activity.

2.7 Public–private partnerships

In public–private partnerships, the state doesn't use its coercive power. Instead, it lowers itself from its position *above* the other actors and places itself at their same level, making cooperative agreements to jointly carry out a certain activity. Generally, the agreement is with companies (e.g. to build and operate a hospital), but sometimes the agreement is with individuals (e.g. opening a museum to display an artist's work that is owned by the artist's heirs).

Just as in any agreement, all options are available at first. In the example of building a highway, perhaps the government builds it while a company manages it, or vice versa. The agreement can be more restrictive concerning only specific aspects of either construction or management. The infrastructure can be owned by either party or initially be owned by one and later transferred to the second after a certain number of years. This may or may not come with payment obligations (from the government to the business, or vice versa), and if so, the obligations can be unconditional or be due only if certain clauses have been met. The agreement can be for a set amount of time or indefinite as long as one of the parties does not renounce it.

The terms of public–private partnerships are usually defined by a contract, which is generally subject to private law (rather than public). This fact is important not only because it defines the law applicable to contractual obligations but also because it determines the competent jurisdiction for litigation that may arise in the case of noncompliance with the agreement by either party.

3 Policies used to organize economic activity

Even if private initiative is given total responsibility for organizing economic transactions, putting in place a minimum set of rules of the game and ensuring that those rules are followed would still be necessary. The organizational role of the state is manifest in these kinds of policies.

In real economies, the rules of the game are never a "minimum set". Neither are they neutral rules; indeed, neutrality is impossible. No norm is completely void of ideological content. When choosing between organizational options, decision makers always have a certain economic model in mind, even though it might not be openly manifested. Therefore, even if these policies are grouped in this section under the heading "organization", they also implicitly or explicitly serve other ends.

3.1. Property protection policy

Even the most steadfast supporters of reducing government functions accept one reason for its existence: to defend private property. A market economy cannot exist without private property. Therefore, the primary structure required to organize a mixed economy is defining property rights and organizing ways to guarantee them. This structure must guarantee the rights of people and also of businesses to obtain, possess, use and transmit capital and goods. That said, the right to property is not absolute or inviolable. The state can deprive a natural person or legal entity of a good through expropriation or even privatize an entire industry. It can also limit the transmission of certain goods. For example, certain medicines require a prescription, while uranium cannot be purchased, and certain goods classified as cultural heritage cannot be freely sold. Gifts and inheritances can be received only by following precise requirements. In fact, that is the key: although the right to property can be limited or conditioned, that must be done, except in highly exceptional cases, only in well-defined circumstances and by following a regulated procedure that provides security to the owners.

Not just tangible goods are protected. Industrial property rights protect trademarks and brand names, industrial designs, patents and also designations of origin. Intellectual property guarantees the rights of authors and other rights holders (e.g. actors and producers) over their work and the benefits derived from its creation; such creations can be literary works, films, musical compositions, works of art, drawings, paintings, photographs and sculptures, architectural designs, and source code for games and computer programs.

Now that the importance of political doctrines' defending the *social ownership of the means of production* has diminished, private property (and the need to protect it) is acknowledged even in countries that still nominally follow an ideology contrary to its existence (the paradigmatic case, China, recognized private property in a 2007 law). A different issue is the opinion on the extension of the public or communal domain. The property protection policy has nothing to do with whether more or fewer assets or industries are publicly owned or with the state's role as direct provider of goods and services.

READING 4.1   A PROPERTY RIGHT THAT WE GIVE UP? OUR PERSONAL DATA

Most people don't let strangers walk into their homes or give away their cars. If someone tries to take these assets, strict laws protect such private property. On the other hand, most people often give up (or directly give away) their personal data. The laws that protect privacy are not nearly as strict as those just mentioned. This is "normal" because data is *something else*, different from a car. Or is it?

Beyond the obligation to disclose them in certain situations, personal data, like vehicles or real state, are (should be) the property of their owners. Like vehicles or real estate, today personal data are an economic asset. And they are not just any asset. The use of personal data by companies is certainly not a new phenomenon, as knowledge of the customer has always served to develop techniques for building customer loyalty or selling other products, but on the web, data collection is carried out on a different scale, immediately and much less expensively. Personal information has thus become an asset of such value that its exploitation is at the basis of the development of many markets in the digital economy. The business model (revenue) of many of the Internet giants is based exclusively on exploiting their users' data for advertising purposes.

Do we protect our data with the same zeal as we protect our other belongings? Sometimes our information is "recovered" from the traces left by our online activity. But on many other occasions, it has been disclosed voluntarily. Sometimes, it is done in an interested manner because just as data serve to personalize advertising, they also serve to personalize applications and services and to make them more useful and attractive; furthermore, advertising, and specifically targeted advertising, supports, don't forget, the *all-for-free* model on the Internet. In other cases, the benefit of disclosure is linked to a perception of social or psychological reward; social networks are the best example of this. However, on many occasions, disclosure is made without receiving (or even expecting to receive) anything in return; it responds to mere laziness or to the fact that no importance is attached to ceding the data, which, given its economic value and that the cession is in no way altruistic, is, in economic terms, an irrational act. On the whole, although individual behaviours (and concerns) are disparate, society as a whole has relaxed its patterns of protecting the personal sphere. Actions in which we expose ourselves that today are considered absolutely normal and that are carried out on a daily basis would have been unacceptable only a few years ago. Certainly, when one's own life is sometimes almost broadcast, there are good grounds for considering that the perception of intrusion into one's privacy has been altered, which undoubtedly influences how one reacts in situations where one is asked for information or where one risks being robbed of it. Alongside increased permissiveness, or even indifference, is often a mixture of ignorance about what is happening to our data and about possible ways of protecting them.

What is the role of states in this situation? Governments are, first and foremost, responsible for protecting the rights of their citizens and, therefore, for pursuing those practices that endanger their privacy. But their role is not merely that of an autonomous police force unaware of what is happening. They are also part of the game, and protection must extend to their practices as well. After all, public administrations are the actors that store the greatest amount of personal data. Even more important is the conflict between privacy and security. As several recent news stories have shown (many more than any citizens would like), governments can also invade our privacy. This is a different debate, but one linked to that of data protection: in the face of increased controls *for security reasons*, where is the limit? Does the end justify any means?

Another variable in the equation is the momentum of the digital economy. The most important companies that are growing and expanding thanks to data collection are from the United States and China. These two countries have data protection regulations that in other areas (particularly in the European Union) are considered lax. The issue is that these companies are at the core of the information-based innovation economy that all governments see as one of the safest and most stable routes to future economic growth. Would all governments maintain the same discourse or the same degree of severity with regard to the use of personal data if these companies were based in their territory (or conversely if they left)?

3.2. Competition policy

As seen, in any mixed economy, the market is the primary mechanism to organize trade, and competition drives the market. Economic theory posits that competition benefits consumers, because it lowers prices and provides more choices. Competition, however, is not good for businesses. This theory teaches us that when competition is solid, companies may become *price takers*, which means that they cannot do anything but accept the prices imposed by the market, but if they have market power, they can sometimes become *price setters* and so obtain extraordinary profits. As a consequence, businesses have incentives to hinder the development of competition. Competition authorities monitor the market to make sure that such a hindrance does not occur, and they pursue cases of unlawful behaviour.

Competition policies (sometimes called antitrust legislation) cover three main areas:

- They lay out when to prosecute collusion. *Collusion* is defined as any informal (or even tacit) agreement between two or more companies that seeks to impede or restrict competition by limiting the rivalry between the colluding companies or by putting in practice joint actions that obstruct the activity of other companies. Collusion usually includes an agreement to set prices but also may limit production, control distribution chains or divide a market geographically. Companies must carry significant weight in the market in order to be capable of carrying out such actions; in fact, an oligopoly is the market structure with greatest propensity for collusion. Petrol stations and telephone companies are examples of companies that are often suspected of coordinating strategies. Collusion also exists in smaller markets (even if they are rarely subjected to inspection when not affecting national markets), such as when *by coincidence* every restaurant in a tourist destination has the same prices for their set menus.

The term *cartel* is also sometimes used to describe these situations, although it is more frequently used when an agreement between companies from several countries tries to control international commerce. Because it involves investigating outside of national jurisdictions, cartels are always difficult to prosecute. Prosecuting them is simply impossible to do when they are formed by governments, because there is no supranational commercial court; this is the case of the best-known cartel: the Organization of the Petroleum Exporting Countries (OPEC). Fines are the most common punishments meted out in cases of collusion.

- They prohibit abusive practices and dominant positions in the market. In this case, a single company puts *sufficient competition* in a market at risk. As in the case of collusion, for this to happen, a company must be in condition to do so; that is, it must have "significant market power".

As a rule, being dominant in and of itself is not prosecuted, but rather only if the company takes advantage of its dominance for its own gain. However, there are exceptions in which ex ante regulation imposes obligations on companies that have been designated as having significant power through a market analysis, without need for further inspections. Thus, in the example used earlier regarding the telecommunications services market, those companies subject to ex ante regulation can be forced to rent their networks to their competitors (the price for rental may even be set) due to the suspicion that if they are not forced to do so, they will impose prices or conditions that preclude viable competition. However, in the case of the Internet platforms operating over these networks (sometimes as near monopolies but subject in this case to ex post regulation), action is taken only if they are shown to use their market power in a way that perpetuates it or extends it into tied markets.

There is an exception in which barriers to competition are considered legitimate. This is the case of patents. A patent is a set of exclusive rights over the exploitation of an invention (it can be a product, a procedure or even an improvement on a procedure). This exclusivity allows the owner of the patent to exploit it as a monopolist during the time that the patent is in force. In exchange, the invention must be published, allowing general access to the technical innovation, once the patent expires.

- They monitor market concentration. Mergers and acquisitions between companies that reduce the number of offerors in a certain market or that concentrate a significant percentage of sales or production in a single company must be reported before being carried out and are subject to audit.

In this case, state action is always only preventative, as these transactions do not involve illegal behaviour. However, if an audit reveals a danger of market concentration, the transaction can be blocked or authorized only after certain requisites have been met.

READING 4.2   EUROPEAN COMMISSION FINES

The Directorate-General for Competition of the European Commission imposes sanctions in demonstrated cases of collusion, for anticompetitive practices that abuse a dominant market position or when companies receive nonsanctioned state aid.

Its website does not provide detailed statistics in all cases classified as offences. The most comprehensive information is on cartels:[1] in the period 1990–2020, fines were imposed for the formation of cartels on 140 occasions (880 companies involved) totalling EUR30.1 billion (reduced to EUR27.7 after the appeals granted by the courts). The following are the ten largest cartel fines ever imposed by the European Commission, already adjusted (i.e. after possible amendments by the courts):

- Medium and heavy truck producers (2016/2017)—EUR3.807 billion imposed on MAN, Volvo/Renault, Daimler, Iveco and DAF for colluding on truck prices (during 14 years) and agreeing to pass on the cost of meeting stricter emission rules to consumers.
- Television producers (2012)—EUR1.409 billion imposed on a score of producers for colluding to fix prices of cathode ray tube monitors.
- Banks (2013/2016)—EUR1.276 billion imposed on Deutsche Bank, Societé Générale, Royal Bank of Scotland, JP Morgan, Citigroup and the broker RP Martin, and later on Crédit Agricole, JP Morgan (again) and HSBC, for manipulating the LIBOR and Euribor interbank interest rates in the financial derivatives market; Barclays and UBS also participated in the cartels but came to agreements with Brussels to pay punitive fines.
- Car glass manufacturers (2008)—EUR1.185 billion imposed on Asahi, Pilkington, Saint-Gobain and Soliver for colluding on prices and dividing the car glass market between them.
- Banks (2019)—EUR1.068 billion imposed on Barclays, the Royal Bank of Scotland, Citigroup, JPMorgan and MUFG Bank for participating in two

cartels in the foreign exchange market; UBS participated in the cartels but was not sanctioned, because it received "leniency" for revealing the scheme.

- Car and truck bearing manufacturers (2014)—EUR953 million imposed on two European companies, SKF and Schaeffler, and four Japanese companies, JTEKT, NSK, NFC and NTN, for price collusion.
- Positions seven to ten of the list include activities as diverse as producing elevators and escalators, selling vitamins, running aircraft fleets and again banking.

The following is a second list showing the highest-profile sanctions handed out by the European Commission, which were imposed for anticompetitive practices hindering the development of the digital economy. This list is ordered chronologically, starting with the most recent:

- July 2019—Qualcomm was fined EUR242 million for selling chipsets for 3G communications at prices below production costs in order to drive competitors out of the market.
- March 2019—Google was fined EUR1.49 billion for abusing its dominant market position by imposing a series of restrictive clauses in contracts with other websites that prevented competitors from placing advertisements on those sites.
- July 2018—Google was hit with a EUR4.34 billion fine for bundling its search engine and Chrome apps into the Android operating system.
- September 2017—Google was fined EUR2.42 billion for abusing its market dominance as a search engine to give advantage to its comparison shopping service for online purchases.
- May 2017—Facebook was fined EUR110 million for providing incorrect or misleading information during the Commission's 2014 investigation of its acquisition of WhatsApp.
- March 2013—Microsoft was fined EUR561 million for not allowing its users to easily choose their preferred web browser, giving priority to Internet Explorer.
- May 2009—Intel was fined EUR1.06 billion for offering hidden rebates to computer manufacturers on the condition that they only bought their processors from Intel.
- February 2008—Microsoft was fined EUR860 million for not disclosing information which would allow rival vendors to make their products compatible with Windows in a reasonable timeframe.
- March 2004—Microsoft was fined EUR497 million for refusing to eliminate Windows Media Player from its Windows operating system.

At the time of this reading, no resolution has been reached on the four investigations opened against Apple (three relating to restrictions on access to the App Store and one more for favouring its Apple Pay application) or on the two against Amazon (for using confidential data of vendors using its platform and for giving preferential treatment to certain offers, in particular those of its own branded products).

1 https://ec.europa.eu/competition/cartels/statistics/statistics.pdf.

3.3. Labour policy

Labour policy is made up of a set of norms that regulate the relationships in the labour market. It should not be confused with employment policy (see Section 6), whose main objective is to facilitate access to employment to those who are unemployed or at risk of becoming unemployed.

Labour policy can establish work hours, conditions for access to employment (e.g. a minimum age or maximum age), health requirements for a job, salary levels, dismissal costs, obligation to pay social insurance taxes or, in general, organize any aspect of the relationship between employers and employees.

Labour policy is probably the most conflictive among all the policies organizing economic activity. For its detractors (proponents of reducing it), compliance drives up the price of the work factor and is therefore a main cause of unemployment. In their opinion, the intrusiveness of norms and agreements makes reaching the equilibrium price (salary) that a *free* labour market would achieve only more difficult. For instance, the introduction of a minimum wage would lead to a new equilibrium with a higher salary, but labour demand would absorb fewer workers. If state action were reduced to the minimum, salaries would drop to the *competitive equilibrium* and increase employment. Minimizing the labour policy is the backdrop for what is known by the euphemism *labour market flexibilization*. This perspective is opposed by those who do not consider a *free* labour market a panacea against unemployment. In contrast, when salaries diminish, the purchasing power of the workers does as well, which negatively affects aggregate demand; if the demand for goods decreases, the demand for labour is also reduced, leading to the worst possible scenario, in which unemployment is combined with low salaries.

3.4. Consumer protection policy

As the name consumer protection policy indicates, such a policy includes a group of public actions designed to protect consumers or users in a general way but also, in greater detail, in their relationship with businesses that operate in particular markets of goods and services. The main area of this policy is regulation, which grants and safeguards certain rights of individual consumers. It covers a wide range of issues, such as protection from fraud, unfair business practices, abusive contractual clauses, establishing the responsibility of sellers of products and services, the availability of effective means of resolving controversies and compensation, controlling incomplete or distorted information (which could include the prohibition of false advertising, the inspection of labelling and the way prices are displayed), controlling payment methods and protecting personal data. Consumer protection is reinforced in the purchase of certain sensitive products: foods, toys, pharmaceuticals, cosmetics and financial products.

Regulation can be completed with additional measures, in particular in the area of education. The most protected consumers, except in cases of apathy, are those who know their rights and the instruments at their disposal to enforce them.

3.5. Environmental policy

Considered globally, economic activity should have a limit that maintains the conditions that ensure that the activity can continue. Environmental destruction threatens that continuity, and therefore, its protection should not be contemplated in a particular policy but rather form part of the organization of the economic activity itself.

The most visible measure of environmental policy is limiting the emission of toxic gases, but just as serious is stopping deforestation; the pollution of aquifers, rivers and other aquatic environments; and the destruction of the coastline and of land in general, which is subject to aggressive practices and overdevelopment.

As occurs in other cases in which the public sector considers acting necessary to mitigate negative externalities, the two most commonly used tools are legislation and taxation. Thus, certain provisions can prohibit or condition particular industrial or agricultural practices. The same polluting practices could be subject to specific taxation.

However, governments can take alternative or complementary approaches. To obtain authorization for certain activities, an environmental impact assessment may need to be conducted first. At this same administrative (nonlegal) level, environmental audits can be required. For consumers, education is again essential: understanding the environmental, social and economic consequences of their choices creates better-informed and hopefully more-responsible consumers. This is the objective of institutional publicity campaigns.

Finally, governments have attempted to introduce market mechanisms into environmental policy. Emissions trading involves permits that allow the owner to discharge a specific quantity of pollutant. Because the permits can be traded, any company with a licence to participate in the market can buy and sell them. The proper functioning of the system depends largely on the number of emission permits in circulation and the criteria used for their initial allocation.

4 Policies used to promote economic activity

As seen in the previous chapter, economic growth can hide many situations. The desired type of growth comes from increasing the productive capacity of the country, as this ensures that the growth will continue over time (or at least that the conditions exist for it to continue). Production can be improved by increasing resources or by using them more efficiently. Traditionally, the resources of an economy were divided into the categories of land, labour and capital; contemporarily, they are defined as natural resources, physical capital and human capital, to which technology is added. Although natural resources may seem unalterable, in reality they can be depleted (a fishing ground), they can increase (the discovery of a new gas field) or, more frequently, their value can change, sometimes dramatically, if they are no longer used (guano) or if new uses are found for them (coltan). That said, policies meant to boost economic activity focus on increasing physical capital and human capital and on better exploiting technology.

Infrastructure policies deal with physical capital, while education and training policies focus on human capital. The objectives of research and development policies are transversal, although they are usually tied to technology usage. The recent, but increasingly pivotal, policies to develop the information society are directly related to the use of information and communication technologies. Finally, the *formulas* offered to developing countries continue referring, although increasingly less often, to development policies, where all the policies mentioned earlier, along with others that deal with adjusting imbalances, are integrated.

4.1. Infrastructure policy

Some types of investment in physical capital (or, as it is referred to in economics, formation of physical capital) are considered vital for the progress of the entire economy. The size of the investment is sometimes so large that private initiative is not interested in undertaking the project, or at least not interested with the characteristics sought by the state—for example, in what refers to the extension of the networks. For this reason, the state becomes involved in the construction, maintenance or improvement of these infrastructures.

Basic physical capital includes the following areas: transport (highways, railroad lines, ports and airports), energy (dams, high voltage power lines and gas pipelines), hydric infrastructure (water supply networks, collectors and wastewater treatment plants) and telecommunications (repeater stations, telephone networks and, today, fibre optic networks). As we shall see later, almost every one of these activities also has its own sectorial policy. Although promoting networks is part of them, the main objective of sectorial policies is to organize the markets for services that use these infrastructures. Conceptually, therefore, the infrastructure policy has a different purpose.

Sometimes the state is responsible for every stage: the construction, exploitation and maintenance of the infrastructure. On other occasions, the private sector is in charge but generally subject to regulation because of the classification of the services that run through those facilities as, to invoke the expression used by EU institutions, "services of general economic interest". Such regulation usually imposes public service obligations, particularly regarding the ubiquity of the network and affordability of the service. Between these two extremes, any kind of distribution of tasks and responsibilities is imaginable. In fact, infrastructures are probably the area in which the most public–private partnerships exist.

4.2. Training and capacity-building policies

Human capital—that is, the skills and aptitudes provided by a worker—is a fundamental part of an economy's progress. This is truer than ever today, because a once-industrial economy has given way to a knowledge-based economy and society. This is reason enough for governments to implement programmes that elevate the education of their youth but also of their workers and, in general, of their entire population. Although education is provided on diverse topics, one basic line is to develop the skills and abilities that companies are looking for in the labour market; one aspect that has recently been gaining importance is training in *entrepreneurship*.

The professional training policy clearly overlaps with the education policy. Including education policy within social policies makes sense because access to education has more to do with a societal project than with an economic project, although it could serve both purposes. Training is also present in policies to develop the information society and, as we shall see later, in active employment policies.

4.3. Research and development policy

Research and development policies (contemporarily renamed as research, development *and innovation* policies or R&D&I policies) consist in a set of activities designed to increase scientific and technical knowledge and to apply the results of this knowledge to new products or industrial processes that ideally break with the previous situation. The ultimate goal would be to obtain a comparative advantage in the market versus international competition (and therefore capitalize on it). Conceptually, governments support such research for two reasons: research is seen as presenting positive externalities, and companies do not invest enough in this area.

R&D&I policy has a purely public side and another that seeks to promote innovation by businesses. Public research institutions work on basic research, which is less interesting to businesses that are looking for immediate utility, but increasingly they are also working on applied research and technological development, aspects prioritized by the private sector. Mixed collaboration mechanisms between public agencies or universities and industry are common. The collaboration can extend to the creation of technology companies. Public business *incubators*, one of the tools used to try to meet the innovation facet demanded by R&D&I policies, constitutes one good example.

READING 4.3   INVESTMENT IN RESEARCH AND DEVELOPMENT

UNESCO provides global data on investment in research and development (R&D).[1] Figure 4.1 shows these data for 2018 (with few exceptions, for which the latest available data are used), expressed in percentages of GDP. The ranking is led by the eight countries where this investment exceeds 3% of GDP, namely Israel (4.9%), South Korea (4.8%), Switzerland (3.4%), Sweden (3.3%), Japan (3.3%), Austria (3.2%), Germany (3.1%) and Denmark (3.1%).

By regions, the data are from 2016. In that year, the European Union as a whole spent 2% of its GDP on R&D, although it had set a goal of reaching 3% by 2020. The African Union also had set a goal (1%), which could be seen as ambitious given that in 2016 it had spent only 0.4%. In the rest of the world, in 2016 North America as a whole spent 2.7% of its GDP in R&D, and Latin America and the Caribbean spent 0.7%, Asia spent 1.6% (although national differences were enormous) and Oceania spent 1.8%. Finally, the percentage in Arab countries was 0.5%.

UNESCO also provides a breakdown of the sources of R&D funding.[2] Figure 4.2 shows the percentage of these activities financed by governments. This percentage might actually be higher because the category of higher education institutions includes expenditure incurred by public universities that should be included as government money, although greater detail is not provided. Nevertheless, higher education institutions (of any kind, both public and private) don't contribute more than 5% to the total expenditure in the

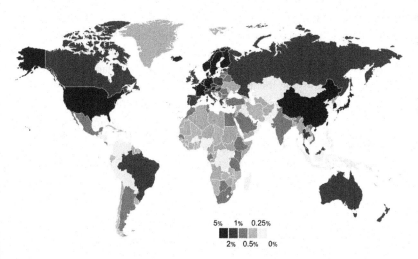

FIGURE 4.1   Global investment in R&D as percentage of GDP (2018 or the latest information available)

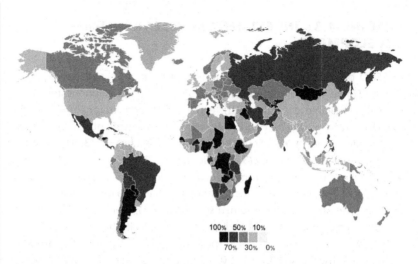

FIGURE 4.2   Government investment in R&D as a percentage of total investment (2016)

majority of countries, so presumably, even without this proposed correction, the results are not distorted.

Therefore, according to only the data provided for the "government sector", the two countries with the highest public contribution to R&D investment, among those that could be considered to have some relevance in global research, are Mexico (77%) and Russia (67%). In the largest countries of the European Union, the percentages range from 39% in Spain to approximately 25% in Sweden and the United Kingdom; between the two extremes are Germany (28%) and Italy and France (32% in both cases). Australia (35%) and Canada (33%) record similar values. In the United States, public investment accounts for only 23%, and it is even lower in the main Asian countries: in South Korea it is 21%, in China 20% and in Japan 15%. Japan is, in fact, the penultimate country on the list, just ahead, curiously, of the one that heads the general classification, Israel, where public investment in R&D is only 11%.

1 UIS (UNESCO Institute for Statistics). http://data.uis.unesco.org/Index.aspx. Indicator: Gross domestic expenditure on R&D (GERD), GERD as a percentage of GDP, GERD per capita and GERD per researcher.
2 UIS. http://data.uis.unesco.org/Index.aspx. Indicator: GERD by source of funds.

4.4. Policy for developing the information society

Adapting the economy to the new paradigm imposed by the emergence of the information society is a key factor in any future economic development. Information and communication technologies, which are at the heart of this revolution, are horizontal technologies: their use is not constrained to a specific sector, so the entire economy benefits from promoting them.

Policies to develop the information society offer all kinds of support to help the economy, and society in general, to progress towards digitalization. A fundamental part of these policies tries to close the so-called *digital divide*. The divide results from not being connected to the Internet (or not having enough bandwidth) or from not having the capacity to obtain the benefits of using digital services or applications. As a consequence, the policies that deal with the problem have two sections: availability (access to the infrastructure) and usage.

- Programmes providing access to the infrastructure have clear connections with the general infrastructure policy and with the sectorial policy on telecommunications. They seek to deploy networks with sufficient bandwidth throughout the territory because, evidently, doing so is necessary for its usage. Other variables could be considered, however, such as affordability.
- Programmes providing incentives to use digital transactions organize training plans and raise awareness about their usefulness; for instance, developing an electronic administration (and even obligating its use in some cases) is inherently useful, but sometimes it is also expected to have a demonstration effect of the benefits of adopting such tools. The programmes are not only directed at individuals; companies (especially small businesses) must also adapt to the new models of online transactions, presence and publicity.

Classifying policies to develop the information society as a way to promote economic activity stems from the belief that closing the digital divide will have an effect on the economy—if not in the short term, then in the medium and long term. That said, this policy, like other policies described in this section, has a social component.

4.5. Growth and development policies

Those countries that do not fall into the euphemistical category of developing countries often have long-term plans to orient the future of their economies. These are guidelines to promote economic growth—or, simply, *growth policies*. Strictly speaking, the concept of *development policies* refers to a set of formulas applied by (frequently suggested to) poor countries to try to stimulate economic development as well as social and political modernization, in order to alleviate their deficiencies in a reasonable period of time.

As for developed (or middle-income) countries, long-term political strategies are increasingly uncommon because of a short-term vision conditioned by economic and electoral cycles. When they do exist, they opt for transversal objectives that affect the entire economy (e.g. reaching a milestone on the usage of *new technologies* or renewable energies by a certain date), or they favour specific industries or activities in which they seek to obtain a comparative advantage over other countries, always with the promise of achieving sustained and sustainable economic growth.

In the case of poor countries, the policies implemented to develop their economies are much less in style now than they were at certain moments during the past century. In many cases imposed ("suggested") by supranational organizations in exchange for forgiving debt or receiving aid programmes, they included (and might still include) reforms of the public sector, privatizations, commitments to open markets and industrial restructuring, and modifying legislation in various areas. *Development economics*, which serves as the theoretical support for this approach, is today less pretentious regarding the effectiveness of the formulas that lead to development and is more open to considering the many facets that such a complex process presents.

Other development policies that have generally fallen into disuse are multiyear plans developed by planned economies. Today, however, some countries that mix a market economy with a centralized economy still maintain similar plans. The primary example is China, which continues to approve five-year plans "for the advancement of the national economic and social development of the country".

5 Macroeconomic adjustment policies

Although the historical tendency of the global or regional economies has been to grow, a closer look at their evolution reveals that growth has never been continuous. Although the lengths of time vary, expansion periods have always been alternated with periods of recession, creating what are referred to as economic cycles. Clearly, recessions are not desired, but neither are sharp expansions, because economies have trouble adjusting. Since the beginning of the 20th century, following the Great Depression, governments have developed countercyclical policies whose long-term goal is to achieve gentle and sustained economic growth.

The two basic policies to carry out this adjustment are fiscal policy, which acts on public revenues and expenditures, and monetary policy, which today is principally used to control inflation. Commercial policy and incomes policy must also be added to the list. Commercial policy, as its name suggests, is concerned with regulating commercial transactions with other countries. Incomes policy may be used to control increases in wages and prices. For orthodox economics, these are the fundamental economic policies. In fact, many textbooks see them as *the only* economic policies. Although such a perspective is erroneous, macroeconomic adjustment policies are given special attention.

5.1 Fiscal policy

Public sector activity generates expenditures. To defray those costs, the state obtains revenue from individuals and companies or borrows money. Given the weight of the public sector in modern economies, any variation in the structure or quantity of its expenditures, or in the mechanisms that it uses to collect funds, affects the entire economy. This impact is the basis for fiscal policy, which consists in the intentional alteration of government spending and revenues. The adjective intentional is necessary because, as we shall see, the evolution of the economy already alters public revenues and expenditures, without need for any policy changes.

Fiscal policy is used to drive economic growth, often by stabilizing or correcting imbalances that arise. However, this is only one of the final objectives that this policy can pursue. The second is redistribution. To provide greater coherence to the description of fiscal policy, this section also studies this function, even though it does not fit at all in the definition of an adjustment policy.

5.1.1 Fiscal policy as a stabilizer of the economy

Government spending generates income directly (through the salaries that it pays) and indirectly (by the goods and services that it acquires). This revenue (or at least part of it) goes to consumption, as the recipients also purchase goods and services, thereby creating a spending chain. Because of this amplified repercussion on revenue, government spending is said to have a *multiplier effect*. This means that public expenditure can be used to increase aggregate demand and, by extension, economic activity, employment and, ultimately, national income. Or, in a negative sense, a reduction in government spending would have an amplified effect (greater than the reduction itself) on the contraction of demand. Similarly, altering taxes (or fees or public transfers) also affects economic activity, as it immediately increases or decreases the income available to those affected and has a similar indirect expansion effect.

Given that the government decides the exact amount of the public budget, the moment in which a new budget is drawn up offers an opportunity to try to steer economic activity in accordance with the state of the cycle. In recessions or economic dips, the government seeks to boost demand, which requires an expansive policy that increases government spending, lowers taxes and increases transfers. In principle, these actions cannot be carried out simultaneously (spending cannot be increased while lowering taxes) unless the government takes out loans. During expansive periods, when growth in macroeconomic demand puts upward pressures on inflation, the inverse approach is recommended: restrain public spending and raise taxes. This approach would generate a surplus that can be used to pay off debt contracted at other times.

Various tweaks have been made to the general rule for how countercyclical policies work:

*   Strictly speaking, only discretionary public action is fiscal policy. Automatic economic stabilizers also act to dampen the economic cycle, softening its effects without the need for outside intervention. For instance, because taxes are proportional to revenues (or progressive in the case of some taxes), during recessions low tax collection helps slow the decrease in disposable income and the consequent fall in consumption. On the contrary, when the economy

expands, tax collection increases, which attenuates the gains in disposable income, thereby moderating the negative effects of rapid growth (essentially raising prices). Transfers and subsidies are also automatic stabilizers. Of course, a tax or the conditions required to receive a subsidy can be changed, in which case, we would enter into the area of fiscal policy.

- Economists largely agree that expansive policies are effective only if the economy is far from its potential level of production: if they are applied when the economy is close to full use of resources, government spending will mainly overheat the economy by increasing prices. Monetary wages, which are not usually sensitive to demand–pull inflationary pressures in situations of unemployment, go up when the economy is near full employment.

- The instruments used to apply fiscal policy are sometimes not selective enough. For instance, setting the objective of increasing demand in general is too vague, because not all sectors of the economy will be in the same situation: the national economy or even the world economy could have bottlenecks (think, for example, in energy or commodities markets), and the supply in certain markets could need some time to satisfy a growing demand. All these circumstances could cause price increases in some markets. The situation could be even worse, depending on how important the affected market is for the economy to function. This ties in with the earlier argument that part of the intended boost might not materialize and could even lead to an increase in inflation. The solution to this problem is to employ fiscal measures directed at specific objectives. However, this is not an easy task, because of the reason that the next point expands on.

- Fiscal policy measures can affect both supply and demand, generating unforeseen consequences. For example, if taxes affecting production factors are modified, the use of these factors in productive activities could be modified, thereby changing the expected results. Think about an increase in compulsory social insurance contributions: it might discourage labour demand and activity in certain sectors, which would lead to lower government revenue from other sources, thereby cancelling out the extra income that was sought by raising the contributions.

- Along these lines, the Laffer curve illustrates how government revenue varies when taxation rates are modified. Arthur Laffer's work, which was in vogue in the 1980s, stated that increasing rates of taxation does not always lead to an increase in tax revenue. Tax revenue, which starts at zero revenue at a 0% tax rate, would increase along with the tax rate until it reached a maximum and would then decrease until it again reached zero at a 100% tax rate (in the understanding that if taxes would take all income, nobody would have an incentive to do anything). Above the maximum, economic actors would presumably look for strategies to avoid paying taxes, such as moving part or all of their activity to the informal economy or black market or moving it to other countries.

- The rational expectations theory provides a comprehensive criticism of employing fiscal policy. If agents are able to anticipate state behaviour, they will take actions that will make fiscal policy ineffective, no matter how it is executed or how the extra income is financed. For example, if the government decides to increase spending through debt, taxpayers will realize that they will have to pay higher taxes in the future, so they will need to save additional money to be able to pay them; these savings would lead to a contraction in the demand that would exactly compensate for the additional public spending, leaving aggregate demand unchanged. This is what textbooks refer to as *Ricardian equivalence*. The policy would be successful in the short term only if the government avoids announcing its purposes, but it would provoke long-term distortions because of the growing uncertainty transmitted to the rest of the economic agents.

  A less radical version of this expectations theory states that even if people and businesses do not totally anticipate the direction that fiscal policy will take, they at least will have an idea and take actions in accordance. Although the effect of fiscal policy is not completely neutralized, it is reduced, barring a completely mistaken forecast.

- Finally, a broad area of controversy surrounds the deficit that is possibly associated with fiscal policy measures. The first criticism is what is known as the *crowding out* of investment: if the public sector needs to go into debt, it must turn to the credit market and it therefore sucks up a part of available savings that cannot be used for other purposes; this is truer for more closed economies whose governments have fewer possibilities of using international credit markets. The second criticism revolves around whether maintaining a budget deficit year after year until the level of public debt becomes a significant part of the country's GDP is admissible. This is such an important issue in current political debate that it deserves its own section.

5.1.2 The adverse effects of fiscal policy: public sector debt

Paradoxically, although one of the main uses of fiscal policy is to stabilize the economy, one of its possible secondary effects, a budget deficit, can become one of the most destabilizing elements of an economy. When loans are taken out to finance the deficit, they have to be paid back in the future, with interest. If the debt grows uncontrollably, a point may come at which these payments consume a large part of revenues (leaving the economy without these resources to take care of other needs), and even so, new loans have to be taken out, which would only make the situation worse.

As seen in Chapter 3, we have many ways to measure a deficit. The same is true for measuring debt, because certain kinds of debt can be treated differently, such as that of certain public bodies. Leaving aside the differences that these criteria can introduce, the indicator that marks the gravity of the situation is not the absolute quantity of the debt but rather the percentage of GDP that it represents. This percentage may grow year after year because the economy is immersed in a long recession (in which government revenue diminishes and spending, particularly social, increases), because of an imbalance in government revenues and expenditures (which is defined as a structural deficit) or because the interest rates on the debt are high (as a general rule, if the average interest payment rate is larger than the economy's growth, the debt will increase).

Although various rules have been proposed, no fixed guideline indicates the ratio between debt and GDP that can be considered unsustainable. The response depends on the composition of the debt, its origin (proportion between budget deficit accumulated each year and interest on old debt), the interest rate (and its tendency), the foreseeable evolution of the economy, the possibility of refinancing (and the refinancing conditions) and the changes in inflation, as inflation affects the real value of financial assets and liabilities.

That said, the interest rate at which countries obtain financing is, somewhat perversely, higher the greater its debt; therefore, once a certain level of dependence on external financing is reached, reducing the debt becomes unavoidable. If a government decides to alleviate the situation immediately (or if it is obligated to do so), it has three conventional options: increase revenue (through tax reform or privatizations), reduce spending (by paralysing investments, reducing the welfare state or reducing the size of the public sector) or restructure or renegotiate the debt. A fourth option is to "print" money to be able to deal with the payment (referred to as seigniorage). Today this fourth option is used less because of the imbalances (inflation) that it produces in the entire economy, although inflation is what reduces the real value of the debt (the government would be charging an "inflation tax"). The inflation tax can reduce the annual deficit but in the case of debt, it only has an effect if it is expressed in the national currency.

If the government decides to try to reverse the situation and avoid out-of-control debt's happening again, the *recipe* includes restrictions in how to finance the deficit (through limits on the emission of bonds) and balanced budget laws that set limits on modifying it during the fiscal year and that introduce expenditure ceilings in some areas.

READING 4.4   THE BURDEN OF DEBT

The World Bank, using its own data and data provided by the International Monetary Fund, provides a time series that displays interest payments made by governments over time, expressed as a percentage of public revenue.[1] This includes "interest payments on government debt—including long-term

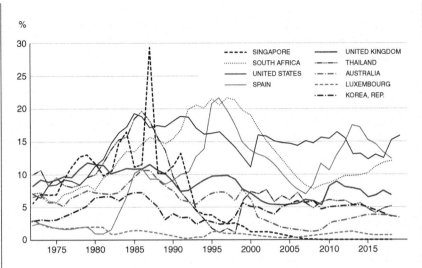

FIGURE 4.3 Interest payments made by governments, in percentage of revenue (1972–2019)

bonds, long-term loans, and other debt instruments—to domestic and foreign residents".

Figure 4.3 displays the evolution of this ratio in nine countries, which were drawn from every continent. The series begins in 1972, just before the first oil crisis (see Chapter 6). At that time, servicing debt was never above 10% of total revenue. From then until the middle of the 1980s, this percentage increased significantly. In the following decades, the upward trend of the curve reversed in some countries, whereas in others it remained at those levels (or even increased). Although this is a small sample of only nine states, peculiar situations can be observed, such as that of Luxembourg, where interest payments have never surpassed 2% or 3% of revenue during the entire period studied, or that of Singapore, where after growing to nearly 30% in 1987, interest payments have been reduced to nearly zero since 2007. In the United States, on the other hand, interest payments have hovered at around 15%. As explained in the text, revenue dedicated to servicing debt is, obviously, not available to be spent in other areas.

1 https://data.worldbank.org/indicator/GC.XPN.INTP.RV.ZS.

5.1.3 Fiscal policy as a redistribution instrument

The specific structure and characteristics of the instruments used to obtain revenue or to spend public money affect the distribution of wealth between groups and even between individuals. Indeed, starting with taxes, they enable selectively influencing the distribution of income. When a tax system is described, both the quantitative aspects (how much is collected) and qualitative aspects (the type of taxes, whom they are applied to, on what activities or situations and in what amounts) must be included. The responses to these last questions determine how well the system has been defined for redistribution.

Generically speaking, the system is progressive if the wealthiest pay the most and regressive if the opposite is true or if people with different incomes pay the same. This distinction can also be made for specific taxes. In this sense, a value-added tax or sales tax is regressive because a millionaire and an unemployed person pay the same tax on a tin of sardines. To put it simply, tax systems with more-direct taxes produce greater distribution (assuming that they are progressive). However, a number of clarifications could be made here. For example, income that was transformed into property is commonly considered more "unassailable" than uninvested or recently obtained income; in other words, taxation on income is usually much higher than taxation on property.

The final impact of a tax is not always immediate. In reality, to effectively ascertain how a certain tax affects the income of different groups, we should be able to trace its effect on the entire economy. As already pointed out, the interdependencies between markets can be subtle and, on occasion, generate unwanted effects. A reduction in the tax on labour, along with an increase in capital tax, could, paradoxically, provoke a loss of jobs because of the closure of some industries or capital flight. Results obtained using the ceteris paribus assumption are not the same as those generated in the always-dynamic real economy.

A related question is if a plan for social justice through taxation can or cannot alter the incentives to carry out or abandon certain activities. If we look exclusively at theoretical models that define rules for optimal taxation, all taxes generate a distortion because they interfere in the decisions of economic agents. From that theoretical perspective, taxes with a general purpose are less efficient than those with a specific aim (e.g. correcting an externality). An additional condition required to maximize efficiency is for taxes to be fixed amounts that do not depend on contingencies or specific situations and that also cannot be altered by the reaction of taxpayers towards said duty.

Efficiency is precisely the main argument used by those opposed to using taxation for redistribution. They argue that possible gains through this channel are cancelled out by the loss of efficiency, which could end up producing a negative result. In the 1970s, Arthur Okun proposed the famous image of a leaky bucket: money is carried from the rich to the poor in a leaky bucket; part of the money is lost because of administrative costs, because of costs incurred from complying with obligations, and because of the distortions in the incentives to work, save and invest. If taxes met three technical requisites, at least two of the holes in the bucket could be sealed: ease of collection (reduction in management costs), simplicity (reduction in the costs incurred by taxpayers to meet their tax obligations, which also reduces fraud) and flexibility (possibility of relatively easily introducing changes, making tax collection adjust automatically).

As said at the beginning, income is not the only instrument of fiscal policy that can be used for redistribution purposes. The composition of public spending (*on what* and *where* certain items of the budget are allocated) also affects the resources (monetary or nonmonetary) to which certain groups or regions have access. In fact, an analysis of annual budget spending allows a hierarchy of priorities to be established between social groups and geographical areas.

Tied to spending (specifically to its financing) is the intergenerational aspect of redistribution. When public spending is financed by selling government bonds, in the future the state will have to obtain extra income to pay the interest and the principle on the bonds. This is not a problem if fiscal policy is viewed as a perfect mechanism in which the surpluses during periods of growth compensate for the deficits during recessions. But if we go to the other extreme and accept the theory that fiscal policy has no real effect on demand, debt would need to be entirely covered by future taxes. Even if this were not fully the case, if the present deficit cannot be compensated by a future surplus, the government will need to raise taxes. Depending on the time given to complete the operation, a "burden of debt" could be left for the following generation (even for various generations). This intergenerational redistribution would not occur if the *Ricardian equivalence* were satisfied, which based as it is on rational expectations, supposes that families will leave inheritances to their children that are large enough to compensate for the taxes that the children will have to pay *for them*. Intergenerational redistribution occurs also in the expenditures themselves, not just in how they are paid for. There are investments without time limits, such as hospitals or highways, which can be used by future generations if they are properly maintained. Perhaps only the future generations will receive certain benefits, such as when a product is developed at a later time thanks to current investments into research and development.

A "golden rule" has been proposed as a principle of intergenerational equity: operational costs should be financed through taxation and investment expenditures through debt. The validity of this principle is not, however, absolute. If the debt decisively affects savings, if it is unsustainable over the long term or if the investments do not obtain the expected social profitability, financing the cost of investment by using debt could reduce instead of raise the welfare of future generations.

READING 4.5   WHO PAYS MORE IN TAXES—BUSINESSES OR INDIVIDUALS?

The Federal Reserve Bank of St. Louis offers on its website FRED Economic Data the possibility to consult, supposedly, more than half a million time series that include data mainly from the United States but also international data.[1] An interactive tool allows various series to be displayed on a single graph. This tool was used to create Figure 4.4. This graph shows four series, starting in 1960, whose first quarter is taken as the reference value of 100 in all of them: taxes on corporate income, personal current taxes, corporate profits and disposable personal income. The shaded areas represent economic recessions in the United States.

Side by side comparisons of these series reveal some astonishing facts. The tax burden on private individuals has grown much more than it has on legal entities. By the beginning of 2000, the ratio of growth in both tax collections had already tripled compared with the 1960 figures (values 2,668 and 890). Since then, the gap has grown increasingly wider, although until the crisis in 2008–2009, the curves had at least shown similar tendencies. After the crisis, however, personal current taxes have grown at a faster rate than before, while tax on corporate income has stagnated or even decreased. The last figure in the series before the pandemic caused by COVID-19 (first quarter of 2020) reflects the widest difference in the whole period: no less than a ratio of 50 to 8 (value 4,972 compared with 795). In other words, compared with the base year (1960), personal current taxes had grown more than six times than tax on corporate income: in the first quarter of 1960, tax revenue from corporations was approximately 50% of what was obtained from individuals ($22.7 and $45.3 billion), while in the first quarter of 2020, it was only 8% ($180.5 billion compared to $2,252.4 billion)

Curiously, while revenues from taxes on corporate income have declined over the past few years, corporate profits have exploded. Although the corporate profit curve has always been well above that of taxes on corporate

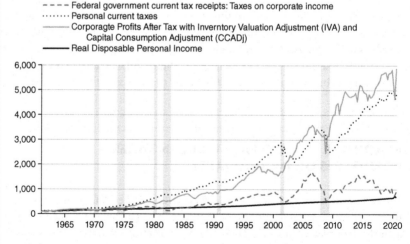

FIGURE 4.4 Tax revenue (payments of businesses and private individuals), corporate profits and disposable income—evolution in the United States (1960–2020)

income, the difference has become abysmal in the final year of the series, reaching a ratio of almost 7 to 1 (5,166 compared with 795, always using 1960 as the base year). The data on corporate profits are after tax and include adjustments for depreciation and other concepts. Disposable income could be considered an equivalent indicator for private individuals. If we look at the curve representing disposable income, its growth has always been below that of tax revenue from individuals, just the opposite of what happens with corporations. The divergence has been growing increasingly larger, and by the end of the series, the values had reached 4,972 (personal taxes) and 663 (income); that is, taxes have multiplied by 50 while income has only increased by a factor of 6.5. Finally, if we compare the growth of corporate profits in 2020 with that of disposable income, the final values are 5,166 and 663. To gain some perspective, corporate profits reached a similar value as disposable income (674) already in the fourth quarter of 1983! In summary, from 1960 to 2020, corporate profits have grown eight times more than disposable income has, but revenue from taxes on corporate income has grown only 13% of what individual tax revenue has grown; this means that the amount received for corporate taxes is 62 times less than what could have been collected if the 1960 proportion had been maintained.

How widespread is the United States model? The OECD provides time-series data from 1965 to 2018[2] for tax on corporate profits[3] and on personal income.[4] Apart from possible problems with the data sources, the second series considers tax on personal income and not personal current taxes, which was the concept used before (therefore including other taxes such as social insurance contributions and those imposed on assets). The data are presented as a percentage of GDP or percentage of total tax revenue (neither of these options is offered by the tool provided by the Federal Reserve Bank of St. Louis, which would have helped with the comparisons). The first option (a percentage of GDP) has been chosen. Figures 4.5 and 4.6 show the evolution of this indicator in six countries, including the United States. The black line in each graph is the OECD average. As we can see, the average taxes on corporate profits have grown from 2.14% GDP to 3.14% (with a peak of 3.59% in 2007, just before the crisis that started the following year); meanwhile, taxes on personal income have grown from 6.77% to 8.30% (with a peak of 10.30% in 1988).

The figures for the United States at the beginning and end of the two series are 3.86% and 1.00% (with a peak of 4.32% in 1967) in business taxes and 7.50% and 9.90% (with a peak of 11.90% in 2000) in personal income taxes. Therefore, whereas individuals in OECD countries generally pay much more than corporations do, the situation in the United States is extreme. A closer look shows that each country has had a different evolution. The model most similar to that of the United States (from the shape of the curves) is Germany; the furthest is Sweden, where the evolution has been just the opposite.

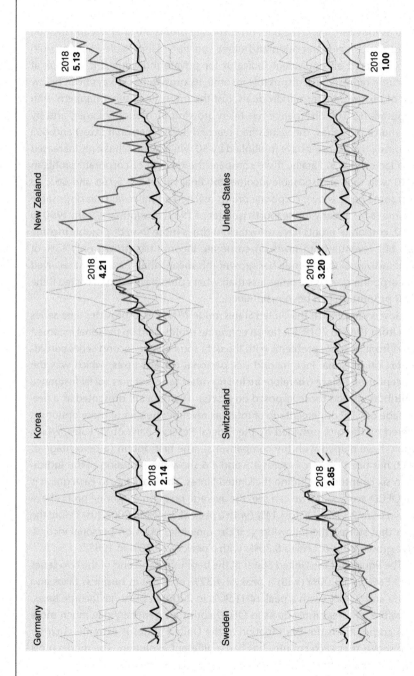

FIGURE 4.5 Tax on corporate income in percentage of GDP—evolution in various countries (1965–2018)

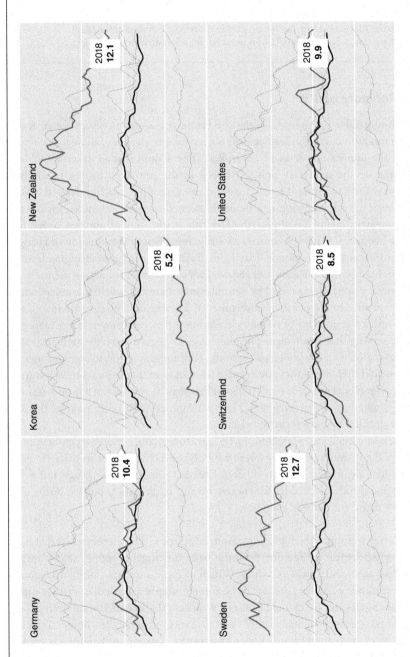

FIGURE 4.6   Tax on personal income in percentage of GDP—evolution in various countries (1965–2018)

1 FRED Graphs. https://fred.stlouisfed.org/ Series B075RC1Q027SBEA, W055RC1, CPATAX and DSPIC96. All the data comes from U.S. Bureau of Economic Analysis.
2 2015 in some cases and for the global average.
3 https://data.oecd.org/tax/tax-on-corporate-profits.htm#indicator-chart.
4 https://data.oecd.org/tax/tax-on-personal-income.htm#indicator-chart.

5.2 Monetary policy

Maintaining stable prices is one of the conditions considered necessary for an economy to function correctly. To meet this objective, the amount of money in circulation or the interest rate must be controlled. The actions that are taken to achieve this make up the monetary policy. As seen in the previous chapter, controlling inflation is not (and should not be) an end unto itself but rather a derived objective. This is why the inflation rate should be related to other indicators, such as the unemployment rate or GDP growth. This rule is sometimes forgotten, as has frequently been seen in many countries recently: regardless of the situation or changes in other indicators of economic activity, maintaining a certain unchanging level of inflation has become the only and *almost-sacred* objective of monetary policy.

Monetary policy is executed by central banks, many of which are independent of the executive branch of their governments. The reason why they are independent is so that the amount of money circulating in the economy is never managed for self-serving and short-term purposes (e.g. to reduce debt through increased inflation, as seen in the previous section). Relinquishing control over monetary policy would then reveal that governments do not trust themselves. However, apart from the problems inherent in all independent regulators, this separation raises the question whether monetary policy can be unaligned with other policies that are directly decided by the executive branch.

As stated earlier, two variables can be used to articulate monetary policy: control over the quantity of money (money supply) and control over its price (interest rate). They are related to each other (in market conditions, quantity and price are not independent variables for money or any other good), but we distinguish between them, for didactic purposes:

• Money is not just the bills and coins in circulation. Many other assets that have varying degrees of liquidity fulfil the basic functions of money (e.g. a means of payment and a store of value). Which of these assets are classified as money determines what we consider to be money supply. In practice, various monetary aggregates are defined that start with cash (legal tender or monetary base) and progressively includes other assets that are increasingly less liquid. Tracking some of these aggregates has been the control instrument traditionally chosen by central banks.

If the money supply is increased—that is, if money is *injected* into the economy— and everything else (production, demand) remains constant, upward pressure on prices would be expected. In this case, monetary policy is expansive. On the contrary, if money is *extracted*, prices should drop. Now monetary policy is restrictive. This option is taken when inflation is considered to be too high; inversely, an expansive monetary policy is used during economic downturns.

The money supply can be augmented by increasing the monetary base (more money is issued), reducing the ratio of cash reserves that banks must maintain on hand to meet customer demands (the reserve requirement), or by using open market operations. The latter are operations in which the central bank buys and sells securities (in particular, government debt) on the financial markets. When the central bank sells debt, it reduces liquidity, given that the buyers give up cash (or liquid assets) in exchange for much-less-liquid debt (more difficult to quickly convert into cash or another means of payment). Inversely, buying public debt increases the liquidity of the system. Over the past few years, open market operations have been broadened and made more flexible in terms of the type of debt involved and in terms of the purchasing conditions.

• The price of money (interest rate) is the second way to control inflation. When the interest rate applied by the central bank to lend money to commercial banks increases, the banks will borrow less cash, and consequently, their capacity to provide credit or loans is diminished. With less money in the hands of businesses and individuals (alternatively, with more expensive financing of expenditure), pressure on prices should be reduced. Therefore, an increase in the interest rate implies, following the definition provided in the previous point, a restrictive monetary policy. A reduction in interest rates supposes the opposite: an expansive policy.

Although we usually talk about the "price of money", in singular, there is no single type of interest, not even officially. The rates also depend on the term given for repayment. The term could be years, or it could be as short as a day, as is the case of the "standing facilities" that the central bank provides to credit institutions to ensure their liquidity or to momentarily absorb any overnight liquidity that they may have.

The efficiency of monetary policy is probably one of the most, if not the most, controversial issues among all macroeconomic adjustment policies. Whereas for some schools of economic thought, its role should be subordinated to that of fiscal policy, for others, it is key to the evolution of the main macroeconomic indicators.

The neoclassical economic paradigm, dominant since the last quarter of the 20th century (even in versions that include some degree of eclecticism), generally considers the amount of money to be inefficient to modify the real variables of the economy (national income or employment level) in the long term, but it does determine the level of prices (inflation). It would have real short-term effects (via the relationship between the amount of money and aggregate demand) as long as the changes in the monetary policy were not anticipated by the economic agents or if the agents were not able to quickly adjust their behaviour to the new policy. From this perspective, states should abstain from discretional intervention in the monetary markets and adhere to a rule of action: in the past, the rule was to maintain a constant rate of growth of money supply, and today it is to maintain a steady inflation rate.

Critics of inflexibly applying this rule argue that the inflation rate should not be the final objective, but rather it should conform to whatever is most convenient for the current economic situation. They also point out that because the same rate of inflation can have different causes, its significance is relative; if, for example, inflation is "imported" from a rise in the price of energy and commodities on the international markets, the policy applied should be different from that when the inflation is caused by internal tensions in the national markets.

READING 4.6 CONTROLLED INFLATION?

Figure 4.7 is based on data from the World Bank on the variation of prices for a basket of goods and services (consumer price index).[1] It shows the evolution of inflation from the start of the 1980s. This was the period after the *Great Inflation of the 1970s* (caused by the oil crises; see Chapter 6), when price stability became a priority for economic policy. In 1980, the second oil crisis was still a recent memory, and few countries had inflation lower than 3%; in fact, double-digit inflation was not uncommon. By 1993 the situation had already changed in the wealthiest nations (Central and Northern Europe, United States and Canada, Australia and New Zealand) although many other states around the world continued to struggle with inflation sometimes greater than 25%. In 2006, just before the crisis, inflation was generally under control (compared to where it had been), although there had been a slight upturn in some rich countries. In 2019, with a few exceptions (Argentina, Iran and Turkey), only countries in Africa had inflation above 10%.

In reality, the World Bank data series begins in 1960. Figure 4.8 shows how the inflation rate has changed in eight countries for which complete data during the entire series is available and also which never experienced inflation greater than 25% (Germany, Italy, the United Kingdom, Sweden, Japan, Thailand, the United States and Australia). More important than the specific values is the observation that inflation changed at similar rates in each country. In the first decade shown in the figure, from 1960 to 1970, inflation did not go much beyond 7%–8% in the worst of cases. In the 1970s, the percentages surpassed 10% and even 20% in the worst moments of the oil crises. In the 1980s, inflation receded, but in 1990, the rates were still high. Since then, with some ups and downs, inflation has been under control and always under 5% (except

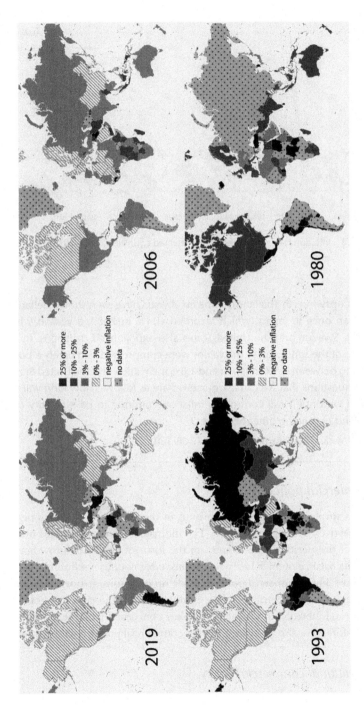

FIGURE 4.7   Inflation rate, consumer prices (2019, 2006, 1993, 1980)

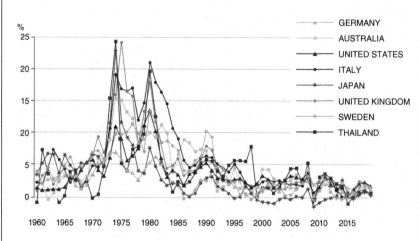

FIGURE 4.8 Inflation rate, consumer prices, selected countries (1960–2019)

for a few upswings in Thailand); some fiscal years have even shown deflation, more than once in Japan (which recorded -1.4% in 2009, a year in which Thailand, Sweden and the United States also experienced deflation). In the final year of the series, 2019, the values were compressed into barely a point, oscillating between 0.5% in Japan and 1.8% in Sweden and the United States.

The questions that we can ask ourselves are as follows: How long will this situation continue? Will controlling inflation continue to be a priority over controlling or guiding other objectives?

1 https://data.worldbank.org/indicator/ FP.CPI.TOTL.ZG.

5.3 Commercial policy

Obtaining a surplus (or at least equilibrium) in the balance of trade is one of the derived objectives set by governments. The ultimate objective is for this surplus to bring greater prosperity to the country in the form of economic growth and job creation. The balance of trade has two columns: what countries sell abroad and what countries buy. The commercial policy is made up of actions destined for both sides of the balance. In all external trade, the relative value of the currencies of the two countries is undoubtedly important. The policy concerned with the exchange rate, which therefore must also be included in the commercial policy, is studied separately.

5.3.1 Traditional commercial policy

According to the traditional theory of international trade, countries tend to specialize in the production and export of goods in which they are comparatively more efficient than other countries—that is, in goods that they produce at a lower relative cost. This is determined by comparing in every country the cost of production of that good with those of other goods. That is, as explained in basic textbooks, in the *country specializing in chairs*, five chairs can be made with what it costs to make a lamp, while in other countries, they can make only four or fewer. It is not that the absolute cost is the lowest in the world: even if the production cost of a chair in the country with the lowest relative cost is EUR6 and in other countries EUR5, these other countries will not produce chairs, because producing (and exporting) products in which they have the advantage in relative cost and buying chairs from the specialist country are together more profitable for them. This is called the theory of comparative advantage. The reason why countries have the comparative advantage in the production of a good is because they are endowed with more of the factors needed to produce that specific good. Following this reasoning, countries specialize in industries that use the resources they possess. If a country has low salaries, it will produce goods or services that require a great deal of labour; if a country has natural resources, it will specialize in products that use those resources.

In accordance with this theory, exchanges generated under conditions of unimpeded trade would provide the greatest supply of goods at the lowest possible prices to consumers of every country. In return, commerce would stamp out the national chair industry of every country specialized in other products. This situation, or the disparities in the balance of trade that could be associated with it, has not been accepted by states, which have traditionally tried to protect their industries or improve their external balances. Therefore, the original basis of commercial policy is essentially disbelief in the benefits of free trade or an attempt to undo the unwanted effects that it may have. This fact is so out in the open that few arguments have been put forth to defend the existence of commercial policy actions. The most common among them is that of the nascent industry: states make use of this argument when they decide to temporarily support new industries until they are big enough to deal with international competition; logic states that such industries either are considered viable once they have been consolidated or generate externalities in the rest of the economy (e.g. by developing a technology or expertise that allows other sectors to progress).

A set of actions has been used (and are used)—with or without its relying on any theoretical arguments to justify it—to curb imports and another set to favour exports.

Protecting national production sectors from imports

A tariff is a tax on imports. Adding this tax causes the price of foreign goods and services to increase, thereby favouring that national alternatives substitute the imports. Tariffs can be *fixed*, such as when they add a specific amount of money to the price of each unit of the good imported, or *ad valorem*, such as when they are calculated as a percentage of the value of the imported goods. A tariff can be disguised as an inspection fee or another customs service fee.

Tariffs are justified when a foreign company is using illicit strategies to sell their product for less than the "normal price" or even below cost (usually termed *dumping*) to eliminate competing national companies and take control of the market. If the cause of the abnormally low price is a subsidy given in the country of origin, the measures adopted are termed *countervailing duties*. In these cases, a minimum sales price is sometimes established instead of a tariff.

Tariffs are the oldest instrument of commercial policy. They were so important that they were once a fundamental source of income for states. In fact, until "modern" taxes were introduced (on income or sales), the governments of some countries obtained a large part of their income from tariffs. However, the importance of tariffs has dropped dramatically in modern times, mainly because of trade agreements that restrict their use.

A long list of nontariff barriers to trade might also be prohibited (or at least conditioned) in the text of those agreements but still be used in practice, as it is often more complicated to oversee them than to monitor tariffs.

- Import quotas are restrictions on the quantity of a good that can be imported. A common way to articulate a quota is through the concession of licences (an official authorization to carry out certain commercial operations and conditions imposed on those operations).

  A variant is voluntary export restraint. The reason behind this "voluntary" self-restriction is simply the behest of the importing country, which the exporter accepts in exchange for other trade-offs or at least to avoid *the response* threatened by the importer.

- The most radical measure among quotas is an embargo, which impedes trade in a certain kind of good, regardless of its origin or destination, or which can be imposed on specific products from, or supplied to, certain countries.
- A local content requirement imposes that a fraction (in terms of units or value) of the final product be produced within the country.
- An extensive set of barriers can be derived from an excessively rigorous interpretation or application of norms that a priori have legitimate purposes. The list includes health and plant-health standards, quality norms, intellectual or industrial property rights, protecting designations of origin, labelling and packing requirements, and consumer or environmental protection norms. The barriers can be found not just in limits or the conditions in which the norms are applied but also in the process of evaluating if rules are being complied with (e.g. tests, certifications, stamps and inspections).
- Finally, other measures (different from those referred to so far) are used discretionally and always with the purpose of controlling de facto the quantities or conditions of imports, such as the obligation of using certain commercialization chains or of hiring authorized resellers (who can be government commercial businesses), requiring a certain insurance to be taken out, restrictions on handling currencies or employing every sort of strategy to create administrative or bureaucratic delays at customs.

READING 4.7   HOW HIGH ARE TARIFFS?

Figures 4.9 and 4.10 show the tariffs applied by each country (on average) on agricultural and nonagricultural products, respectively. The data come from the World Trade Organization and refer to 2016, with a few exceptions. Although more-recent data were available at the time of writing, data from 2016 have been used because at the end of that year, following presidential elections in the United States, a trade war broke out on several fronts (although the most prominent was the "relationship" between the United States and China) in which tariffs were the main weapon. Because we do not know for sure whether tariff increases will be consolidated or returned to pre-dispute levels, we thought it more appropriate to present data for a year of *peace*.

For each product, the "most-favoured-nation" tariff, defined as the "normal, non-discriminatory tariff charged on imports (excludes preferential tariffs under free trade agreements and other schemes or tariffs charged inside quotas)", is used. It is expressed as a percentage of the value of the goods (ad valorem tariff).

Starting with the agricultural products, tariffs in Europe and South and Central America were (except for a few exceptions) between 10% and 15%. In North America, the United States was at the lower end (5.19%), whereas Canada had higher tariffs (15.61%). The situation was less homogenous in Africa and Asia. Australia and New Zealand applied among the lowest tariffs on the planet (1.19% and 1.38%, respectively). The global ranking was headed by

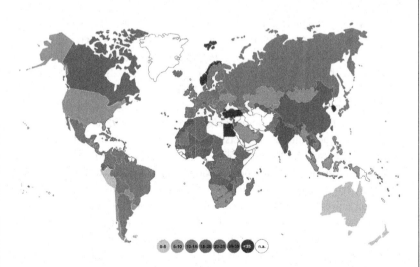

FIGURE 4.9   Average tariff imposed on agricultural products (as a percentage of the value of the goods) (2016)

FIGURE 4.10 Average tariffs on nonagricultural products (as a percentage of the value of the goods) (2016)

Egypt (just over 60%), followed by South Korea, Turkey, Bhutan and Norway (almost 40%); Switzerland, India, Tunisia and Thailand also surpassed 30%.

The tariffs for nonagricultural products were generally much lower. Europe (except for Russia), Canada, the United States, Australia and New Zealand were all in the 0% to 5% range. They were higher in Asia (between 5% and 10%, except for outliers such as India) and even higher in South and Central America. Once again, Africa presented a heterogeneous picture. The world ranking was headed by the Bahamas (with an astonishing 35.58%) and was trailed at a distance (with less than 20%) by Bhutan, Algiers, the Central African Republic and Chad; these were followed by more African nations until reaching positions 11 to 14, occupied by Argentina, Uzbekistan, Brazil and Bangladesh (with average tariffs around 14%).

A comparison of the two tables reveals curious cases, such as Norway, which had the fifth-highest tariffs on agricultural products (39.92%) but the fourth-lowest on nonagricultural products (0.47%). The situation in Switzerland was similar (34.16% and 1.69% respectively). The opposite occurred in Brazil, which applied an average of 14.12% on nonagricultural products (which was a comparatively high value, placing them 12th in the world ranking) and 10.01% on agricultural products (which placed them at 96 out of the 138 WTO members).

High tariffs in both sectors could be found in some African countries, like Zimbabwe, Algiers, Chad and Ethiopia. Low tariffs in both sectors existed in Hong Kong and Macao (as low as 0%) and also in Singapore (0% for nonagricultural products and 0.1% for agricultural products); Australia and New Zealand also imposed low tariffs on all kinds of products.

1 https://data.wto.org (Category: Tariff indicators—Applied duties).

Stimulating exports

Exports are driven directly by providing subsidies, tax reductions or aid in obtaining credit for businesses that sell their products abroad.

Indirectly, any action directed at reducing the production costs of national companies will increase their capacity to sell abroad. The traditional approaches are to control wages and introduce greater competition in markets where it is required, in particular those in which basic, or highly used by exporting sectors, inputs are negotiated. Starting in the 1950s, with the popularity of the term *productivity*, the search for competitiveness in foreign markets began to be complemented with policies to promote productivity. Another indirect way of stimulating exports is through marketing campaigns, either general campaigns lauding the virtues of the country's products or campaigns promoting specific goods or services.

5.3.2 Exchange rate policy

If a factor determines the magnitude of external trade, it is the exchange rate between the country's currency and other currencies. Controlling (or at least influencing) the exchange rate constitutes the exchange rate policy or foreign exchange policy.

The exchange rate is fixed when the exchange ratio between two currencies is fixed. With a fixed exchange rate, when a country wants to make its national products less expensive and foreign ones more expensive (stimulate exports and curb imports), new exchange ratios with other currencies are established that make the national currency weaker. This is referred to as devaluation. When, on the contrary, the national currency is strengthened with new exchange rates, a revaluation has occurred.

Flexible or "floating" exchange rates are more common today. Different currencies can be bought and sold on the foreign exchange market, and the prices of currencies fluctuate because of various factors: the publication of macroeconomic indicators of different countries, inflation rates, interest rates and expectations regarding the evolution of each. With a floating exchange rate, a currency is said to appreciate or depreciate in relation to others.

In reality, the foreign exchange market is not pure, and some exchange rates are managed float regimes (sometimes referred to as "dirty floats"). Indeed, states do not resign themselves to not influencing variations in exchange rates. Sometimes they act directly (buying or selling currencies or various assets in foreign currencies), and sometimes they manoeuvre their own money markets, modifying interest rates, buying different kinds of assets or in general carrying out actions that *signal* to the currency market that they are prepared to protect or combat a rise or fall in their currency. Because intervention in the currency market affects the country's money supply, central banks sometimes carry out internal operations and external ones (they buy assets in one and sell in another or vice versa) to neutralize this effect; this action is denominated a "sterilized" intervention in the exchange market.

Finally, sometimes various nations form a trade bloc (or at least have strong trade ties among them) in which one of the partners has a strong currency. In these circumstances, the rest of the countries commonly try to "associate" their currencies with the strong one, establishing a practically fixed exchange rate with it and fluctuating with those of countries outside the bloc at the same rate as the strong currency. This leads to a hybrid situation with an almost fixed exchange rate with a set of currencies (those belonging to the bloc) and a floating rate with the rest.

5.4 Incomes policy

In contrast to the other adjustment policies that we have discussed, which are always applied everywhere, the incomes policy is used only in exceptional circumstances. Such circumstances are generally high inflation that cannot be controlled by using traditional mechanisms (particularly monetary policy). If this is the case, the state can take the initiative to fix some prices (or set increase limits), specifically wage levels. This public action is known as an incomes policy.

"Take the initiative to fix" was written instead of directly fix because the extreme of actually fixing wages is not always reached. More commonly, the government publishes price guidelines or brings management and trade unions together to reach an agreement in line with the government's wishes, offering trade-offs to facilitate negotiation (e.g. in social or fiscal policy).

READING 4.8   THE MONCLOA PACT

The grave situation of the Spanish economy at this time, as well as the manifest need to profoundly reform its institutional aspects to be more in line with the criteria and principles of a modern market economy, have been acknowledged by all political forces with parliamentary representation and stated in the economic agreements signed by the government and those forces. In these agreements, incomes policy plays an essential role in the process that must be urgently and unavoidably undertaken to overcome the current economic crisis. And within the framework of that incomes policy, moderating the rate of salary growth, to keep pace with the forecasted rise in prices, is key to overcoming the crisis. In a market economy this policy must not simply use legal prohibitions, but rather, on the contrary, it must use everything in its power to re-establish the proper functions of trade unions and the business community in a context of freedom of contracts, and in which the state only uses economic policy instruments to orient the free action of individuals.

This was the introduction to Royal Decree-Law 43/1977 on wage policy and employment, published in the *Boletín Oficial del Estado* (BOE), the official gazette of the Kingdom of Spain on 26 November 1977. As stated in the cited text, it is one of the laws that defines the agreements reached a month earlier, on 25 October 1977, between the government and the representatives of the main political parties, trade unions and business associations (although the final document was signed by only the government and the political parties). They are known as the Moncloa Pact.

The Moncloa Pact is one of the most successful examples of an incomes policy. Suffering from inflation that had skyrocketed to 19.8% at the close of 1976 and that almost reached 30% in the summer of 1977, the trade unions promised to not ask for salary hikes greater than 20% (22% in some cases); all parties also agreed that social security contributions would not increase over 18%, and limits on rental income from certain dwellings and business premises, and in benefit sharing among boards of directors, were also set. The result was that inflation closed the year at 26.4% (despite much higher forecasts) and decreased to 16.5% in 1978 (up to 10% could be considered a reasonable inflation rate during that period).

In reality, the pact went much further. In the spring of 1977, Spain was walking a tightrope. The still-incomplete transition to democracy initiated only a year and a half earlier was tangled up with (and seriously threatened by) a deep economic crisis. It was just an episode of the global oil crisis, initiated in 1973 but amplified by the political situation and the economic structure of the country: inflation galloped out of control, unemployment also began to climb, exports were only 45% of imports (and the growing debt was already three times greater than the gold and currency reserves) and tax revenue (which was no greater than 20% of GDP) was not sufficient to cover the services wanted to be provided as part of what was thought to be a modern state.

In addition to the "Agreement on the economic reform and correction programme", the "Agreement on the political and legal action programme" was signed. An income tax was created that increased the tax burden up to 35%, pensions were increased and unemployment benefits improved, funding was increased for education, land was made developable to tackle speculation and labour reforms were made. Moreover, freedom of the press was broadened, along with the rights of assembly and association; the power of military justice was limited; and adultery and cohabitation were decriminalized (!). After decades of stagnation, Spain began to look like a European country.

6 Social policies

The social policies put in practice by a country define the size and scope of its welfare state. A broad welfare state should produce a more cohesive society with fewer imbalances. Critics of these policies focus on the cost of maintaining them and also accuse them of distorting incentives for individuals. Specifically, those in favour of greater *individual responsibility* argue, for example, that receiving unemployment benefits makes people not seek work with the same zeal that they would if they did not have them; similarly, being assured of having a pension and health insurance would cause people not to save.

As already occurred when studying other groups of policies, we again point out that although for didactic purposes we separate various social policies, some of them are connected and even overlap each other.

6.1 Social protection policy

Social security is the most common name for social protection schemes. According to the International Labour Organization's definition, social security "is the protection that a society provides to individuals and households to ensure access to health care and to guarantee income security, particularly in cases of old age, unemployment, sickness, invalidity, work injury, maternity or loss of a breadwinner". Therefore, social security, where it exists, provides in kind (basically medical services) and also monetary (subsidies and pensions) benefits. Access to healthcare is part of the health policy that will be studied in the next section. The monetary benefits last for a specific time (subsidies that are provided in the face of certain contingencies that temporarily interrupt obtaining income) or lifetime (retirement, widowhood, disability or incapacity for work pensions).

Public social security systems are usually financed (at least in largest part) by taxes raised from the working population. These contributions are used to pay for some of the benefits that the workers receive while they are part of the labour force but also to fund retirement pensions. This leads to intergenerational solidarity: the current active population funds the pensions of older generations in the belief that the following generations will fund their retirement pensions. The increase in life expectancy (and therefore the average number of years that retirement pensions are paid), along with a drop in the birth rate and high unemployment rates, place the system's sustainability at risk (understood here as offering the same benefits and that it continues to be financed mainly by contributions, without needing to look for other sources of income).

Social insurance systems convert individual risk into collective risk. States that do not have public social protection systems can pursue a similar objective through regulation. Obligatory affiliation to mutual insurance or the requirement to pay for health insurance or pension plans are ways of providing private coverage for some, if not all, of the risks covered by social security. Public systems can never be totally substituted, though, as they are intended to be universal while the alternatives described only cover the active population: a person who has no income cannot be obligated to pay for an insurance policy.

6.2 Health policy

The health policy is tied to the social protection policy. In fact, the definition of social security policy presented in the previous section starts with the sentence "the protection that a society provides to individuals and households to ensure access to health care". The first and most important question concerning health policy is, therefore, whether individuals and households are in fact ensured access to healthcare and whether the access is universal The following question concerns the conditions under which health service is offered.

Indeed, a public health service may or may not exist. It if does exist, access to services could be universal or nearly so (covering all residents or only nationals) or be restricted to certain groups. If it is restricted, one of two opposing policies will be adopted: those that offer the service basically to the working population who contribute to financing the system or, on the contrary, those that offer it to certain groups that would not otherwise have access to healthcare (which is based on the idea that workers or their companies would be able to pay for a private insurance).

The conditions in which the public health service is offered could require some kind of payment or no payment, and the service could cover any illness or leave out certain treatments or medications. The system can be entirely public, private with some kind of arrangement or mixed. A mixed system, in turn, can be limited to certain services or a specific geographic area, and it could be organized under different modalities. In addition to arrangements or agreements are also public–private partnerships to build infrastructures (hospitals and health centres) or to run the health service.

READING 4.9   PUBLIC AND PRIVATE EXPENDITURES ON HEALTH

Global Health 2035: A World Converging within a Generation, a report created by a commission of 25 independent experts, was published in the British medical journal the *Lancet* in December 2013.[1] Figure 3.7 of the report, directly transcribed here with modifications to the format in Figure 4.11, shows two interesting statistics for 11 countries (with disparate levels of economic development): the distribution of total healthcare expenditure between public spending and private spending, and the percentage of total expenditure that is paid out of pocket by users of the healthcare system or covered by some kind of insurance (either public or private). The data are for 2010.

The x-axis (abscissa) represents public expenditure. In France, it was 77%, which means that private expenditure was 23%. For Tunisia, it was 54%, which left 46% for the private sector. The y-axis (ordinate) represents the percentage of spending covered by private insurance. Returning to the two earlier examples, in France, it was 14% of total spending, which by extension implies that 9% of private expenditure (23% total private spending–14% covered by private insurance) was paid out of pocket by users. That is why France is in the upper area, where nearly 100% of spending is covered by some kind of

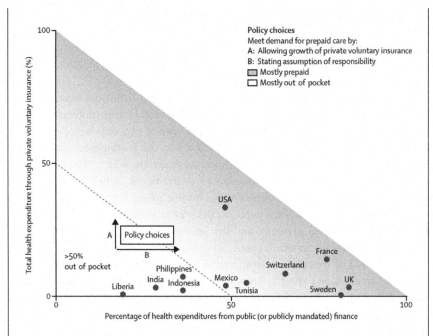

FIGURE 4.11 Expenditures on health services (2010): the distribution between public and private expenditure, and percentage covered by some kind of private insurance

insurance (specifically 91%, the sum of 77% covered by public insurance and 14% by private insurance). In Tunisia, insurance covered only 10% of private expenditure (approximately 5% of total spending), which left out of pocket spending at 41% (100%—54% public coverage—5% private insurance) and that is why it is only slightly above the dotted line that marks 50% (at the start of the greyed out area).

Two clarifications are necessary. The first is made in the appendices of the report: users do not pay 100% of the spending uncovered by insurance. Although this new variable cannot be included in the figure, a percentage of this amount is "other private expenditure", which is defined without more explanation as "spending by businesses and nongovernmental organizations on health". Although this spending is not significant in either France or Tunisia, it is in other cases (in the United States, it was 7% of the total, which means that 19% of spending apparently not covered by any kind of insurance was actually only 12%; presumably, some workers had some kind of agreement with their employers beyond paying part or all of their insurance).

The second clarification is more important: to this point we have talked about only spending and not about the percentage of the population covered by one of the coverage schemes, which would undoubtedly be more interesting. There is no direct relation, because it depends mostly on how the two models function, specifically on the efficiency of the public programmes. Let us return to the example of the United States, where public spending was 48% but where only 31% of the population was covered by some kind of government plan in 2010, according to the U.S. Census.[2] Even worse, the report explains that public insurance and private insurance are not mutually exclusive, and only 19.7% of the population depended exclusively on public plans. On the other side, 55.3% of the population had private insurance tied to their job (compared to 9.8% that had paid out of pocket), although this was the only insurance for only 45.8% of the population; the rest complemented it in some way, which clearly shows the variety of coverages and rights that the different kinds of insurance offer. It also reveals that when no obligatory minimum standards are established, having insurance does not necessarily mean you are completely covered for any contingency. Finally, perhaps the most shocking information in the report is that 16.3% of the US population was uninsured in 2010. The uninsured population have no option but to pay out of pocket. However, out of pocket spending includes not only the expenditures of the uninsured but also the co-pays made by the insured population, as well as spending on health services not covered by their insurance plan. Therefore, given that out of pocket spending was 12% of total health expenditure, we can infer that uninsured people spend much less on health than the insured population. That people in the former group are simply healthier is a possible but not plausible explanation. At least that is not what the Obama administration seemed to think when in 2010 it pushed for healthcare reform through the Affordable Care Act, commonly known as Obamacare.

1 Reprinted from Jamison, D.T., Summers, L.H., et al. (2013). "Global health 2035: A world converging within a generation". *The Lancet*, vol. 382, no. 9908, pp. 1898–1955, with permission from Elsevier—which can also be found at http://www.globalhealth2035.org/sites/default/files/report/global-health-2035.pdf.
2 DeNavas-Walt, C., Proctor, B.D., & Smith, J.C. (2011). *Income, Poverty, and Health Insurance Coverage in the United States: 2010*. U.S. Census Bureau, Current Population Reports, P60–239. Washington, DC—which can be found at https://www.census.gov/prod/2011pubs/p60-239.pdf.

6.3 Education policy

The education policy organizes a country's education system. This organization is not neutral in the sense that classifying the education policy as a true social policy is determined by the extension and quality of the system and by the conditions required to access it (ultimately, by the equal opportunities to access quality education). An education policy answers three basic questions: who teaches, who is taught and what is taught.

*   Regarding who teaches, the policy defines the degree to which the state is involved as an education provider. Education can be public, private or mixed,

in the latter case articulated around a wide range of agreements or arrangements. The education system might not have only one model but instead vary depending on its different stages.

As seen in the health policy, public provision (public education) does not necessarily mean free education. Inversely, private or mixed education can be free if the state subsidizes private centres. The early stages of the system area always more likely to be free (basic education). Obviously, when the state directly offers education, it has to facilitate and organize the spaces (or directly build them) where it will be taught.

- Who is taught is defined by the ages that can or the criteria to access different education levels. Frequently, some stages of education are made obligatory, which means that access to them must be universal. When the system is not universal (a reduced number of places, which normally occurs in higher education or in schools that provide certain kinds of education), the norm must specify the criteria used to select students. So that people who meet the requirements are not excluded for economic reasons, a scholarship system is commonly established (if tuition must be paid or if there are associated residence costs).
- What is taught is regulated in norms that define the structure and organization of each curriculum and in greater detail in the programmes for areas, modules and materials. In some types or levels of education, this design is highly detailed; in others, the centres are allowed to organize their education plans in any way they see fit (within a general framework).

6.4 Employment policy

Employment policies are made up of a set of actions meant to help people outside the labour market or who are at risk of being left out. Active policies try to facilitate access to a job. Passive policies intend to make sure that unemployed people maintain a certain level of income.

Passive policies are benefits and subsidies that, in the event of unemployment, provide the receiver with income that substitutes wages. They are part of the social security policies seen earlier. In contrast to active policies, they do not affect the labour market, because they do not modify the profile of potential workers (labour supply) or the demand for labour.

As just stated, active policies attempt to adapt labour supply to *what the market demands*. In fact, these policies are particularly important when a mismatch between the skills of the population and the requirements of businesses occurs—that is, when structural unemployment occurs. However, they are not necessarily directed at unemployed people: for some programmes, participation is open to anyone (unemployed or not) or even specifically directed at certain groups of active workers. In spite of this, the priority is usually to provide work for unemployed people and specifically for groups that have greater difficulty in entering the labour market (young people, women, people who have a disability, long-term unemployed people and people older than a certain age). In any case, beneficiaries are always individuals, although these policies also favour companies indirectly, in that actions increase the skills of their current employees (if they had benefited from some action) or at least allows companies the possibility of hiring a better-prepared labour force. Various actions are available:

- Training is oriented towards practical skills such as teaching workers how to operate tools but can also provide other kinds of knowledge that could help unemployed people enter the labour market, help active workers remain employed or even help active workers advance in their careers by *retraining* them in new skills.
- Some actions facilitate geographic mobility, whether within the country or internationally through *migration policies*.
- Some actions encourage an entrepreneurial culture and mindset. In general, this is achieved through actions that "accompany" whoever takes this option.
- Tax measures may include reducing what companies must pay when they hire workers with a specific profile (long-term unemployed, older workers) or reducing taxes on freelance workers.
- Legal obligations may require, for instance, companies hiring one person who has a disability per a certain number of workers.

6.5 Territorial policy

The term *territorial policy* is ambiguous in that it can refer to the political-administrative organization of the territory, to planning and land use (simplifying a great deal, what the land is used for; this could be categorized as organizing policy) and to cohesion policies between different regions or different areas in the same region, which are regarded here as social policy. Therefore, this chapter includes actions meant to alleviate the problems of economically depressed regions (with a high rate of unemployment, which can be due to general causes or the recent closure of an industry) or regions whose characteristics impede developing new economic activities or maintain existing ones (mountainous or insular areas, isolated or poorly connected areas, rural areas and areas with an ageing population).

In general terms, territorial policy is articulated by creating special chapters in policies used to promote economic activity (especially those related to infrastructure and training—lately both take into special consideration aspects associated with the progress of the information society), in other social policies (improving health or education services) or in sectorial policies that will be described later (with specific attention to industrial or tourism policy). The precise actions taken depend on the exact circumstances that make differentiated treatment necessary (or advisable); often, various such circumstances can occur at the same time (poorly connected rural areas with a high unemployment rate and youth emigration).

Territorial policy, therefore, is not its own entity in the sense of introducing actions different from those of other economic policies, but rather, as occurs with other social policies that focus on specific groups (e.g. women, youths and elderly people), what makes it an independent policy is that it deals jointly with the needs of a particular group of citizens. In the target areas, territorial policy has a dual objective: to deal with the problems present but also, in the medium term, to make sure that these places, which are generally in danger of depopulation, have enough services and economic opportunities to tie the current residents to the region or even to attract new ones.

6.6 Housing policy

The *housing policy* seeks to ensure access to housing to various groups that may have difficulties finding a home. The most common tools used are direct provision, regulation (including direct intervention on prices) and taxes.

- The state offers housing directly when it builds public housing (social housing) that it sells or rents below market prices or when it rents housing that has already been built (either publicly owned or that have in turn been rented to the state by private owners).
- Regulations can impose all kinds of conditions for housing sales or rental contracts to be valid. They can even fix prices, particularly through rent controls.
- By using taxes, the state can, for example, provide incentives to buy housing or penalize owning uninhabited homes that are not put on the rental market.

6.7 Other social policies

Women, young people, elderly people and disadvantaged minorities are groups whose conditions require special attention, which public administrations sometimes provide through isolated actions or, if the government is more ambitious in its objectives, through policies that try to consistently and comprehensively deal with their disadvantages or particular needs.

- The *gender policy* tries to reduce inequalities suffered by women, specifically in the labour market, including compatibility between work and maternity. It also deals with other specific problems such as domestic violence or retirement for women who have not worked outside the home.
- Although the term *youth policy* is not always used, sometimes plans or programmes are put into action directed at adolescents or young adults. Some of these actions overlap with other social policies (e.g. education, employment and housing). Others are specific, such as encouraging participation in social activities and the formation of associations, prevention (drug-use education, road safety education and sex education), assistance in emancipation, facilitating mobility and access to entertainment.

- The government can also craft a *policy to care for elderly people*. Many of the actions that make up such a policy can be included in the health policy. The services provided in situations of dependence constitute another of its basic pillars. The third group of actions is concerned with "active ageing", encouraging leisure and participation in various activities.
- People who have a disability, ethnic minorities, socially marginalized people (homeless people), immigrants, and people with addiction problems are groups that can be attended to with specific policies.

Other social policies include *family policy* (which is concerned primarily with reconciling family life and work life, and also with providing incentives for having children, generally through assistance during childbirth and later for taking care of children), *cultural policy* and *sports policy*.

7 Sectorial policies

In certain sectors of the economy, the state does not resign itself to merely accepting the results of market operation. This is usually the case when a sector is considered key to the country's economy but also when the *free play* of market forces could put the resources that an activity uses in jeopardy; sometimes both circumstances occur at the same time.

Governments have particular policies for each essential utility (e.g. an energy policy, a telecommunications policy and a water resource policy) and usually have a transport policy, an industrial policy, an agricultural policy, a fisheries policy or a tourism policy. Sometimes they include *subpolicies* within these broad areas. For example, governments could have a natural gas or nuclear energy policy within its energy policy or a steel or automobile policy within its industrial policy.

The tools used in these policies are highly varied and span practically the entire gamut described in the first section of this chapter.

- In the past, public provision was the first option in some industries, particularly for basic utilities, which were considered a natural monopoly. Although the public ownership of large electric or telecommunications companies is not unheard of, it has become uncommon, at least in countries that have opened these sectors to competition (the majority today); when working, public operators are usually restricted to regional and local markets. On the contrary, the public ownership of water supply companies is much more common.

  For those services deemed essential where universal coverage is aimed to be achieved (without this obligation's being placed on private operators), many public companies subsist (or have been created) to provide service to areas where private companies do not operate. A cost is associated with providing service to those areas (if they were profitable, the private sector would cover them), one that must be paid for as just another public expenditure; when public companies provided service in the entire territory, cross-subsidization was used or (less frequently) the profits obtained in profitable areas were reinvested.

- Today, regulation is the main mechanism used for public action in almost all sectorial policies. Legal norms can require obtaining a licence to operate (e.g. a fishing boat or a hotel), establish certain conditions that the activity must meet (e.g. separation of railway infrastructure and transport operations), impose public service obligations (e.g. those included in the universal service for telecommunications), establish a technical code or quality standards (e.g. manufacturing steel) and any other requirement imaginable.
- Along with direct provision and regulation, the imposition, exemption or reduction of taxes, providing subsidies and other types of assistance, fixing sales prices or setting minimum or maximum price limits, and contractual agreements with the private sector are all options used to make the market behave in a way that the authority in charge of public policy feels is appropriate for the country.

READING 4.10   TELECOMMUNICATIONS POLICY

The telecommunications sector has been in the crosshairs of governments around world ever since the first networks were laid over a century ago. This fact suggests that *guiding* the activity of this sector has always been seen as beneficial, regardless of the political party in power. The result is that what could be considered, in a generic sense, a sectorial telecommunications policy has persisted over time.

In the early stages, from the first commercial rollouts, but in particular in the period spanning from the end of World War II to the crises in the 1970s, telecommunications was a *public matter*. The service was usually controlled by a monopoly, which in most countries was a public operator. The main argument for maintaining monopolies was based on the market situation: telecommunications was assumed to be a natural monopoly. Other, less-important arguments included its influence on industrial and technological development and, in particular, the protection of national industries (equipment providers), and equity, although in many cases (and for a long time) the commitment to extend the network was more theoretical than real.

At the end of the 1970s and the start of the 1980s, the situation began to change radically. The extraordinary transformation was driven by not only various technological and economic factors but also political ones: at that time, privatization and globalization were on the rise, while doubts began to be raised about the public sector's capacity to efficiently provide services such as telecommunications. Reform plans included privatizing the monopolies, gradually opening the markets, and *re-regulation* (not deregulation). The final point reveals how opening the market up to competition was a guided process that was viewed in the long term. And yet once the dust had settled, telecommunications had become a private enterprise. The public sector limited its role to that of intermediary. The reason for public action continued being the market situation, but with a different argument. Competition could not be quickly established just by removing legal obstacles. The moment that the market opened up, the monopolies had advantages that would be difficult for their new rivals to overcome. Introducing total freedom suddenly, without rules, would have allowed the monopoly to abuse its dominant position. Even in completely open markets, their networks continued to be an "essential facility" required to develop competition; therefore, allowing other operators to access and use these networks was regulated ex ante.

As the socioeconomic paradigm shifted towards an information society, the telecommunications sector entered a new stage. Because telecommunications has been a fundamental part of this change, programmes designed to promote the information society have overridden sectorial policy. The most obvious consequence is that, in a way unthinkable years ago, the public sector has reappeared as a direct actor, investing funds in the deployment of

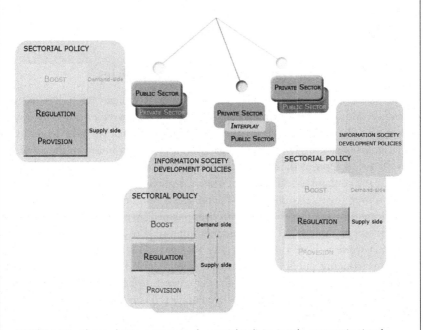

FIGURE 4.12   The evolution over time of sectorial policies in telecommunications[1]

broadband infrastructure, especially (but not only) in places where private initiative had not yet reached.

In any case, this is not the only way that public action takes place in the new scenario. Plans also include other initiatives in which the public sector plays an indirect role, such as providing incentive for demand or supporting the activity of private operators in certain areas or under certain conditions. And, of course, it maintains its role as intermediary, as specific sectorial regulation has not disappeared, despite the promise made years ago that after a time it would be replaced by generic ex post competition analyses. Accordingly, the list of reasons that justify public action has grown longer, to include telecommunications as a merit good (tied to the fact that markets don't always guarantee the supply needed to ensure that the innovation promised by the development of the information society is not inhibited), the context of the competition (many markets remain not completely competitive, in the opinion of regulators) and equity (the fight against the digital divide). As an important corollary, these arguments, along with the larger role assumed by the public sector, provide more possibilities to establish new types of relationships between the public sector and the private sector, including contractual agreements.

1 Reprinted from Gómez-Barroso, J.L., & Feijóo, C. (2010). "A conceptual framework for public–private interplay in the telecommunications sector". *Telecommunications Policy*, vol. 34, no. 9, pp. 487–495, with permission from Elsevier. The text is a summary of the discussion found there.

8 The coordination and subordination of policies

As we stated several times in this chapter, economic policies rarely have a single objective. Although they frequently have a priority goal, various others are associated with it. For example, the structure and content of what we have denominated social policies also imply a certain organization of the economy, in the same way that the orientation of the policies that we have included in the organization section already contains a declaration of *how social* public action is meant to be.

Moreover, the interconnectedness of policies is reinforced (and at the same time complicated) by the fact that the objectives pursued by public action in the economy are not just interlaced but sometimes impossible to achieve at the same time. We don't seem to have a magic formula for generating growth while containing inflation, reducing public debt and maintaining external balance all at the same time. Even more difficult would be for that growth to be sustainable and to redistribute wealth. That these objectives are connected is reflected in how economic policies are articulated, and this connection reveals that simultaneously executing any imaginable set of policies is impossible or that implementing one possibly obligates modifying others. For example, suppose that a government decides to increase the coverage of a certain social policy. This will presumably be accompanied by a large increase in spending. The government would have two options to obtain funds: cut spending in other areas, which could mean renouncing other policies (or diminishing them), or increase income by introducing changes into its fiscal policy. If the latter option is chosen, taxes must be modified or the debt must be increased. Modifying taxes would likely alter demand, and that would come with repercussions that would be felt throughout the economy. On the other hand, if the deficit is increased, it could affect the interest and currency exchange rates. These alterations will in turn generate other effects on fiscal balance and, depending on the economic situation, subsequent effects that could lead to new changes in other policies.

All the arguments presented in the preceding paragraphs can be condensed into two basic conclusions. The first is that the different policies presented in the previous sections are not isolated elements without connection among them. On the contrary, they form part of a single machine, and they must work in harmony. Although occasional inconsistencies can occur, conceptually two policies cannot work in antagonistic directions. Every economic policy must be in line with (or at least not contradict) the general conception of what the state's role in the economy should be. This general conception is determined largely when certain objectives are prioritized over others or, by extension, when certain policies are prioritized over others. This ties in with the second conclusion: every model of organizing economic life must decide how to distribute and in what to employ the scarce resources that it has. If part of this organization is in hands of the state, the state is obligated to choose between different alternatives. Given that, as illustrated by the previous example, precisely predicting the effects that an economic policy can unleash is almost impossible, we should instead talk about choosing between different expected results. Making the right decisions and exercising good management are the keys to achieving final results that are close to sought-after outcomes.

9 Assigning responsibility in policy design and implementation

In any state, the set of governing bodies is territorially structured on three layers: the central government, the governments of the supramunicipal territorial divisions into which the country is divided and the local governments. In reality, the situation is often more complex in that the last two levels can be further subdivided. In France, the regions are divided into departments (and these in turn, although without legal entity, into districts and cantons), and the *communes* (municipalities) can be made up of *arrondissements*. China features a first category made up of provinces (or, where appropriate, autonomous regions, municipalities under central jurisdiction or special administrative regions); then prefectures or districts; and finally cantons, ethnic cantons and villages (and, in some cases, other subordinate levels such as villas, subdistricts or hamlets).

Leaving aside the particularities of each country, we are interested here in the degree of subordination that the governments of the lower strata have with respect to the central government. If the autonomy granted to the two lower levels, and specifically to the intermediate one, is scarce, we are talking about centralized states. In federal states and confederations, on the contrary, this autonomy is (should be) broad. Between the two extremes are all kinds of situations. Moreover, what is important is not so much the de jure situation as the de facto situation. The central government of a federal state might have been given considerable powers or might simply exercise coordination tasks and legislate in a limited number of areas. Some states are not constitutionally federal, but its regions (whatever name they adopt) have been given a decision-making capacity similar to, or even greater than, that retained by the governments of the territories which are part of a federal state.

This decision-making capacity can be extended to a large part of the policies analysed earlier. Different education, infrastructure or environmental policies can coexist within a country, to cite just three examples. In all these cases, the powers exercised may be legislative or merely executive and might or might not be shared with the central government. Decentralization has a limit: these are the policies linked to the common currency (in particular monetary policy and exchange rate policy) and those which, conditioned by international relations and agreements, often require a single orientation for the whole country (e.g. the rest of trade policy).

A key point in the distribution of responsibilities is undoubtedly the fiscal issue. The answers to two questions determine to a large extent the capacity for action granted to each level of government: on the one hand, who collects the revenue and who decides how it is obtained (in particular, what taxes are levied and what type of rate is applied) and, on the other, who decides on what and how the expenditure is executed. What is most appropriate and what implications arise from each situation are the subjects of study in the branch of public economics known as "fiscal federalism". Simplifying and synthesizing the analyses carried out in this field, the contrasting arguments are as follows:

- The main reasoning in favour of decentralization is based on the idea that the levels of government closest to citizens are more aware of their needs and preferences. If, following this logic, these levels are given the power to draw up and manage their own budgets, the principle of correspondence or co-responsibility concludes that, for expenditure to be judicious, they must also be responsible for collecting their own resources.

  In addition, the argument goes, when revenues and expenditures are managed locally or regionally, each vote has greater weight in the election of the government that is in charge of this management, and, the argument continues, citizens are therefore more involved in contributing to its control.

- Against the fiscal sovereignty of noncentral authorities, the criteria of equity are put on the table, and furthermore, a warning is given about the merely *opportunistic* shifts in economic activity that heterogeneity can generate. With regard to the first aspect, not all territories are equally rich, so their capacity to obtain income is not the same, and therefore, their capacity to offer services or provide funds for specific policies would not be the same. Equity could also be undermined by the imposition of different taxes or by the application of different rates and conditions to the same taxes. If this happens, it brings us to the second issue: those individuals or companies who have the means to move to the constituency that is most favourable to them from a tax point of view will be tempted to do so. "Having the means" means that it is not exactly the lower classes or small businesses that have the easiest time of all to change residence or headquarters; nor do they have the greatest incentive to move, which brings us back to the (intensified) problems of equity. And if these movements end up creating geographical poles where wealth is accumulated, the inequalities will become even more apparent.

Fiscal decentralization presents two further problems. The first is that the impact of activities which generate externalities, whether positive or negative, on territories other than the one in which they occur can be underestimated; with a global vision, governments could appropriately incentivize or punish them fiscally, but the territory in question, in whose calculation of costs and benefits these externalities do not enter, will probably not do so. The second is that economies of scale can be lost, and unnecessary duplication can occur; this is the case if, for example, each tax unit develops its own application for tax payment or if two hospitals are built in neighbouring areas (but belong to different jurisdictions) which could be served by a single common hospital.

• This is neither an argument for nor against fiscal co-responsibility, but what degree of autonomy is given to each jurisdiction in terms of debt capacity must be carefully decided, also taking into account that access to credit will not be on the same conditions for all of them.

Governments have ways of trying to overcome the drawbacks of decentralization without giving up its benefits. The first is to harmonize tax figures, criteria and procedures. The second is to accept that some kind of adjustment between territories must be made through direct transfers from one to another or, more commonly, by creating "solidarity" funds to be shared among those who, for one reason or another, are disadvantaged.

In practice, fiscal decentralization is never complete. Often the central government maintains, even in federal or quasi-federal countries, control over a large number of taxes and then distributes part of the revenue to one or more of the lower layers of government. The many nuances of this general pattern can lead to diverse, sometimes extraordinarily complex, realities.

The discussion on fiscal federalism has been illustrated here, as it usually is, by considering the central government of a country and the powers hierarchically dependent on it. However, it can be extended to the situation of any pair of governments that have a political relationship of subordination. This would be the case of a municipal government and the provincial or regional government on which it depends in some specific fiscal aspects. It is also the case of states that have agreed to cede part of their sovereignty to a supranational body; remember, for example, that the European Union has a single monetary policy but not a common fiscal policy and that it has not made progress even in the eternally pending tax harmonization.

READING 4.11   THE COST OF PUBLIC GOODS

A significant number of public goods are provided by the levels of government closest to citizens. The website cited in Reading 2.1 (Gobierto[1]) categorizes the expenditures of Spanish municipalities into six large areas. One of them is basic public services. Although not all items included there are public goods, many of them can be defined as such.

The category of basic public services is organized into four subcategories:

1   Urban safety and mobility includes activities such as public security and safety, traffic safety, civil protection and fire prevention and firefighting.
2   Housing and urbanism includes items such as urban planning, access to population centres, public street paving and protected buildings.
3   Community welfare includes sewage, potable water storage, waste treatment, street cleaning, cemeteries and funeral services, and street lighting.
4   The environment includes budgets for parks and gardens and for environmental protection and improvement.

Figure 4.13 displays individual (smaller maps) and overall (large map) spending on the four categories, always in euros per inhabitant. These expenditures refer to the 2018 budget.

From a global perspective, 729 municipalities (of a total of 5,454) spent more than EUR750 per person on these services, 428 of them spent more than EUR1,000 and only 92 spent more than EUR2,000. On the other end of the table, 241 spent fewer than EUR100 per resident, 569 fewer than EUR150 and 1,087 fewer than EUR200. When this expenditure is viewed as a percentage of the total budget, the results are absolutely disparate (from more than 80% to just a few percent), but in general, the numbers are not far from 50%. Public goods are not free.

The breakdown in Figure 4.13 reveals that environment generally has the smallest budget of the four subcategories. The next on the list is urban safety

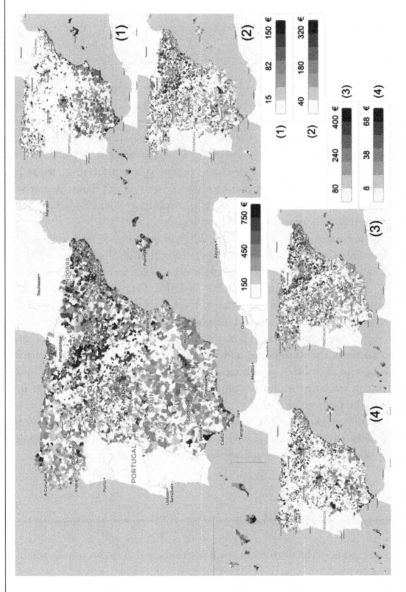

FIGURE 4.13   Spending per resident by Spanish municipalities on basic public services (in euros, 2018)

and mobility, which had no budget at all in many interior areas. Housing and community welfare accounted for large percentages of many municipal budgets in Spain.

1 https://presupuestos.gobierto.es/.

Summary

Once the objectives pursued by public action in the economy have been set, this chapter explained how action to fulfil them is carried out. The state has a *toolbox* including various instruments that it can employ. The most common (and perhaps the most flexible in modulating its scope and impact) is its capacity to establish the rules governing general economic activity (or a specific activity). The state also has the power to impose taxes and levies or to provide aid and subsidies. It can also establish incentives for certain agents or reach different kinds of agreements with the private sector. Finally, it can act even as a substitute for the market, setting prices or even directly providing goods and services.

Any of these measures can be used for different purposes. A tax can be used to redistribute income, reduce the volume of a certain kind of exchange or simply generate income that can be applied to other objectives. At the same time, various measures can be used to pursue a specific objective. Economic policies are made up of consistent sets of measures directed at reaching a (generic or specific) goal or to orient a certain economic sector. One possible way to classify economic policies divides them into policies that organize economic activity, policies that promote economic activity, macroeconomic adjustment policies, social policies and sectorial policies. Economic policies, which must work in harmony, always play an instrumental role in reaching the ultimate objectives pursued by public action, which we analysed in the previous chapter.

The decision-making capacity can be decentralized. Who collects the revenue, and who decides on what and how the expenditure is executed are the questions that determine the capacity for action granted to each level of government.

Overview

This chapter contained the following:

- A description of the instruments available to the public sector to take action in the economy.
- A description and analysis of the economic policies whose goal is to organize and promote economic activity as a whole or only in specific sectors of the economy.
- A description and analysis of macroeconomic adjustment policies (e.g. fiscal policy, monetary policy and commercial policy).
- A description and analysis of social policies and sectorial policies.

- A discussion about the necessary coordination of policies and about fiscal federalism.

Self-assessment questions

The self-assessment questions are meant to evaluate how well you have understood the information presented in this chapter.

1   What conditions are required for a public company to provide a service?

    a   It must be free and universal.
    b   It must be free, but it doesn't have to be universal.
    c   It must be universal, but it doesn't have to be free.
    d   It doesn't have to be free or universal.

2   Which of the following is correct?

    a   Ex ante regulation is always stricter than ex post regulation.
    b   Ex post regulation is always stricter than ex ante regulation.
    c   Ex ante regulation can be more or less strict than ex post regulation; the strictness of the obligations imposed has nothing to do with when they are applied.
    d   Ex ante regulation is always equal to ex post regulation; they are differentiated only by when they are applied.

3   What does the crowding out of investment refer to?

    a   If the public sector goes into debt, it shouldn't invest in infrastructure until it liquidates the debt.
    b   If the public sector goes into debt, it needs to take out loans that will no longer be available for businesses.
    c   If the public sector goes into debt, future generations will have to pay for the investments made in the present.
    d   If the public sector goes into debt, public investment is reduced and shifts into priority areas.

4   Monetary policy is expansionary _____

    a   If the monetary base is reduced.
    b   If the central bank buys government bonds from individuals.
    c   If the interest rate at which the central bank lends money to commercial banks increases.
    d   All the above.

5   What policy seeks to help unemployed people adapt to the job profiles that companies are searching for?

    a   Active labour market policy.
    b   Passive labour market policy.

c   Employment policy.
d   Social security policy.

Questions for reflection

The answers to the following questions are not in the text; they require you to search for additional information or to apply to real cases what you have learned in this chapter.

1   The text provides various examples of public action that can be considered nonmonetary incentives. Think of more examples.
2   Do you believe that prolonged and well-endowed unemployment benefits discourage beneficiaries from looking for a new job? In light of your answer, what characteristics (length, amount) should such benefits have?
3   Although today the traditional distinction between *right-wing* governments and *left-wing* governments is less clear than it was in the 20th century, what economic policies do you believe would today be prioritized by one or the other type of government? In what specific policies do you think the main differences reside?

5

CONCLUSION

State or market?

1 Introduction

In this book, we've studied the reasons, objectives and tools that shape how and why public activity in the economy is carried out. Although this could be enough to understand the relationship between the state and the economy, this analysis would be incomplete if we did not reach some kind of conclusion. Any conclusions reached in economics must include the criteria of whoever presents them, at least to some degree; after all, economics is a social science. In the matter at issue, this simply must be the case because, as we to a greater extent demonstrate in this chapter, neither theory nor observation can perfectly resolve the state/market dilemma or even provide an answer that can be accepted by the majority, without controversy. In this situation, trying to remain neutral is unreasonable. Defining the limits and, in general, the relations between the private sphere and the public sphere, between free market and government action, is one of the main, if not the main, tasks of any economist. Therefore, although in previous chapters an attempt was made to maintain a positive economics approach at all times, describing actions and criteria as aseptically as possible, in the second half of this chapter (Sections 4 and 5), some positions and specific situations are defended and others criticized.

However, that is the second half of the chapter; the first one serves as a preface to the conclusion. The government's role as an alternative to the market is derived from the market's shortcomings when organizing economic life. But until now we have not considered if that role could be restricted by its own limitations. The following two sections describe the state's shortcomings from theoretical and practical perspectives, respectively. After completing this analysis, we will have material to come to a conclusion.

DOI: 10.4324/9781003173731-5

2 Public action in the economy: a priori objections

From a theoretical perspective, three aspects of public action in the economy can raise doubts about its appropriateness. The first refers to the difficulties that members of a society can have in reaching an agreement about what is preferred. The second, once agreement has been reached, is to evaluate the restrictions that elected representatives might encounter when attempting to carry out their mandate. The third is how to determine whether the agreed-on actions provide the expected results.

2.1 The limitations of collective decision-making

At the start of Chapter 3, we saw why we cannot establish selection criteria to automatically decide which among various alternatives is preferred from the perspective of social welfare. The underlying problem is that several definitions of social welfare are available, because measuring individual utilities is impossible and even less so is aggregate utility. Therefore, adopting a positive approach and studying what processes a society, either as a whole or through its representatives, uses to make decisions seems to be a reasonable approach. The social choice theory provides work that has been done on this aspect.

If not the only, then the main, interest is to understand the mechanisms that govern democratic societies. In a dictatorship, the only criteria imposed are those of the dictator. On the other extreme, in full democracies, the criterion would also seem to be simple: if a referendum was held to resolve every dilemma, we would be able to clearly discover the majority opinion. This would indeed be true if we always had only two options to choose from, but when we have more than two, which is quite common, a referendum does not guarantee that the one chosen was undisputed. At the end of the 18th century, Nicolas de Condorcet had already revealed the limitations of the voting process: the order in which the alternatives are presented to the voters and the voting procedure itself condition the result. In the middle of the 20th century, Kenneth Arrow further formalized this result in his "impossibility theorem", which posits that no procedure whatsoever can convert the ranked preferences of individuals into a community-wide ranking while also adhering to certain criteria of rationality *and* democratic values. This second point is important because such a system method could exist if someone were to order the preferences—that is to say, if a dictator were to make the decision.

Arrow's theorem has a second reading: every democratic public sector will have to figure out how to coherently include the preferences of its citizens in its decision-making process. If the situation arises in which, even after voting, the majority opinion remains uncertain, what criteria should guide the government when ranking the priority of different economic policies or different parts of the same policy (e.g. when assigning budgets)? Furthermore, this is all based on the supposition that individual citizens have precise (and rational) preferences on each and every one of the matters that the government makes decisions on and, in

addition, that the government somehow receives the information on those preferences. The restrictions already imposed by Arrow's theorem on public decision-
making become even more severe in the real world, where individuals do not
always have opinions on every issue or behave rationally and where the opinions of
all interested parties cannot reach the government.

READING 5.1   DOES ALL OF SOCIETY PARTICIPATE IN DECISIONS? HOW DEMOCRATIC ARE WE?

Are all societies free to decide how they organize themselves, including how
to organize their economies?

The Clio Infra project has set up historical databases of a large number
of social, economic and institutional indicators, generally from the start of
the 19th century to the start of the 21st century. One of those indicators is
the *latent* (inferred, not directly observable) *democracy variable*,[1] an index
that summarizes seven other indicators. Figure 5.1 presents the results in a
box-and-whisker diagram. We are not interested in the details but rather in
a global vision: the median grew until 1985 (though in 1920 and in 1960, it
reached values greater than the following in the series), but with a great deal
of dispersion; after 1990, the dispersion was reduced, but the box's median
and upper limit (which marks the third quartile; the lower limit marks the first
quartile) were in decline, and many atypical values appear in the background
of the graphic. Translated into plainer language, this means that in the final
years of the 20th century, many countries with *poor democracy* had improved
their score on this indicator, whereas a few had plummeted; on the contrary,
democracy was eroded in many of the countries that were at the top of the
table. The image at the start of the 21st century is that of a planet that is
more closely clustered at lower levels of democracy than 15 to 20 years earlier,
although a few states display extremely poor levels of democracy.

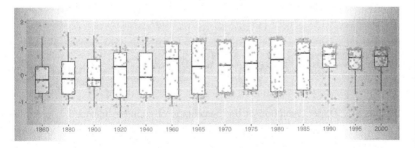

FIGURE 5.1   Evolution of the "latent democracy variable" (1860–2000)

Has this tendency changed in the new century? The veteran nonprofit organization Freedom House created a summary indicator on the level of freedom (understood as civil liberties and political rights—not to be confused with the Index of Economic Freedom, presented in Figure 1.2). With the results of this indicator (denominated "freedom in the world"), they grouped states in three categories: free, partly free and not free. In its 2020 report,[2] the NGO presented the number of countries that have been in each of the three categories since 1989 and in intervals of ten years until 2019. With all the caution needed when comparing two different indicators (and also taking into account that the thresholds that separate the three categories are arbitrary;

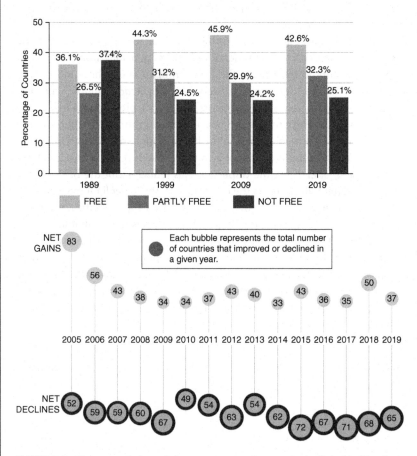

FIGURE 5.2 Upper: evolution of the percentage of countries included in the three categories of the "freedom in the world" indicator (1989–2019). Lower: number of countries that declined and improved in the same indicator (2006–2019)

other cut off levels could lead to different results), the image of global democ-racy at the end of the 20th century that emerges is more favourable than the one offered by the "latent democracy variable", as can be seen on the upper part of Figure 5.2. Conversely, the last decade studied clearly shows that the state of things has worsened, as can be seen in more detail on the lower part of the same figure, which shows the number of countries (in absolute value, not percentage) that from one year to the next have improved or declined in the "freedom in the world" indicator.

1 https://clio-infra.eu/Indicators/LatentDemocracyVariable.html. Data from Fold-vari, P. (2014). *A latent democracy measure 1850–2000*, Utrecht University, Centre for Global Economic History, Working paper n° 59.
2 https://freedomhouse.org/sites/default/files/2020-02/FIW_2020_REPORT_BOOK LET_Final.pdf.

2.2 The limitations of government actions

Although important, the criticism of public action in the economy derived from Arrow's theorem is not the only one that can be made. Tied to (or as a consequence of) the advances made by the social choice theory, a school calling itself *public choice* was developed, which raised further objections to possible government activity in the economy. Conceptually, the most interesting is the argument that nothing like a "col-lective preference" or "general will" exists. It postulates that the axiom in which indi-viduals always behave to maximize their own utility remains valid even when they hold public office. Therefore, elected politicians (generally representatives chosen through a voting process) and political appointees would manage the public budget to satisfy their personal interests, and optimizing the well-being of society remains secondary.

These and related arguments are the basis of a theory on *government failure*. In fact, just as Chapter 2 listed the conditions that must be met for market action to obtain an efficient result, we can also talk about the exact requisites for govern-ment action in the economy to reach its objectives—that is, for such action to be, if not efficient (the resources assigned to it are not considered), at least effective. Chapter 2 also revealed that the difficulties in meeting the conditions required for the market to be efficient constitute a substantial part of the criticism made of it as a mechanism to organize economic activity. Likewise, the failure to meet the basic requisites for government action in the economy to be effective provides solid arguments against such action.

The following points detail the requirements that must be met for public sector action to be effective. Each is followed by a second paragraph presenting the (theoreti-cal but also practical) objections that can be made regarding meeting these conditions.

• Those in charge of designing and managing economic policies seek the com-mon good, not their own interests.

If the rationality of individuals implies that in their private activities, they pursue their own interests, we have no reason to believe they would behave differently when in public office. In fact, reality teaches that it is not uncommon for public officials to work for personal gain, whether monetary or other. They have many opportunities to do so because they handle public funds and decide between options that impact various actors differently.

- The previous point mentions *the common good*. This concept is defined well enough, and political authorities know how to orient their work to comply with this definition.

Lacking a single definition of social welfare, the government is supposed to act as a *benevolent dictator* capable of identifying what is best for society. But we have no reason to believe that the public administrator knows what theory cannot determine. In practice, no criterion, accurately or not, is employed as a rule. In certain situations, individual interests are not aligned and can even be opposed. Which request is finally accepted often depends on spurious criteria, such as the pressure of political lobbies or how socially or politically close certain collectives with a vested interest are to the decision-making body.

- The authorities designing the public action are presumably qualified to do so: they correctly understand how the economy functions and are capable of identifying and evaluating objectives and the ways to reach them.

Access (at least politically) to public responsibility is not restricted to people with proven expertise. Those who reach public office are not obligated to read this book (perhaps fortunately for them). Not even having *technocrats* in public office ensures that the measures taken will be adequate for the economy in a given moment.

- The same authority in charge of designing public action also has the information required to do so.

The public sector also suffers from the problems caused by imperfect information. Generally speaking, it cannot access all the information available to citizens and businesses, either because that information does not reach the government or because those agents hide it deliberately. One specific problem that affects some public decisions is the lack of prices to guide them. After all, price is an indirect method of learning the preferences of those demanding the product, which is essential to knowing how to employ resources in the best way possible.

- The public authority is free to make the decisions that it deems necessary.

  This limitation is not insurmountable if collective or planned models are chosen to organize the economy. However, mixed economies have safeguards that limit the transfer of property rights, which in turn imposes restrictions on the design of many policies, specifically those based on equity criteria or that require redistribution.

- Honest and efficient public employees objectively and competently implement the policies decided on at upper levels. In this way, those responsible for economic policies maintain control over the objectives.

  The information that reaches authorities regarding the work of their subordinates is not perfect. Their relationship could then result in a *principal–agent problem or agency dilemma*. This occurs when coordination between representatives and who they represent or between boss and employees is not achieved. The use of mechanisms to align the interests of both parties is required in such cases. In this regard, public employees can be tempted to modify the conditions of plans and projects in a way that maintains or reinforces their status within the administration. In addition to all this, inefficiencies are generated when the bureaucracy is rigid or unnecessarily complex.
  The agency dilemma can also occur at the higher level. Political authorities can be not only the principals in relation to their subordinates but also the agents in relation to the people who voted them into office to carry out the measures that they had promised to implement.

- Decisions are always reversible. So public employees can be fired when they are no longer necessary, the salaries of government employees and pensions can shrink as well as grow, infrastructures that become unnecessary can be abandoned and incentive programmes can be easily discontinued if they are not achieving the proposed objective.

  Many public actions cannot be *rolled back* or, if practicable, the way for undoing them is not the same as the way by which they were rolled out. The measures presented in the preceding examples are not always easy to enforce, or at least the time needed to put them into practice can be much greater than the time spent in adopting the previous, opposite decision.

- The policies are consistent with other policies, and those that are promoted at different decision-making levels are not contradictory.

  That local, regional and national policies will be coordinated is not guaranteed. Moreover, in some cases, even coordination between different bodies of the same government is absent or lacking. Some studies dealing with this issue cite a prime example in which for a time the US government was subsidizing tobacco farmers while promoting antismoking campaigns.

- Consistency is not only territorial or functional but also temporal: short-term policies and long-term policies are also consistent.

One administration cannot obligate successive administrations to continue the first's policies; each may not even have similar objectives. This inconsistency can even be (and is) observed over the course of the same mandate, as the political cycle forces a government to change its priorities when new elections approach, focusing on actions thought to be more beneficial electorally.

READING 5.2   HOW WELL ARE GOVERNMENTS DOING THEIR JOBS?

Measuring effectiveness, and even more so the effectiveness of a government, is difficult. An approximate way to evaluate it is to look at what its citizens think about its performance. This is not exactly scientific, but it is still useful information; in fact, in a democratic society, public opinion is more important

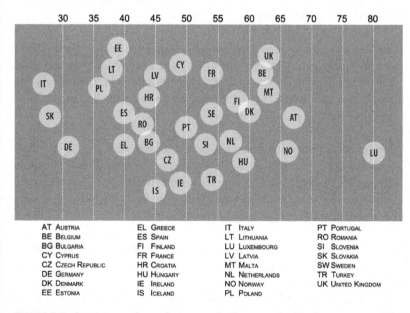

30	35	40	45	50	55	60	65	70	75	80

AT Austria	EL Greece	IT Italy	PT Portugal
BE Belgium	ES Spain	LT Lithuania	RO Romania
BG Bulgaria	FI Finland	LU Luxembourg	SI Slovenia
CY Cyprus	FR France	LV Latvia	SK Slovakia
CZ Czech Republic	HR Croatia	MT Malta	SW Sweden
DE Germany	HU Hungary	NL Netherlands	TR Turkey
DK Denmark	IE Ireland	NO Norway	UK United Kingdom
EE Estonia	IS Iceland	PL Poland	

FIGURE 5.3   Percentage of people surveyed who agreed with the statement "The administrative services of my city help people efficiently" (2015)

than any other indicator. Eurostat, the European Union's statistics office, carries out surveys called *eurobarometers*. In 2015, it published a eurobarometer titled "Perception of quality of life in European cities". One of the questions was "The administrative services of my city help people efficiently", to which the people surveyed had to say how much they agreed or disagreed (on a four-point Likert scale). Figure 5.3 presents the sum of the percentages of those who answered "strongly agree" or "somewhat agree".

As can be seen in the figure, Luxembourgers were, by far, the most satisfied with their local administration. They are followed by Austrians and Norwegians (the survey was also carried out in European countries that are not members states of the European Union). On the other end, all the countries who reported below 50% satisfaction with the local services are from Eastern or Southern Europe, with the exceptions of Ireland (at the 50% limit), Iceland, and Germany, which somewhat surprisingly is third from last on the list, where only slightly over 30% of people report that they were satisfied. Slovakia and Italy had the dubious honour of closing out the list.

1   https://ec.europa.eu/eurostat/cache/BubbleCapital/index.html?lg=en#tableCode=
    urb_percep-11.

2.3 The limitations to measuring public action

If a government takes action in the economy, it supposedly does so in the belief that the result obtained will be closer to what society wants than what the market will produce on its own. This assumption should later be confirmed by some type of evidence, which will also reinforce the justification for later actions.

However, finding such support isn't easy, because measuring the results of public action is complex. For example, how modifying regulations alters the dynamics of a market can sometimes be evaluated only in the long term and probably not incontrovertibly, as the regulation will certainly not have been the only factor in the market's evolution. In addition, it will generally lead to indirect effects on other areas of the economy whose impact is even more complicated to accurately estimate.

In the case of public projects, their success is commonly measured through cost–benefit analyses. However, most of the time, such projects provide nonmonetary benefits that are difficult to calculate. Accounting conventions must be used that can produce quite different results. In the criticisms of inflation measurements presented in Chapter 3, we saw how difficult evaluating the quality of services is, and the public sector offers mainly services. On the costs side, the difficulty emerges from the fact that public bodies almost never have homologous institutions to which they can be compared (international comparisons can never be totally reliable). Therefore, verifying the merit of the accusation that public institutions and companies have no incentive to reduce their costs is almost impossible, because they have no profit and loss account to protect.

The difficulties involved in calculating the results of public actions impede evaluating the degree of truth in specific criticisms made of them. This is clearly the case of the consequences of the crowding-out effect, which, as we saw in Chapter 4, the public sector is accused of generating when it goes into debt. If this effect does in fact occur, we would first need to know what the money borrowed is used for. If at least part of it increases some areas of public expenditure, we would have to estimate the gain in social welfare tied to those increases and later compare it with what would have been generated if that money had been available to the private sector (taking for granted that it would have been used in productive activities or in consumption, which is not necessarily true, given that both businesses and individuals could also have used it for speculative investment).

A related argument is that voters lack the incentive to monitor the performance of their representatives (of their agents in an agency model) or to follow the execution of the public budget and committed expenditures. Such oversight functions as a public good: nobody would be excluded from the benefit that it would provide, and of course no reduction in individual utility occurs if the entire country receives the information. But it requires time and a certain level of commitment from volunteers. Therefore, most people can easily just let "someone else do it".

3 Public action in the economy: practical difficulties

In a global and globalized world, the capacity for governments to take action in their economies is seriously conditioned. The same is true of the effectiveness of the measures that they might take.

First of all, governments have voluntarily ceded part of their autonomy. Supranational or bilateral agreements they have signed obligate them to assume commitments that limit their ability to manoeuvre. Agreements or treaties can be negotiated in different forums, refer to different subjects and have varying scopes. That said, the most common are preferential trade and *free trade* agreements. Although these agreements may seem to affect only commercial policy measures (negotiation of tariffs and quotas), their content is usually broader and includes commitments regarding labour rights, property rights, consumer rights, health or environmental regulations, and even the management of public services. Even more important is that states sometimes renounce their capacity to settle disputes, by transferring the competence of ordinary courts to arbitration courts created ad hoc. On the basis of arguments such as eliminating trade barriers and "protecting investors", these treaties generally tip the government–market scales in favour of the market.

When states go beyond mere trade agreements to undertake integration processes, the transfer of sovereignty is obviously greater the further along the process is (establishing a customs union, single market and currency union would be stages before political integration). Taking for example the European Union in its current state, the majority of the economic activities have common (or at least *harmonized*) regulations, and the leeway given to member states to take direct action is also significantly limited; even the circumstances in which public funds can be given without being considered *state aid* incompatible with treaties has been established. It also has a single monetary policy, not only for member states who have adopted the single currency. On the other hand, EU member states have a bit more margin to act on fiscal, economic stimulus and social policies.

Second, beyond signed treaties, states have in practical terms lost a large part of their autonomy, with the exception of those (few) countries that have voluntarily remained outside the global economy, in particular outside the free movement of capital. This is due to a subtle but unrelenting pressure for economic policies to be aligned with *what is expected*. Even who sets the current orthodoxy is not clear, opposing it is almost impossible. This situation is manifested in the case of monetary policy. If a, shall we say, "unconventional" policy is followed, *the markets* will react by *punishing* that country with pressure on its currency exchange rate and adding a premium to the interest rate that is applied to its debt. The chain reaction that this would generate could neutralize or even revert the impact expected from the original measure. A similar result could happen if other measures are adopted, such as a highly expansionary fiscal policy that tried to significantly increase public spending. The conclusion is that no country *would dare* to implement policies that are too far from what is considered adequate, and as a result, their independence is far from absolute. The situation is even more complicated if we look at it in greater depth, because sometimes it's not even actual data but rather the mere expectation of what is going to happen or what *must* happen that sparks the *reaction of the markets*.

On a global level, other private agents also condition what states can feasibly do. This is true in the case of credit-rating agencies, whose ratings on the solvency of national and regional governments restrict their borrowing capacity, or certain audit or consulting companies, whose reports sometimes have greater repercussions (even credibility) than official government publications do.

We also have to remember the role of certain international or supranational organizations in defining economic orthodoxy and, therefore, in determining what *must be done*. This affects the least developed countries, which have had entire lists of tasks imposed on them in order to receive aid or debt relief. But some of the recipes have also been *suggested* to developed countries: to participate in the global game, for instance, they must open their markets to international competition and privatize public companies. One area that appears obligatory to liberalize is the financial sector. The consequent elimination of almost any barrier to the free flow of capital has only reinforced the effects described earlier.

The third and final reason restricting public action on the global stage that began to take shape half a century ago and has been consolidated by the progress of the digital economy is the effectiveness of economic policy measures.

Indeed, one of the basic conditions for public action in economy to achieve its objectives is that the rest of the agents (individuals, businesses) do not circumvent the obligations that can be derived from the action. This refers specifically to the income the public sector needs to fund its activity—that is, to paying taxes. In addition to the underground economy and fraud are *grey* operations, involving difficult-to-trace cash outflows to other jurisdictions that are not always willing to collaborate with the governments of countries from which the money is sent. Less frequent, but increasingly common, is the real or fictitious transfer of residence. All this is possible because neither people nor especially capital face the obstacles to crossing borders that they may have encountered decades ago.

In the specific case of taxing business activity, one basic problem is that some countries have low tax rates (or are directly tax havens). In the past, companies maintained links with territories that were difficult to conceal. In the *material* world, many processes have today become international and clarifying how much added value is generated in each step is difficult: a business can manufacture in various places, assemble components in another, subcontract a certain process in a third, use a subsidiary to move the final product and sell it in dozens of markets. In the *immaterial* world, the situation is more extreme: nominally, the headquarters of many digital economy companies can be almost wherever its owners want (and they usually want places where they will pay the least taxes).

The first sentence of the preceding paragraph ("countries have low tax rates") does not diminish the responsibility of companies who follow *questionable* practices, but it does introduce a nuance, in that they could not carry them out without the complicity of some governments. But, above all, the sentence calls attention to another important obstacle for public action in the economy to achieve its goals: the competition between states to attract economic activity. In the present global scenario, rather than enforce their own laws, many countries have entered into a race to the bottom to offer *more-favourable conditions* to businesses and entrepreneurs. This refers not only to taxes but also to the context (regulation) in which the activity takes place. The principle of comparative advantage, which has traditionally been the basis of international trade, is no longer valid. Businesses do not produce where it is comparatively cheaper to do so but rather where it is cheaper to do so in absolute terms. And this involves searching not only for lower production costs, especially in labour, but also laxer health and environmental regulations. So the country that chooses to adhere to stricter standards runs the risk of some companies' leaving the country or, as they say euphemistically, *offshoring* their production.

In the light of the above, it is concluded that the main issue of the ineffectiveness of economic policy measures is the difficulty (either directly or indirectly because of less activity) in obtaining income. The lack of funds impacts the government's capacity to carry out its policies, policies that, in a kind of vicious circle, will most likely be less effective because of its not having sufficient resources. This has a significant impact on policies that promote economic activity and on social policies. Reforming (cutting back) the welfare state has been on the table since the 1990s, as states constantly search for a viable model. This also affects the sustainability of public companies, especially those in which the state has become a complementary provider (rather than a substitute) to private providers.

READING 5.3   LEPRECHAUN ECONOMICS: THE LEPRECHAUN LIVED IN AN APPLE

In Reading 3.3, which presented Ireland as an example of the disparity that could exist between measuring a country's economic growth with GDP or with one of the other indicators derived from it, a *not-so-official* version of the origins of said results was promised. We now tell that story.

It is a long story, but its defining moment came when the Irish government published that the country's GDP in 2015 had grown 26.3%, only to a few months later revise that number to 34.4%. Prominent economist Paul Krugman, in his *New York Times* column, described the phenomenon as *leprechaun economics*. If this had happened in some other part of the world, Krugman would have thought of other kinds of fairies; since it happened in Ireland, it was no doubt *leprechauncraft*.

Everything started in the 1970s, when the following was generally accepted: businesses that owned patents (usually on intellectual property) could turn them into intangible assets in their accounting and also include a fee for the royalties associated with those assets in the final price of the products they sell. This is not unreasonable at first glance, but given that these are intangible assets, determining how high the fee in question should be is difficult. This being the case, a company who sells a phone could arbitrarily say that the royalty is equal to its theoretical profit, thereby converting the profit to zero. Regardless, this would not be a problem for the country where the phone was sold (and which wants to tax the profit), because royalties are also subject to taxation. The real issue is that this tax is paid in the country where the company is licensed to use the patents. If this second country was a tax haven, the first country would not allow the company to pull such a stunt, but if it was a *reputable* country, it would have no choice but to accept the *global rules of the game* and allow the tax to be paid in that *reputable* country. But the company with the licence to use the patents (a subsidiary of the big phone company in the *reputable* country) could also have been granted its use by another company, the real owner of the patent, which is registered in a tax haven and, what a surprise, is also owned by the phone company. This *reputable* country might have obligated the company established in its territory to comply only with a few formal requirements and, moreover, allowed it to transfer the money that it collected through royalties to the company that owns the patents (the one located in the tax haven)—and all this at a tax rate close to zero. The scheme could fall apart if the tax authorities in the country where the head office of the phone company is located trace the activity (and profits) of its affiliates. But even then, the company still has a remedy: if the legislation of the *reputable* country had the particularity of allowing for a national company to be exempt from taxes if it is controlled and directed from a foreign country, a second subsidiary, controlled from the tax haven, can be created to buy the first subsidiary; next, the first subsidiary transfers money to the second so that it in turn can send it to the tax haven. The first subsidiary is no longer an affiliate of the parent company but rather of a company of the *reputable* country, so it can avoid the reach of the tax authorities in the parent company's country. If the tentacles of the tax authorities brush against the second subsidiary, officially it can be set up as an independent company. If the company still has any risk of having to *pay the bill*, more intermediary steps can be introduced, such as passing the money through yet another country, a country that receives and returns it with no questions asked (and, of course, without excessive taxation).

If all this was possible and the *reputable* country was Ireland, we would be talking about the *Double Irish* arrangement (sometimes combined with a *Dutch Sandwich*). If we think of companies that sell mobile phones, we could have been talking about Apple.

Ireland was already listed as a tax haven in one of the most important articles (because it was pioneering) on the subject published in 1994.[1] The progress of the digital economy (which gives greater weight to intellectual property) and the globalization of markets has only led the country to allow these types of permissive practices to proliferate (and perhaps become more refined). This all went on in certain normalcy until the European Commission started an investigation in 2014, which in August 2016 concluded that Apple had received illegal state assistance from the Irish government (in 2014, for example, the company paid an effective corporate tax rate of around 0.005% on its total European profits, which it had transferred to Ireland, when 12.5% would have been the normal rate); Apple received a fine of EUR13 billion for back taxes from 2004 to 2014 (although it had been proven that its relationship with Ireland had started at the end of the 1980s). However, before the sentence Apple had already prepared for the new scenario in which the *Double Irish* technique would fall under the spotlight. In 2015, Apple transferred, from Jersey, its intangible assets tied to intellectual property to its Irish subsidiary, which resulted in the country's GDP's increasing more than 30%. Although Ireland's Central Statistics Office altered its way of doing things, to hide the operations behind this incredible result, after almost three years, it admitted the truth: the Irish economy's leprechaun had emerged from an apple.

Apple's movement in 2015 is part of a new strategy of *tax engineering*, the *Green Jersey*, another corporate tax tool among the many officially listed under the flashy name of base erosion and profit shifting (BEPS). And those who don't like jerseys have another way to keep warm: the *Single Malt*, another structure that can easily be used to modify the *Double Irish* arrangement. For whoever is thirsty, the bar is open.

Of course, Ireland is not the only country that follows practices lacking, shall we say, moral integrity. In addition to the many small states (curiously, often islands) listed as tax havens in that article from 1994 mentioned earlier were also *serious* countries such as Switzerland, Singapore and Luxembourg, the same Luxembourg that in Reading 3.3 championed the divergence between GNP and GDP, an interesting coincidence. When *Luxembourg Leaks* broke, revealing that 1600 companies were registered at the same address, a four-storey building at 5 rue Guillaume Kroll street, it was another interesting coincidence that the consultancy firm PricewaterhouseCoopers, experts in creating "complex tax structures", was located next door.[2]

On its turn, Apple is also far from an isolated example; instead, it is in many ways a kind of pioneer. A Wikipedia entry lists the companies that have used the *Double Irish* arrangement (according to information from specific news articles denouncing the practices of these companies),[3] which includes globally known firms such as Adobe Systems, Airbnb, Facebook, General Electric, Google, IBM, Johnson & Johnson, Medtronic, Microsoft, Oracle, Pfizer, Starbucks and Yahoo! To complete the list of Internet giants, Twitter was included in the list of companies using the "holy grail of tax evasion" by Forbes,[4] before the possible change caused by the European sentence. This list is undoubtedly much longer. The names appearing in the headlines provided by the International Consortium of Investigative Journalists regarding the *Luxembourg Leaks* include Pepsi, IKEA, AIG, Coach, Deutsche Bank, Abbott Laboratories and the Walt Disney Co.; and the list of consulting firms specializing in tax loopholes includes names such as Ernst & Young, Deloitte and KPMG, in addition to PwC.

In light of these *public–private schemes*, who has the moral authority to ask Irish citizens to meet their tax obligations and to remember to ask for an invoice including all applicable taxes from the professional who is fixing up their house? What they can be asked is to change their brand of smartphone or tablet—if anyone was able to assure them that the new brand would not behave in the same way as the first.

1 Hines, J.R., & Rice, E.M. (1994). "Fiscal paradise: Foreign tax havens and American business". *The Quarterly Journal of Economics*, vol. 109, no. 1, pp. 149–182.
2 International Consortium of Investigative Journalists. It states that many firms that moved to Luxembourg have paid less than 1% on their corporate profits: https://www.icij.org/investigations/luxembourg-leaks/.
3 https://en.wikipedia.org/wiki/Double_Irish_arrangement.
4 https://www.forbes.com/sites/robertwood/2013/10/20/twitter-follows-apple-google-facebook-to-irish-holy-grail/.

4 So, state or market?

The belief that the private sector is more efficient than the public has become an axiom that has dominated economic and political thought from the last quarter of the 20th century up until the present day. *Market forces* minimize costs, improve quality and provide a balance between supply and demand. Or, seen from another perspective, the public sector is not as capable, as the market is, of allocating resources in line with the desires of the majority. In this setting, "the public sector must be cut back" has become an endlessly repeated mantra.

But is this true? What conclusions can we reach after reading this book?

If we are basing the conclusion on a theoretical analysis, remember that an entire chapter was dedicated to analysing the reasons why the market doesn't obtain the efficient result that theory predicts it will once certain conditions have been met. The final section of that chapter, however, explained that a strict definition of efficiency is adopted, but most importantly, that section clarified that just because a possibility opens up for public action does not mean that the state is obligated to act. No theoretical work can demonstrate that public action leads to a better (more efficient) outcome than the market would produce by itself.

Furthermore, in the first section of this chapter, a series of criticisms was presented that raises doubts about the (possible) effectiveness of the public sector. Acknowledging this, we must point out that many of those same objections can be made of the private sector. Just as there is a public choice theory, there could be a *private choice theory*. Models sustaining the conclusions of economic theory assume that businesses exclusively pursue profit and that, by doing so, they contribute to selecting the best use for scarce resources. But this is not always the case. It should be so when the business owner also manages it. However, today businesses are not usually directed by their owners. As businesses grow or become conglomerates, their structures become more similar to those of the public administration. Most importantly, in such structures, the incentives of private managers are not necessarily different from those of a public administrator. Just as individuals have no reason not to pursue their own interests when managing in the public sphere, so too they do not have any serious reason not to do the same when managing in a private sphere (other than their own). In other words, if personal interest takes precedence over social interest, it should also take precedence over other people's interests (specifically the interests of a company's owners). The corollary is that each and every one of the criticisms of public management have an equivalent in private management: the employee is an agent whose interests are not necessarily aligned with those of an owner who acts as the principal; internal bureaucracy may grow, and the objectives of middle management may also be inappropriate (to control the largest part of the budget or have more subordinates under them, regardless of whether it's beneficial to the company); the ability of managers is not guaranteed; the information that they have is not perfect; the decisions that they make are often conditioned by nonbusiness factors; and they are not completely reversible and may not be consistent with what is done in other departments of the company or with the strategy that the company will follow in the future.

Another common criticism is the supposed low productivity among public employees. But, again, a parallel counter argument emerges: evaluating the work carried out by a single employee in a company is difficult. In any organization (public or private), the overall result masks individual behaviours. Although, in theory, the private sector uses more-expeditious and simultaneously more-flexible methods to monitor particular tasks in order to reward more-productive employees or punish those who have not carried out their respective jobs well, the truth is that whoever applies those methods can make mistakes or do so unfairly for various reasons (e.g. disinformation, personal bias and concealing their own responsibility).

In reality, an organization is not efficient because it is public or private. What is truly important is proper organizational design, along with good management that sets up a system of incentives and some sort of mechanism to control indolent, negligent and corrupt behaviour. Take privatized companies as an example: there is no conclusive proof that the improved results (when they have occurred) came from the internal restructuring generally carried out or from the changes in market conditions which usually accompany the sale (e.g. opening up to competition or new regulation). If it is due to restructuring, no insurmountable obstacle prevents a public company from undergoing such a change. Despite the inertia that is usually present and the fear that those in conditions to do so have of tackling the problem, the public administrations and bodies that depend on them can also be reformed, not just cut.

READING 5.4 ARE GOVERNMENTS MORE JUDICIOUS IN THE USE OF RESOURCES THAN THE MARKETS ARE? THE ARAL SEA

In Reading 2.3, we saw how palm oil plantations are contributing to the deforestation of large swaths of tropical jungles around the world, particularly in Indonesia and Malaysia. Companies that produce this oil are interested only in maximizing their profits—economic rationality in its purest state. But these companies are not the only ones responsible for this situation. Far from placing impediments to these plantations, the governments of these countries promote palm cultivation; they do so in non-transparent ways and not always honestly.[1] And some palm oil producers even have public capital.[2] The governments of Indonesia and Malaysia are not, however, isolated cases. Other governments also approve of expanding palm cultivation, sometimes directly promoting it.[3]

However, sometimes the states not only *cooperate* in private activities that put the sustainability of the country's resources at risk but would be the only defendant if a suit in defence of the environment were brought. One of the most commonly cited examples is the Aral Sea, because its shocking nature.

The Aral Sea was not a sea but rather a lake (the fourth largest in the world) so large that it deserved its name. It is (or was) at the border between what are today Kazakhstan and Uzbekistan. In the 1970s, the Soviet Union decided to convert adjacent areas into cotton fields, for which it carried out irrigation projects on the rivers that fed the lake (i.e. dams, dikes and canals). At a certain point, so much water was diverted that the amount of water evaporating from the lake became greater than the amount reaching it, so it began to shrink. By 1989, a small part in the northeast, in Kazakh territory, had separated from the rest of the *sea*, and thanks to a later intervention (the construction of a dike with international help), it is the only part of the body of water that remains today; the rest of it, as seen in Figure 5.4, has completely dried up.

The Soviet plan was successful if we consider that even today Uzbekistan is one of the largest exporters of cotton in the world (although with certain problems in its production that are resulting in its replacement by rice, a crop

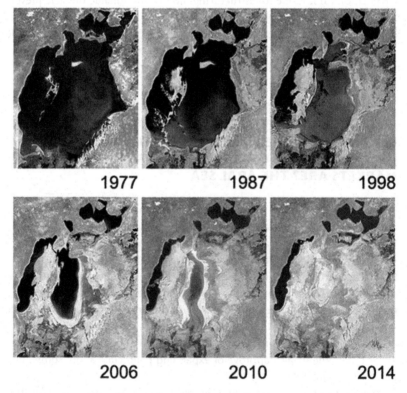

FIGURE 5.4 Satellite view of the Aral Sea—variations from 1977 to 2014[4]

FIGURE 5.5   Boats abandoned on what was once the shore of the Aral Sea[5]

that requires even more water resources). But the ecosystem has been devastated. The region's climate has become more extreme. Strong winds, frequent in Central Asia, generate salt and dust storms that circulate the pesticides and fertilizers that are used upriver (and that for decades had been deposited in the sediments in the lake, precisely because it was a lake and its water was not renewed) and also the remains of an abandoned microbiological war testing site, on what was once an island in the lake. Plant and animal species have disappeared, and the local population, who have seen how their traditional way of life disappeared (especially fishing), have emigrated. Those who remain suffer from one of the highest rates of respiratory disease and throat cancer on the planet.

1 Although many news articles have reported on the role of the Indonesian authorities, see, for example, *Indonesia for Sale* on the Gecko Project website, an investigative journalism initiative promoted by the Earthsight NGO: https://the-geckoproject.org/indonesiaforsale/home.

2 Around 6.5% of Indonesia's production comes from Big State-Owned Plantations (BSOP), according to https://www.indonesia-investments.com/business/commodities/palm-oil/item166?.

3 See *El avance de la palma africana en seis países de Latinoamérica* (The growth of African palm in six Latin American countries) a report published on the environmental journalism website Mongabay: https://es.mongabay.com/2017/12/especial-avance-silencioso-la-palma-africana-seis-paises-latinoamerica/.

4 Aerial images from a U.S. Geological Survey: https://earthshots.usgs.gov/earthshots/node/91.

5 NASA Earth Observatory. *Aral Sea abandoned boats*. Photograph courtesy of Ismael Alonso (2011)—downloaded from https://svs.gsfc.nasa.gov/10862.

After this long digression, we now find ourselves at the same starting point. We do not seem to have any criterion that allows us to know what should be reserved for the market and what space should be made for public activity. The reality is that there is no possible solution. Theoretical models are useful (necessary) for guiding any decision, but they cannot provide an irrefutable answer. In the real world, economic agents are not always rational or perfect optimizers, and their expectations on the evolution of the economy can be mistaken; neither is the government an omniscient and aseptic corrector of all possible problems. In the real world, government and the market are not opposite poles along an axis. The market is made up of a multitude of businesspeople, workers and consumers, and the state distributes its power across public administrations at diverse levels of responsibility and operating in different parts of the territory, in addition to autonomous institutions. The acumen and performance found throughout that web of competences, as well as the behaviour of the individuals who make up that web, will be far from uniform. In the real world, different interests and opinions aren't added together or imposed, but rather, they adapt to a negotiation that takes place within a certain institutional and historical framework. In the real world, effectiveness, when mistakenly reduced to merely lowering costs, is not the only parameter that interests society. In some services, the cheapest option is not always preferred if it means less quality in the service or if the reduced cost comes at the expense of the rights of those who provide it. In the real world, sometimes a decision has to be made between what seems more useful in the short term and what is more convenient for the future. In the real world, a decision has to be made on how people who for personal circumstances have been excluded from regular economic exchanges will participate in the economy.

The conclusion is that how to best allocate resources, organize production and fairly distribute what is produced depends on the specific time, place and circumstances in which the decisions are made. Does this mean that public action is advisable or admissible in any sector or by using any method? The answer is no; after all, an entire chapter was dedicated to knowing when public activity makes sense. Ultimately, this pragmatic approach requires rejecting overly rigid dogmas and instead examining each case to find what is presumed to be the best way to obtain the result desired by society (by *a* society, as a neighbouring community might desire something different). It also means that, unfortunately, no formula can determine the right decision. In addition to "environmental" or contextual elements (which are becoming increasingly uncertain because of technical and social change) are factors that are impossible to introduce into the equation. The government's supposedly corrective role becomes more than questionable when a public administrator carries out actions that are clearly flawed and also takes control of public funds. But if the board of directors of a bank bankrupts the institution because of disastrous risk management, thereby affecting the financial system of the entire country, and still allocates exorbitant financial compensation to its members, then the *invisible hand* of the market is not guiding the economy down the best path.

READING 5.5 BAD TIMES FOR LYRICAL POETRY

Who is more trustworthy—those who run governments or those who run businesses?

Periodically, the nongovernmental organization Transparency International publishes an edition of *Transparency International's Global Corruption Barometer* series.[1] The ninth edition, from the end of 2017, presented the results of a questionnaire given to 162,136 adults from 119 countries about how they perceived corruption in their own countries.

One of the questions was, "How many of the following people do you think are involved in corruption, or haven't you heard enough about them to say?" They were asked about a president/prime minister and officials in their office, members of parliament, government officials, local government councillors, police officers, tax officials (like ministry of finance officials or local government tax collectors), judges and magistrates, religious leaders and business executives. The respondents could choose from five possible answers: none, some of them, most of them, all of them, don't know/haven't heard. Adding all the answers (from around the world), the percentage of answers of "most of them" added to those of "all of them" are presented in Figure 5.6.

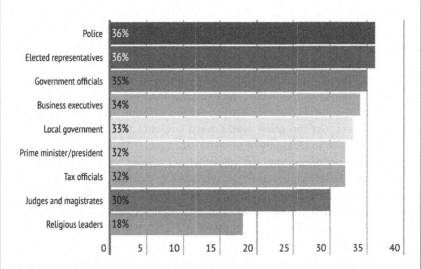

FIGURE 5.6 Percentage of people surveyed around the world who answered that all or most of the members of the groups indicated were involved in corruption (2017)

In light of this graphic, we argue that the answer to the question posed at the start of this reading is "neither—don't trust anybody". Around the world, the same level of dishonesty seems to be perceived in the public sphere as well as the private. Only religious leaders escape the fire (but not completely).

The report highlights the countries in which the public sector is seen as more corrupt. A "public sector" is calculated by taking the average of every category except for business executives and religious leaders (although doing it this way includes judges, who, strictly speaking, do not belong to the public sector). The ranking is headed by Moldavia (69% of respondents answering that all or almost all the people working in government and public administrations are corrupt), followed closely by Yemen, Lebanon, Liberia and Venezuela. At the other end of the list are Germany (6%), Switzerland and Sweden (8%), Australia (10%) and the Netherlands (11%). In these data (as well as those in Figure 5.6), direct percentages from the survey were added without making adjustments to the answers "don't know/haven't heard".

Examining the database allows for many interesting comparisons to be made. Here are two of them:

- Those who see the greatest corruption in businesses (answering "all of them" or "most of them") are from Mali, Benin and Lebanon. South Korea (60%) is in the sixth position, and Chile (56%) is in ninth. Those who most trust business executives (largest percentage of "some of them" or "none" answers) are the French (82%), followed by the Swedes and Australians. If the percentage is adjusted by eliminating the "don't know" answers (which in countries like China account for 30%), the preceding list doesn't change much; one exception is Moldavia, which rises from the fifth position to first, but South Korea is still sixth with almost two-thirds (63.8%) of the responses indicating "all of them" or "most of them", compared to one-third consisting of "some of them" or "none" answers. On the other side, Estonia becomes the country that most believes in the integrity of business executives (89% answered "some of them" or "none", after the adjustment), followed by China (85.7%), Sri Lanka, Sweden and France (all over 80%). In Australia, this percentage is 79.4%; in the United Kingdom 77.9%; in Italy 74.2%; in Spain 68.4%; in the United States 64.3%; in Germany 61.1%; in Russia 60.0%; in South Africa 59.6%; and in India 56.8%.
- The countries that perceived the most corruption among government officials were Yemen, Lebanon and Moldavia; South Korea is in the fifth position (69% answered "all of them" or "most of them"), but Chile is in the middle of the table at 40%. Those who most trust them are Hong Kong (86% answered "some of them" or "none") and Australia, the Netherlands, Spain and Sweden (all over 80%). If we again adjust by

removing the "don't know" answers, little changes at the top of the list (Moldavia, Lebanon, Yemen and South Korea are the first four), whereas at the other end, Germany moves to the top (92.4%), followed by Sweden, Hong Kong, China and Switzerland. If we return to the countries that we had provided the data for earlier and list them in the same order, in Australia the percentage is 87.5%; in the United Kingdom 73.7%; in Italy 55.6%; in Spain 83.7%; in the United States 67.0%; in Germany 92.4%; in Russia 46.5%; in South Africa 50.0%; and in India 50.6%. In addition, for China, the percentage becomes 90.2% and France 67.4%.

Taking into account all the misgivings regarding the data source and that only government officials have been used for the comparison, we conclude that Sweden and Australia believe more in the honesty of people who are working in the public sector than of those working in the private sector, a perception that is heightened in Spain and especially in Germany. In contrast, India, South Africa and France see business executives as more honest, and in Italy and Russia, much more honest. The United States, the United Kingdom and China show no significant differences. If we look at absolute values rather than relative (and not factor in countries that have unstable socioeconomic situations), the Swedish and the Chinese seem to be the ones who are most trusting of human honesty, wherever they work; the Koreans, in contrast, seem to be the ones who have the most difficulty in believing in the decency of their compatriots.

1 httpps://www.transparency.org/news/feature/global_corruption_barometer_ citizens_voices_from_around_the_world.

5 How societies can regain their freedom of choice

We closed the previous section by concluding that what ultimately counts are the specific circumstances of the moment in which societies make a decision about how to organize their respective economies. The current circumstances not only are complex but also place obstacles, even impede, such a decision from being made freely. If the private sector is given preference over the public, it should be based on a collective reflection that first decides what exactly the preferred option is and then defines the profiles and limits to the organizational model that is in the best interests of the society. It's not just a matter of principle: if the decision is imposed to any degree, this will not lead to long-term stability, because reactions will arise reclaiming lost independence.

Four pillars would need to be constructed in order to return to unsubordinated collective decision-making. This of course does not mean that we have to curb or revert the social and economic tendencies that characterize the present moment, but rather, we have to contain, or directly neutralize some of the potentially harmful effects that they are generating. Although they are presented separately, for didactic purposes, the four aspects are intimately tied, hindering our delineating the arguments.

5.1 The need for global rules of the game

A world without borders needs rules without borders—at least a minimum set of rules regarding basic rights and obligations. Without them, producers and *capital* will move in search of the most advantageous conditions, and proposing conditions that radically differ from the minimum thresholds will be almost impossible for any country. As seen earlier, this fact significantly limits the effectiveness of fiscal, labour and social policies implemented by governments. As capital, goods and services, and labour markets are getting more integrated, it becomes more urgent to deal with problems on a global level.

Another reason for supranational agreements is the global nature of certain issues. Global warming is a good example. The eventual crises of climate change will be felt everywhere, regardless of the degree of responsibility that can be attributed to each country. A collection of merely national approaches will be condemned to failure. In general, this argument is valid for all the goods that in Chapter 2 were classified as global public goods.

Just as the effectiveness of national legislation depends on whoever dictates it having sufficient legitimacy to convince the majority to respect it and the ability to sanction those who do not comply, the effectiveness of global regulation is conditioned by the legitimacy of the issuing body. In other words, for signatory states (and their populations) to feel committed to promoting compliance, the agreement has to be truly consensual, not imposed, and cannot be at the service of spurious interests.

5.2 The need to recover state sovereignty

The adjective *sovereign* usually accompanies the noun state. In reality, it doesn't modify the noun, as all states are (should be) sovereign. Sovereignty implies that each state has authority over a certain geographic area without being subject to any other state or power. However, in this chapter, we have seen that states have lost part of their autonomy to decide what policies are good for them; in other words, their sovereignty has been limited.

Nothing can be said when competences are transferred to a supranational organization. However, voices need to be raised when, even voluntarily, they are transferred to private entities, especially when not done transparently, such as in the fine print of a trade treaty or agreement. But the situation is much more worrisome when the concession of competences is involuntary. If we return to the *discipline* imposed by *the markets*, this is a preposterous situation. It is preposterous because what drives the huge movements of money (causing, for example, a currency's exchange rate to rise or fall) is for the most part merely speculation. The operations carried out by central banks or companies with *real* businesses constitute only part of these transactions. Computer programs that send out thousands of buy-or-sell orders in seconds in the name of investment funds whose ownership is sometimes opaque seek only to obtain immediate profit, whatever the consequences may be. *Preposterous*, therefore, seems like a good way to describe the fact that the autonomy of states is limited by the private interests of an unknown set of so-called international investors. These investors, paradoxically, are not truly investors if we use the economic concept of investment: to provide resources to increase production capacity. Additionally, despite the fact that they supposedly respect independence, integrity and transparency, certain recent events have demonstrated that the other private agents with global influence on the ability of states to act (auditing firms, analysts and credit-rating agencies that have shareholders that frequently also include investment companies and unit trusts) do not deserve to be, and of course should not be, above sovereign states.

We once again emphasize the following point: the appropriate ratio between government and market in an economy and the activities that should be carried out by the public sector within that distribution should be decided by the society in which those economic exchanges take place. Although individual interests (or of certain groups) are unavoidably mixed into these decisions, a society itself must develop mechanisms to control those interests and to address the various demands. What is inadmissible is for a society's capacity to enact its own rules to be inhibited by a kind of faceless global power. This is not an unavoidable situation, of course, although to correct it again requires a supranational agreement.

READING 5.6   THE WORDS ECONOMY

All textbooks that act as introductions to macroeconomics explain the relationship between the interest rates and a currency's value compared to other currencies: if a central bank raises the interest rate, the financial assets emitted in the currency of that country (e.g. bonds and deposits) become more valuable, which causes the demand for that currency to increase (to invest in those profitable products), the result of which is that the currency appreciates in value; in contrast, the currency depreciates when the interest rate is lowered. This is not a trivial relation: the interest rate is considered to be one of the variables that have the greatest influence on exchange rates.

On 10 March 2016, Mario Draghi, president of the European Central Bank, announced a *stimulus package* for the European economy. The official price of money was lowered five-hundredths to 0% and also raised the massive public asset purchase programme from 60 billion to 80 billion a month, including bonds issued by nonbank corporations. The press coverage at that time

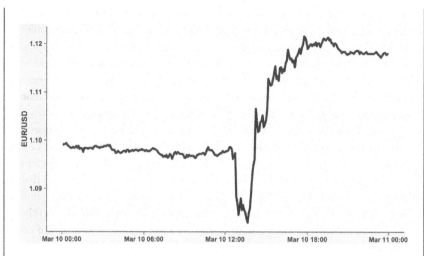

FIGURE 5.7 Changes in the euro–US dollar exchange rate between hour zero and 24 hours on 10 March 2016

commented that the measures went beyond *what financial analysts expected* (Draghi had "fired his bazooka"—a phrase found in articles from various news outlets), and the value of the euro immediately dropped 1.6% versus the US dollar (it had started the day at 1.0997 US dollars to euros and reached 1.0822). Whether this drop should have been bigger or smaller is debatable, but without a doubt, it makes sense according to economic logic, even in a world based on future expectations.

However, traditional economic theory remained standing for a few minutes. In the press conference following the announcement, Draghi cautioned that "we don't anticipate it will be necessary to reduce rates further". This apparently innocent comment led the euro to immediately rally, closing the day at 1.1178 US dollars to euros after having reached a high of 1.1218 (an almost 3.7% increase compared to the low, with an initial, almost instantaneous spike—see Figure 5.7—of 2.5% just minutes after the comment was made). It wasn't a *momentary tantrum* from the markets. The exchange rate remained at that level over the following weeks: it didn't drop again until well into summer, when changes in the real economy and the *anticipated economy* caused it to drop to 1.10, the level at which it had begun on that picturesque 10th of March.

5.3 The need to establish inclusive globalization

The risk of polarizing societies is evident. The transformations associated with globalization and technological change and in general the dominant new socioeconomic paradigm have created a new scenario that features winners and losers—and many more of the latter. In a world without barriers, any person whose task is not sufficiently specialized becomes *dispensable* and suffers downward pressure on their wages and rights. The change affects many who for a few decades had reached middle-class status in rich countries and even in many developing countries. Exacerbating the situation, their governments are cutting back social policies that they benefit from and seem not to have the funds (and sometime ideas) to create programmes to help them adapt to what the new context demands. To make matters even worse, the fiscal obligations on this salaried class has remained the same (or even increased) while they silently and impotently observe how many of the large companies and personal fortunes that have obviously been favoured by the *new economy* find ways to pay less.

The result is growing discontent towards a political class that offers no solutions and towards globalization and the immigration processes associated with it. In democratic societies, this could provoke (and in many cases has already provoked) a greater focus on *alternative* options that could eventually radically alter the balance between government and market. Ironically, workers in the poorest countries, who might feel benefited by the movements of the global economy, do not find themselves in a position to enthusiastically congratulate themselves about their new situations.

In the global market, different labour and social conditions should become equal or should at least converge. And indeed, this is occurring, but in large part towards the lower end. If this tendency does not change and if the benefits continue to accumulate in the hands of just a few who have found the way to wealth, the future is not promising. As discussed in Chapter 2, imbalances in the distribution of wealth are also a market failure because, taken to the extreme, they could threaten the continuity of the mixed economy model and the continuity of the model of society itself.

5.4 The need to recover community social capital

Unscrupulous businesses and corrupt politicians can arise at any place or time. Their behaviour is a problem *for* society. But if such behaviour becomes common, it is a problem *of* society. In any group, *the bad* (like *the good*) are not imported: not only do they form part of the group, but they have probably developed within it too. So when they are not the exception, something in the group itself is not functioning correctly. Its community social capital has deteriorated.

To understand the concept, we must first consider that only in elegant theoretical models do all parties involved in exchanges behave as a benefit or utility maximizer (acting purely in self-interest); in the real world, economic exchanges occur within a social framework in which interpersonal relationships exist and unwritten rules guide those relationships. Social norms are respected because of incentives (e.g. to feel part of the group) or fears (e.g. the stigma of deviating from the norm). In fact, thanks to social norms, externalities can be avoided or resolved (not making noise at night *in consideration of others*), or public goods can even be collectively provided (all neighbours commit to shovelling snow or removing weeds from the pavement in front of their homes).

Even without entering into moral considerations, a society that shares and respects a set of values, where mutual trust prevails, and that is capable of acting in a coordinated manner in benefit of all seems preferable to a social model in which individual action is limited only through coercion. The first of these two societies has greater community social capital, defined as the norms, attitudes and institutions (formal organizations or informal networks) that are capable of promoting coordination and collaboration processes on the basis of reciprocity and trust and that are oriented towards the good of the community.

If social capital shrinks, selfish behaviour becomes more common. This is bad news for public action in the economy because it makes the first criticism of the school of public choice more likely to come true; that is, politicians and public managers look after their own interests rather than the interests of the community. In contrast, for market activity, it would seem to be good news, as self-interest is the basis of the model. However, it only seems so: exacerbated self-interest, which considers only short-term profit, puts the sustainability of the model itself at risk. As we saw in Chapter 2, if the market does not self-control, then public action is justified to establish external control. But that control will not be effective if those who exercise it see it as an opportunity for their own profit. This will lead to a downward spiral of individualism reinforced at every turn, as each case of corruption or lack of solidarity among those whose behaviour is under public scrutiny (politicians guilty of nepotism; large companies who offer squalid working conditions while avoiding their fiscal obligations; and famous people who hide their fortunes in tax havens) discourages average citizens (taxpayers as well) from fostering the common welfare.

Reversing such a trend is complicated. In highly unequal systems, social capital exists only within the group with which individuals identify, probably because they share the same circumstances; there is neither sense of society nor any will do anything for it. Only when conditions become more equal with the spread of better social positions does the aspiration to construct a society in which everyone has a place arise. Of course, some people will always be dissatisfied with the fact that each person does not receive *only what they have earned*, just as altruistic, charitable or philanthropic personal actions occur in highly unequal societies, but that does not radically modify the situation.

In the past century, the growth of macroeconomic magnitudes had generally been reflected in an improvement in the conditions of individual lives. Given the change in model—in particular, after the most recent crises—this is no longer the case. The (apparent) economic improvement is not generating greater social cohesion but rather is often increasing the gap between groups. If, as has been said, globalization does not become inclusive, we will continue advancing towards an "everyone for themselves" model. Those of us who think that an unfettered market is not the model that our societies need now look to the future with concern.

READING 5.7   BUILDING SOCIAL CAPITAL POINT BY POINT

The text says that social norms are respected either as an incentive or out of fear. It is about feeling part of a group or of the disdain that comes with anti-social behaviour. This is probably also what Lyda Judson Hanifan, who is credited with first using the term *social capital* back in 1916, thought. What that state supervisor of rural schools in West Virginia could not have imagined is that "the accumulation of social capital, which can immediately satisfy social needs [of individuals] and potentiality be sufficient to substantially improve the living conditions of the entire whole community"[1] could come from the satisfaction of accumulating points on a card or from the fear of losing them. *Citizenship by points*, like gunpowder, is a Chinese invention. Both are equally explosive.

Many chronicles describe,[2] with more or less rigour, the Chinese concept of 社会信用体系—usually translated as "social credit system", though "trust" or "reputation" would seem to be better translations than "credit". In short, the system works as follows: citizens and companies have an account from which points are deducted in the case of reprehensible or illegal actions and in which points are added if particularly praiseworthy behaviour occurs; there are black lists of untrustworthy citizens and red lists of exemplary citizens that may both be publicized.

The origin of the system can be traced back to the final years of the last century, when speculation began to be made on the introduction of a mechanism to assess the trustworthiness and reliability of companies and citizens (in their capacity as economic agents); the initial aim was to restore confidence in markets that were too accustomed to noncompliance with the rules and to improper behaviour. Since then, different projects have been

FIGURE 5.8   Roncheng's "civilized families" are displayed on public noticeboards[3]

developed, which, while sharing the same basic idea, are different in purpose, scope and the specific procedures by which they are governed. At the time of this book's going to press, local, regional and commercial initiatives (sometimes with connections between them), not necessarily restricted to economic exchanges, were coexisting. This means that no single system is available for the whole country. In 2014, a national strategic plan was published, in the second stage of which (starting in 2021) a unified system could be imposed.

The actions that are rewarded or punished are different in each of the existing programmes and are intended to respond to the objective being pursued. The most curious ones are usually highlighted. Let us put aside the companies and focus on the behaviour of citizens: donating blood, recycling waste and carrying out some voluntary action earn points in some programmes. On the other hand, jaywalking, traffic violations, not visiting family members regularly and not collecting dog waste takes them away; if the offence is serious, such as not paying a debt, you can fall straight into the abyss of the table. On the Internet, praising the actions of the administration and being a reliable buyer or seller are rewarded, whereas being connected to an online game for too long, cheating on it and spreading hoaxes are reprimanded. The prizes given to those who achieve a certain score are as varied as a reduction in the price of a public transport ticket, free use of rental bikes for a while, preferential access to hospitals, better conditions when taking out a loan or exemption from paying a deposit on rentals. Punishment often takes the form of a ban: a ban on access to certain public services, on applying for certain jobs, on buying plane or high-speed train tickets, on sending children to private schools or on buying certain "luxury" items on the Internet. Perhaps the greatest punishment is the public exposure of those blacklisted. Apart from possibly appearing on posters or even in the cinema before a film is shown are mobile phone applications that alert others to the presence of blacklisted people in the vicinity.

We must make a couple points before we assess the system. The first is that many other countries also have blacklists—accessible or reserved, permitted or clandestine. They are common in the financial system but are used in other sectors too or at least companies track down and collect information from *not recommended characters* (for historical data on e.g. rentals, health and insurance). The reasons for being blacklisted are not always economic: remember the famous "witch hunt" in the film industry by the House Un-American Activities Committee or, also in the past, the lists of trade union activists that circulated in some countries; a much more current example is the vetoes that, for various reasons, are imposed on social networks. Increasingly used systems also adapt the terms of certain operations on the Internet (privileging them or hindering them) to a not always clear assessment of the participants. However, the Chinese social credit system has another dimension and could reach even greater proportions if at some point a national system fully connects the public programmes with those now maintained by Internet companies (companies which, as Reading 4.1 revealed, store an extraordinary amount of information about their users).

The second important point is that because of the idiosyncrasies of Chinese society, often not understood outside the country, the system is internally seen differently from the dystopian vision with which it is often described. A survey carried out in 2018 in several regions[4] showed not only that the initiative had a high degree of approval but also that this approval was greater among older people and among a certain social elite (economically well-off, educated people living in cities) who—far from being the most concerned about the potential threats to their privacy, which was what the authors of the survey predicted—considered the system to be an instrument for promoting honest behaviour in social and economic exchanges.

Whether these programmes are promoting honest behaviour remains to be seen. No mention has been made of their effectiveness (which is extremely difficult to measure, on the other hand) beyond presenting almost anecdotal examples that tell the story of someone who made amends for their faults or offences when they knew, sometimes indirectly when a request was refused, that they had been blacklisted. Perhaps in the future, the system will prove to be effective. Perhaps it will be extended to other countries. It may even become widespread. What it will not avoid, in any case, will be a nostalgic look at a past in which the reward for acting for the common good was only the satisfaction of the person who acted in that way.

1 Taken from Woolcock, M., & Narayan, D. (2000). "Social capital: Implications for development theory, research, and policy". *World Bank Research Observer*, vol. 15, no. 2, pp. 225–249.

2 Indeed, many articles and websites deal with the subject. We highlight two here: Mistreanu, S. (3 April 2018), *Life inside China's social credit laboratory* (https://foreignpolicy.com/2018/04/03/life-inside-chinas-social-credit-laboratory/), and Ahmed, S. (2019). "The messy truth about social credit". *Logic*, issue 7 (https://logicmag.io/china/the-messy-truth-about-social-credit/).

3 Photograph by Simina Mistreanu—downloaded from the website mentioned in note 2.

4 Kostka, G. (2019). "China's social credit systems and public opinion: Explaining high levels of approval". *New Media & Society*, vol. 21, no. 7, pp. 1565–1593.

Summary

In earlier chapters, we established a framework within which the state could potentially take action in the economy. Although we will never be able to provide unconditional answers, we must think about when and under what conditions state action would be more beneficial than inaction. First, the mechanisms used to make collective decisions must be reviewed, because they are obviously fundamental not only to determining the circumstances when public action is legitimate or not but also to setting precise objectives and the scope of the action.

When public action is taken, it confronts limitations that could hinder not just obtaining the set goals but even being in a position to pursue the objectives. The theory of public choice formalized the criticism by revealing many *government failures*. Doubts also arise regarding how difficult measuring results obtained by public action is. That said, some of the shortcomings that the public sector is accused of (or that are actually true) are replicated almost exactly in modern companies; moreover, these companies also have to deal with other situations that distance them from the behaviour required in ideal market models. What really counts is not who owns an institution but rather how it is organized.

Even in an ideal and benevolent state that strictly adhered to what is collectively agreed on and didn't add inefficiencies to the process, carrying out independent national economic policies is increasingly difficult. In a globalized world, the limits on what is feasible for governments to carry out sometimes result from the voluntary abdication of sovereignty (supranational agreements), but in most cases, they're limited by their inability to control how certain agents react to policies that those agents don't agree with.

Governments, businesses and citizens are all part of the same society. If economic dysfunction is caused by a reprehensible behaviour of individuals that, even if not generalized, is not uncommon, the problem is social, not economic. Beyond what theory predicts, if an economy lacks community social capital, it will not reach efficiency, no matter how it's organized.

Overview

In this chapter, you learned to achieve the following objectives:

- To identify the impediments to making a collective decision.
- To understand the theory of public choice and categorize the constraints that governments face when trying to meet their forecasts and also when wanting to demonstrate the level of compliance with their stated objectives.
- To describe the difficulties involved in carrying out independent national economic policies.
- To identify the conditions that would have to be restored for democratic societies to retake control of their futures (including economic ones).

Self-assessment questions

The self-assessment questions are meant to evaluate how well you have understood the information presented in this chapter.

1   Arrow's impossibility theorem establishes which one of the following?

    a   An individual cannot rationally rank their own individual preferences.

    b   Whatever the circumstances, no decision-making rule allows individual preferences to be transformed into a community-wide preference.

    c   No decision-making rule allows individual preferences to be transformed into a group's preference, except if a dictator ranks the preferences.

    d   No decision-making rule allows individual preferences to be transformed into a group's preference, except if every individual has carried out a perfectly rational ranking of the preferences.

2   "Individuals behave in a way to maximize their own benefit even when they are in public office" is an argument made by which one of the following?

    a   The public choice theory.

    b   The public impossibility theorem.

    c   The market failure theory.

    d   The theory of externalities.

3   Which of the following assertions is not on the list of requirements that must be met for public action in the economy to be effective?

    a   Public authorities know how to manage in a way that is in line with the definition of general welfare.

    b   Different policies are consistent with each other and those promoted in different decision-making areas are not in opposition.

    c   Public authorities can make any decision deemed necessary.

    d   The actions taken by public authorities must be irreversible.

4   The agency problem or dilemma occurs between whom?

    a   Voters and members of parliament.

    b   The managing board of a bank and the directors of its branches.

    c   The president of a public institution and the directors of its different departments.

    d   All the above.

5   Which of the following statements is false?

    a   Conducting a cost–benefit analysis is the most commonly used method to measure the results of public projects.

    b   That voters monitor the activity of their representatives and try to control budgets and spending works like a public good.

   c   The public sector also suffers from the problems caused by imperfect information.

   d   Private management does not have any of the problems of which public management is accused.

Questions for reflection

The answers to the following questions are not in the text; they require you to search for additional information or to apply to real cases what you have learned in this chapter.

1   Review the list of circumstances that limit the effectiveness of governments. Which of them do you think are affecting your current local government?

2   Try to find the text of a free trade treaty that your country has signed, and evaluate the benefits and disadvantages that it brings.

3   "State or market?" is the title of this chapter. The arguments put forth in the text regarding this question are only *some* answers. What is yours?

6

STATE ACTIVITY THROUGHOUT HISTORY

Theory and reality

1 Introduction

We here reprise the phrase that we used in Chapter 1: states are free to organize economic activity as they see fit. The only constraints are the values that they establish. Therefore, their actions are conditioned by the way society's wishes are determined and by who executes these intentions and how.

In modern democratic societies, elected governments must (should) fulfil the promises that they make in their election manifestos, so the decisions that they make are in this way putatively supported by those who voted for them. Of course, voters cannot predict every action that the government will take in the future, but they can have a general idea regarding the types of measures that it will implement. From an historical perspective, however, this is an exceptional situation. Most of human history has witnessed a correspondence, obviously forced, between the interests of the powerful and the interests of society. Thus, whoever was powerful enough to do so organized economic activity in such a way as to enrich certain groups or families, to dominate other geographic regions and/or to spread a religion. Acting on behalf of the common good, understood as the well-being of the largest number of the individuals who make up society, is a relatively new situation. Similarly, although today the market is almost universally entrusted as the basic mechanism to allocate and employ resources, in other eras the space for private economic activity was more limited.

The historical sequence of different scenarios suggests that although the debate regarding *the public* and *the private* in the economy may not have changed, it has acquired various nuances. Theoretical contributions of the past cannot be directly compared to those made today, because the questions that have arisen in more-recent times were not relevant when those earlier contributions were postulated.

DOI: 10.4324/9781003173731-6

Every era attempts to resolve the issues that are pertinent to their time. Like in any other field, economic thought is a product of its time and place.

Maintaining the focus on state activity in the economy, this chapter will provide an overview of economic history and one of the history of economic thought. To ensure the consistency demanded by the last paragraph, facts and theories are analysed simultaneously. This approach not only is consistent but also contributes to a better understanding of both aspects: the context always influences what is written, but sometimes what is written (some of what is written) manages to influence the context.

The conventional account of both histories is undermined, or at least limited, by the Euro-centric perspective adopted by the majority of authors who have engaged in either discipline (*Western-centric* in the most recent historical periods). This chapter is not an attempt to overcome this deficit; it does not present original research work, but rather, it borrows from already-published work. Its value is not in providing new information but rather in selecting and compiling information related to the theory and reality of state activity in the economy. Despite the importance of this subject, textbooks (almost always general purpose) usually do not clearly identify what the different schools of thought have contributed to the topic or to what degree the economy of a given time depended on public action.

2 Up to the contemporary age

2.1 Antiquity

The transformation of rudimentarily organized human groups into societies with a greater institutional presence gave rise to more-complex political, religious, and economic structures. Of course, this evolution manifested differently in each community and took place at different times and paces. Nevertheless, the various processes have a series of common (or at least widespread) characteristics that help understand the origin of the role of the state (of what we would consider a state today) in the economy. First, political power was centralized. The sovereign and surrounding elites decided what should be done with the community's resources, and for the most part, only their interests were satisfied. At times, this hoarding of wealth began to be organized through taxation or similar duties (often paid in kind). Second, social structures were hierarchical. The lowest layers made up a workforce who had barely any rights—or who had no rights, in the case of slaves. Finally, commerce began to develop, which, in turn, was a factor in the development of the groups who carried it out.

In this context, the economic doctrine (if we can call it such) that has been passed down to us from the most prosperous ancient civilizations revolves around administrative aspects of organizing tax collection, distributing wealth (among elites) and constructing public works. In addition, and despite the limited space that strictly private economic activity occupied in those economies, even prices and compensation for work ("salaries") were sometimes regulated; the Code of

Hammurabi contains a detailed list of "labour situations" and the corresponding compensation required for each case.

The exception came from the Greek thinkers of the 5th and 4th centuries BCE, who developed an initial discourse (at least the earliest-known discourse) questioning the status quo. They did so not only because economics is an aspect of human endeavour whose meaning should be examined by philosophy but also because they lived in an environment in which thinking about economic issues made sense. In the preceding centuries, the Greek polis had gone through a social crisis that led to reforms, as well as what could be referred to as a certain "economic liberalization", which was both a consequence and a cause of the development of commercial ties with the East and of the expansion in the Mediterranean. An important aspect of this situation, as we shall see next, is that many merchants made fortunes and were often seduced by luxury.

Both Aristotle and Plato, who dealt with economics, although they didn't consider it to be an independent discipline, saw the pursuit of wealth by their fellow citizens as a danger to social harmony. To some extent, the economic growth brought by commercial expansion engendered instability rather than happiness, like in the legend of King Midas. As a consequence, both of them called for economic activity to be controlled by the state. Plato believed that supervision should be thorough: those in charge of this task, the guardians (one of the professions required for a "civilized life"), should decide how income would be distributed, although they themselves would have to live austerely and possess only what was strictly necessary. Aristotle did not share his teacher's arguably extreme positions. He was in favour of pursuing self-interest, though always limited to satisfying needs; having needs met would make sure that economic questions didn't interfere with the enjoyment of activities that were *really important*. To ensure this limit, in *Politics*, he proposed the existence of a superintendent whose primary task was to make sure that everyone involved in an exchange behaved honestly and established agreements and contracts in such a way that *order* was maintained; some authors have even suggested that Aristotle believed that these supervisors should set prices. The third Greek author that is usually found in economic history textbooks is Xenophon, though only because he can be considered the father of the term *economics*, because he wrote a treatise on household management by that name (*Οικονομικός*); his work doesn't go beyond the stated objective.

No historian cites a significant contribution to economics by the Roman Empire. However, the formalization of property law in its legal system continues to be the basis for the limits, guarantees and legal effects of modern versions of property rights.

2.2 The Middle Ages

Almost without exception, after the chapter on Aristotle, or ancient Greece in general, economic history textbooks jump ahead around 15 centuries, to the Scholastic period. This immense gap is due to the inexistence of facts (and ideas) worthy of note, primarily as a result of the stability of the decentralized feudal economic model that followed the fall of the Roman Empire. Although the commonly used epithet of Dark Ages is arguably unjust, that period was marked by little margin for intellectual progress in the field of economics. As mentioned earlier, all economic thought is a product of its time, and the issues that had concerned economic theorists in other eras were simply not pertinent (and therefore of no interest) to the feudal mode of production, which was characterized by self-sufficiency, the limited division of labour, the inexistence of breakthrough technological innovations in manufacturing or transportation, and limited commerce that was mostly restricted to local trade.

Perhaps to fill this gap, some textbooks point out contributions by economic thinkers who lived before the scholastics but in *other worlds*, where the economic situation was different from that in Europe. While Europe was steeped in the Middle Ages, Imperial China experienced a period of great splendour—the state playing a much more active role, in building, for example, the colossal trade and transport route that was the Grand Canal. However, the most famous Chinese economist (at least in Western textbooks), Guan Zhong, who provided guidelines for how the state could avoid price fluctuations, predates even Plato. Those who do fit into this time frame were the Arab thinkers (the Greek works were translated to Latin from Arab, not directly from Greek). Abu Hamid al-Ghazali, who in the 11th century studied how to best collect taxes, deserves a mention. Today, however, the contribution made by Ibn Khaldun three centuries later is more highly regarded. Among the economic issues that he examined is what could be called state social spending, which in his opinion favoured not only the recipients but also the state.

Returning to the scholastics, these thinkers re-examined the economic ideas of the Greeks, with all the nuances derived from their different contexts and motivations, and arrived at similar conclusions: the sinful nature of human beings causes, against the will of God, love for oneself to be greater than love for others, and therefore, the result of unregulated individual activity (ergo, the markets) does not conform to divine law. For Thomas Aquinas, carrying out actions for profit (this included not only what we today refer to as usury but just earning any interest on loans) and conducting any trade that did not respect the "just price" were immoral. The intervention of authorities to ensure harmony in the socioeconomic order is, as in the case of the Greeks, a corollary of scholastic reasoning.

The reason why the scholastics were interested in some of the issues for which economists are still searching for answers today is not random. Simply put, in their time, they began to experience the transformations that would lead to the later emergence of a system that could be denominated capitalism: various crafts which had until then been practised by peasants in their homes began to turn into independent trades, and after centuries of general autarky, trade in goods began to re-emerge; as a consequence of all this, a new social class appeared, the bourgeoisie, which in turn furthered the importance of cities as economic centres.

At the end of the period, new economic problems emerged. One decidedly curious but significant problem was caused by certain monarchs who, driven by the need for funds to finance their military campaigns and lifestyles, couldn't resist the temptation to devalue their coin by physically altering it (reducing their weight), leading their subjects to respond with similar ruses. The late scholastics, such as Nicole Oresme, dealt with this episode of general pursuit of self-interest, reminding the authorities of their obligations and suggesting price controls. However, debasing currency had happened before: some authors have included it as one of the factors that led to the fall of the Roman Empire.

READING 6.1   BUBBLES THAT EXPAND AND BURST: THE SOUTH SEA BUBBLE OF 1720

Getting rich quick without much effort is something that all humans seem to desire. It must be in our species' DNA. That may be the reason why the same story is repeated time and again: a seemingly easy opportunity to multiply savings, a fear of missing out on the gravy train that spreads to the point of near madness, the sudden discovery that not all that glitters is gold and the house of cards that collapses, creating a tidal wave that wipes out not only the overly ambitious but also many of the banks involved in the affair, in good or bad faith, and, depending on the size of the wave, the entire country or even a group of countries.

Tulip mania is usually considered to be the first crisis provoked by the popping of a speculative bubble in modern history. This is the story of the apparently dramatic collapse of a first futures market, for tulip bulbs, which occurred in 1637. The adverb apparently is used because, although the first

FIGURE 6.1   South Sea Bubble playing cards (1721)[2]

written narrative that appeared in the 19th century popularized a version of events that has passed from book to book, some modern researchers have greatly clarified what happened, especially the consequences of the incident, which were perhaps not as serious as once believed.

Much more credible, however, is the story of the *South Sea Bubble*, because it has been documented much more carefully. A collection of documents about the subject can be found in care of the Harvard University Library, which has a website dedicated to the incident in its *CURIOSity Digital Collections*.[1] The following is a summary of what is presented on that website.

The South Sea Company was created in 1711 with the promise of obtaining a monopoly on trade with the Spanish territories in South America, in exchange for taking on all the public debt generated by British involvement in the War of Spanish Succession (which began in 1701). The potential profitability of this promise, however, was tied to the result of the war. The Treaty of Utrecht of 1713, which ended the war, limited the company's trade opportunities, as it confirmed Spain's sovereignty over its overseas territories. Prospects grew even worse when the relations between Spain and Great Britain deteriorated in 1718.

Despite the fiasco, the company convinced the British government to convert part of the national debt in South Sea stock. In 1719, the British Parliament authorized a new conversion of public debt. Despite this, in January 1720, the South Sea Company was valued at a modest 128 pounds. In an attempt to generate greater interest in the company, its directors spread false reports regarding their successes and about the wealth of the territories that it was exploiting. In February, the stock price increased to 175 pounds. In March, yet more debt was converted into stock and by the end of the month, with investor confidence strengthened, it soared to 330 pounds.

While this was happening (or as a cause for this to happen), the rush to invest in stocks of companies grew disproportionately. The previous years had brought a wave of enthusiasm to Great Britain, including financial: after the war with Spain, an increase in international trade was foreseen in markets that were increasingly global; luxury was no longer reserved for the aristocracy; consumerism grew and neither class or gender was an impediment to invest in the stock market; the newspapers became sources of information and the cafés were the prosperous epicentres of stockbrokers. In this context, in the middle of 1720 (sometimes known as the "year of the bubble") a large number of projects, some of them absurd, came to the stock market, taking advantage of the speculative frenzy, each creating its own bubble.

In this panorama, the wave grew, and in May, South Sea stock had reached 550 pounds. In June, the "Bubble Act" was passed, which forbade the creation of joint-stock companies without royal charter. The company received the charter, which was seen as a vote of confidence, and by the end of the month, stock spiked to 1,050 pounds.

Suddenly, investor confidence began to wane. At the end of August, stock was still at 800 pounds, but a few months earlier, the company itself had established a plan to lend money to buy stock, and many who had taken out the loans were forced to sell, to cover the first payment that was due at that moment. The market *turned around*, sell orders stacked up and eventually the price collapsed. The result was that in September the stock had returned to 175 pounds, causing the ruin of many people and institutions that had participated in the game. Among the affected people was Isaac Newton (sources seem to confirm that he lost the majority of his fortune) who supposedly had said that he was capable of "calculating the movements of heavenly bodies, but not the madness of people". In 1721, an official inquiry discovered a network of lies, corruption and bribes, and many of those responsible were tried in court, both from the company and from the government.

Who said that history doesn't repeat itself?

1 https://curiosity.lib.harvard.edu/south-sea-bubble.
2 Composition made with three playing cards out of the 52 which form the deck (https://curiosity.lib.harvard.edu/south-sea-bubble/browse/playing-cards). Baker Library Special Collections, Harvard Business School, Harvard University. Record ID: 8001624098_urn-3:HBS.BAKER:228052 (ace of diamonds) and 8001625460_ urn-3:HBS.BAKER:228061 (ten of diamonds) and 8001625464_urn-3:HBS. BAKER:228064 (king of diamonds).

2.3 Modern age

By the 16th century, the political and economic situation in Europe had changed a great deal from that of the previous centuries. First of all, nation-states began to take shape. Second, trade was expanding at a vertiginous rate, and enormous quantities of silver were arriving from the Americas (impacting prices). Third, the social attitudes and ethical principles evolved at the velocity of the times: whereas Luther continued considering usury a mortal sin and advocated for merchants to charge the just price, shortly after, Calvin considered profit a just reward for a businessperson's diligence and dedication in following a vocation that had been granted by God. The School of Salamanca, which can be considered a late continuation of the scholastic tradition, as well as contributing to what today we call the monetary and fiscal branches of economics, already accepted free pricing (market price) for luxury goods and pointed out the effects of competition on prices; in fact, the price of "the things necessary for life" could be established by a "common estimation" if many buyers and sellers were involved.

In this context, concepts appear, such as "national interest"—or, more properly, "state interest". Rather, they adapt to the new reality. Mercantilists believed that this greater interest and not the precepts of justice, whether divine or not, was damaged by the pursuit of self-interest. And given that the principal manifestation of public interest is the accumulation of precious metals, the commercial sector is where the control of private initiative must primarily be directed. This was carried out mainly by controlling imports and exports (establishing tariffs and applying other measures that today belong to commercial policy) and by granting commercial monopoly privileges. Importantly, the mercantilists were not theologians writing manuals on how to reconcile Christian and commercial doctrine or how to interpret the concept of justice, but rather, they were often merchants and businesspeople *converted* into writers or pamphleteers. Through protectionism, they encouraged the search for new markets while safeguarding their businesses and privileges within their own country; therefore, the national interest was clearly in line with their personal interests.

The application of mercantilist approaches in 17th-century France was one of the reasons why the agriculture sector stagnated, leading to supply problems. In response, in the 18th century, the physiocrats claimed the role of agriculture as a primary source of the *produit net*. Because the development of agriculture was hindered by restrictions on exports (designed to keep the price of grains low and, by extension, keep also low the salaries of the manufacturing industries), the physiocrats postulated the abolition of these trade barriers. They praised the virtues of competition in their writing and argued for minimum state intervention. In fact, their thinking is often associated with the expression "laissez-faire, laissez-passer". However, their arguments were not absolutely consistent. For example, François Quesnay, one of the major representatives of this school, advocated for market controls, particularly on agrarian markets, given their special importance. In addition, for physiocrats, the pursuit of self-interest, which led to an excessive demand for manufactured and luxury goods, continued to be part of the problem that had to be resolved.

READING 6.2   BRILLIANT ECONOMIST OR BRILLIANT CROOK?

One of the reasons that seems to have contributed to the burst of the South Sea Bubble was that just a few weeks earlier, in France the Mississippi Bubble had burst (on 17 July 1720). The main actor in that story was the Scot John Law, who lived from 1671 to 1729. John Law was a complex and controversial figure, and the story of his life is told in three *formal* publications, whose titles are almost identical, except for the verbs: "John Law, the Scottish gambler who *rescued* France from bankruptcy"[1], "John Law: the gambler who *broke* France"[2], "John Law, the gambler who *revolutionized* French finance"[3]. The only thing that the writers of these publications agree on about him seems to be that he was a gambler. And his knowledge of probability statistics apparently provided him some benefits in various moments of his life.

FIGURE 6.2 Portrait of John Law[4]

Following closely the entry devoted to him in the Encyclopaedia Britan-nica[5], which describes him as a Scottish monetary reformer and originator of the "Mississippi scheme" for the development of French territories in the Americas, we can summarize the events of his life as follows. Law studied mathematics, commerce and *political economy* (not just *economics*) in Lon-don. After killing a contestant in a duel, he went to Amsterdam, where he studied banking systems. A decade later, he returned to Scotland and wrote his best-known work, *Money and trade: A proposal for providing the nation with money* (edited in 1705 and 1720). He presented a plan for banking reform to Scottish Parliament, but it was rejected. After several other rejections, Law obtained permission in 1716 to implement his plan in France. The French government was heavily in debt as a result of the many wars that it had been involved in under Louis XIV, who had died a year earlier, and Law's project, which promised to reduce the public debt, was attractive. For Law, however, reducing the public debt was secondary. He shared with his mercantilist contemporaries the belief that money is the engine of economic development and that increasing its amount stimulates the growth of the national product and increases the power of the nation. He differed from the other mercantilists in his consideration of the central bank, which for him should be an agency creating money in the form of bills that would circulate instead of the scarce gold and silver. In Paris, Law actually founded a bank that had the power to issue banknotes. He later merged the bank with the Louisiana Company, which had the exclusive right to exploit the vast French territories in the Mississippi Valley in North America. Law's plan worked well for a few years but was complicated by speculative moves and political intrigues, something that was not attributable to Law. As the mastermind of a plan, popularly known as the Mississippi Bubble, Law was in 1720 forced to flee France. He died destitute in Venice.

The central part of this biography refers to Law as an economist. Law has been praised for introducing in modern times paper money on a large scale (Marco Polo had already seen it in use in China) and praised as one of the first authors to discuss the functions of money and to establish a monetary theory. Some have said that his vision of the financial system was so modern that it seems more apt for today than for the 18th century. This statement can be understood when the French part of his biography is explored further, which is without a doubt the most substantial. That is where he put into practice "quantitative expansion" strategies for monetary supply, today considered a heterodox economic policy but still used, and some of the schemes that he came up with (almost no other biography agrees with the Encyclopaedia Britannica that Law had nothing to do with how the events turned out) are similar to modern strategies employed by governments to try to get out of difficult situations. Or it would be more appropriate to say that modern strategies are reminiscent of those developed by Law.

The Encyclopaedia Britannica has also an entry on the Mississippi Bubble in which it provides a broader and less-neutral vision of the incident and the figure, who it now defines as a "Scottish *adventurer, economic theorist, and financial wizard* (emphasis added) who was a friend of the regent, the Duke d'Orléans". In fact, his friendship with the Regent for Luis XV (who had inherited his great grandfather's throne when he was five years old) is what allowed him to receive permission to establish the Banque Générale in 1716, a private bank which was conceded the privilege to issue convertible bearer notes (billets d'état) and, one year later, to create the Compagnie d'Occident, which was granted a monopoly to exploit the French territory of Mississippi. The

FIGURE 6.3   A German caricature of John Law from the period, which reads, "The wind is my treasure, my pillowcase and foundation. Master of the wind, I am master of life, and my monopoly on wind will immediately become the object of idolatry"[6]

strategy to reduce the debt was simple: state creditors could be paid in notes and use them to buy stock issued by the company, stock that promised to be highly profitable. Importantly, this idea to reduce the debt was seemingly replicated by the British government in the South Sea Company episode.

This promise of profitability and also the manipulation by the Banque Royale (the new name after the Banque Générale was nationalized in 1718), in which it bought stocks owned by individuals by using notes that it issued itself, caused the stock price to soar and the demand for notes to grow (which the bank responded to by issuing more and more). This created a vicious cycle in which a growing supply of money was needed to drive up the price of the company stock in order to maintain confidence in the fiat money.

In 1719, the scheme was in its full glory: the stocks that had been sold at 500 livres were worth 18,000. At that moment, Law had taken over the monopoly of all French colonial trade by merging the original company with tobacco and slave trade in the new Compagnie des Indes; he had also been named Controller General of Finances of the King of France and controlled taxes and the minting of new coins. But the system was fragile. News of what was really happening in Louisiana (swampland in which many of the early colonists had died from malaria and other diseases) led to the first solicitudes to convert the notes to gold. One after another, attempts to keep the structure afloat failed. The government's rule on limiting the amount of gold and number of jewels that could be kept at home sent the opposite message than the one intended, convincing people that the gold, not the notes, had the true value. Law's final attempt was to merge the company with the bank. The stockholders had the right to exchange their stock for notes, at the still-generous price of 9,000 livres. But to reimburse the stocks, it had to issue (with no backing) such a large number of notes that it sharply increased the monetary supply. This sparked hyperinflation, which reached a monthly rate of 23% in January 1720. The farce in which the theatrical hiring of 6,000 beggars to parade through Paris pretending that they were miners who were going to Louisiana to work in the supposedly recently discovered gold mines was uncovered, definitively destroying confidence and provoking the collapse of the stock price.

All this led to turmoil, which forced Law to flee. Although Law was the scapegoat, whether all the decisions (especially the disproportionate issuance of notes) were his or those of Phillipe, Duke of Orléans, remains unclear. But of course, he was the architect of the system that collapsed.

The footprint that this episode left on history goes beyond a mere anecdote. The shambles made of the French state's finances (and the impact of the later actions to fix the situation) contributed to the outbreak of the French Revolution in 1789. Moreover, for decades, fiat money was viewed with mistrust; in fact, the link between money and gold was not broken until the 1970s, when the gold standard was abandoned by the Bretton Woods Accords.

1 https://moneyweek.com/30441/john-law-the-gambler-who-broke-france-58412/.
2 https://www.spectator.co.uk/2018/09/john-law-the-scottish-gambler-who-rescued-france-from-bankruptcy/.
3 https://www.ft.com/content/29aff968-a224-11e8-b196-da9d6c239ca8.
4 Portrait painted by Casimir Balthazar in 1843. Today it hangs in the Musée de la Compagnie des Indes, Ville de Lorient (France) under the title *Portrait de John Law (1671–1729), Contrôleur Général des Finances*. This reproduction was downloaded from https://commons.wikimedia.org/wiki/File:John_Law.jpg.
5 https://www.britannica.com/biography/John-Law.
6 Image downloaded from https://es.wikipedia.org/wiki/Archivo:John_Law_cartoon_(1720).png. The translation was taken from https://www.bbc.com/mundo/noticias-42486645.

3 From *The Wealth of Nations* to the start of the 20th century

3.1 The turning point: Adam Smith

While the physiocrats wrote their final contributions to economic thought, an industrial revolution (later known as the "first") was taking place in England during the second half of the 18th century, which would mark the beginning of a new historical era. The technological transformation later became economic and social, converting a rural economy based on manual labour into a mechanized, urban economy in which merchants began to lose influence to industrial entrepreneurs. At the dawn of this new era, *An Inquiry into the Nature and Causes of the Wealth of Nations* was written and published, which was later simply referred to as *The Wealth of Nations*, one of the few books on economics that even laypeople can associate with its author, Adam Smith. It also created a revolution in economic thought which helped to advance the discipline into its contemporary age.

In the opinion of many, Smith's work, with its famous "invisible hand", was the first step in the construction of a system capable of properly evaluating the efficiency of markets or, alternatively, the need for public action. The truth is that arguments of varying degrees of rigour can be found in any chapter of the history of economic thought, including, as we have seen, in earlier centuries.

What distinguishes Adam Smith from his predecessors is that he examined the combined result of individual actions: although individuals act strictly in self-interest, rather than for the common good, the sum of all these actions produces the most benefit for society. We stress the idea of combined actions, because Smith provides in his book around 60 examples in which the pursuit of self-interest leads to consequences that are detrimental to the common good. Moreover, the idea of an invisible hand that infallibly guides the markets is more of a modern interpretation of his idea than the foundation of his work, in which he uses the expression only incidentally and in a way that is associated with the religious and cultural context of his era.

However the metaphor of the invisible hand is interpreted, what Smith makes clear is that public interference could not improve the result of private activity. His lack of trust in politicians and public servants, whose work he described pejoratively, also weighed heavily on his conclusion. Again, here we point out an important nuance: book IV of *The Wealth of Nations* describes three duties that a sovereign in a system of "natural liberty" has to attend to, specifically defence, justice and "the duty of erecting and maintaining certain public works and certain public institutions, which it can never be for the interest of any individual, or small number of individuals". They are not, however, the only exceptions in which the invisible hand must be *assisted*. In addition to these three duties, Smith admits that regulation is necessary in various other areas (including price ceilings on interest rates; retaliatory tariffs; and public health or liquor taxes), all of which has even led some to exaggeratedly refer to him as a "cautious interventionist". To cover government spending, he supported a proportional income tax, arguing that everyone should contribute to supporting the government "in proportion to their respective abilities—that is, in proportion to the revenue which they respectively enjoy under the protection of the state".

Although much of what Smith wrote is open to interpretation, his system of natural liberty clearly posited that the market should be much less guided by governments or religions than in any other doctrine that had been proposed until then. By reconciling the pursuit of self-interest with public interest, he legitimized it morally and scientifically, which had never been completely achieved before.

READING 6.3   THE FABLE OF THE BEES

The medical doctor Bernard Mandeville was born in Rotterdam in 1670, but he spent a large part of his life living in England, where he wrote an allegorical poem titled *The grumbling hive: or, Knaves turn'd honest*, which was published anonymously. In 1714, it was included in a book titled *The fable of the bees: or, Private vices, publick benefits*, in which the poem was followed by a prose commentary on the origin of moral virtues and a chapter of "observations". In 1723, more essays and observations were added, and in 1729, a second part was published.

The work, which already had repercussions in the era in which it was written, has been analysed from various perspectives, including ethics, religion and politics but also from the perspective of economic thought. Some say that it influenced various economists, but especially Adam Smith. Of course, as we shall see after reading a summary of the fable, it represents a magnificent precursor, conceived no fewer than 70 years earlier than the *invisible hand*. Even with the many interpretations that can be (and have been) made of Mandeville's thought (he has been called an anarchist but also a utilitarian), today it has been recovered and reclaimed, especially by those who believe that laissez-faire is the best way to organize economic activity.

The fable of the bees starts by describing a hive (a society) that seems perfect.[1]

A spacious hive well stock'd with bees,
That liv'd in luxury and ease;
And yet as fam'd for laws and arms,
As yielding large and early swarms;
Was counted the great nursery
Of sciences and industry.

Paradoxically, not prudence and frugality but rather luxury and vanity drive the activity of the hive.

Vast numbers throng'd the fruitful hive;
Yet those vast numbers made 'em thrive;

Millions endeavouring to supply
Each other's lust and vanity;
While other millions were employ'd,
To see their handy-works destroy'd.

In fact, every member of that ideal society is vicious and corrupt.

. . . All trades and places knew some cheat,
No calling was without deceit.
. . . The lawyers, of whose art the basis
Was raising feuds and splitting cases . . .
They kept off hearings wilfully,
To finger the refreshing fee;
. . . Physicians valu'd fame and wealth
Above the drooping patient's health,
. . . Among the many priests of Jove . . .
Some few were learn'd and eloquent,
But thousands hot and ignorant
. . . Justice herself, fam'd for fair dealing,
By blindness had not lost her feeling;
Her left hand, which the scales should hold,
Had often dropt 'em, brib'd with gold;

However, and this is a second paradox, all that perversity makes the society as a whole reach the virtues described at the start.

Thus every part was full of vice,
Yet the whole mass a paradise . . .
Such were the blessings of that state;
Their crimes conspir'd to make them great:
And virtue, who from politics
Has learn'd a thousand cunning tricks,
Was, by their happy influence,
Made friends with vice: And ever since,
The worst of all the multitude
Did something for the common good.

The bees are not satisfied with the state of things ("though conscious of his own [cheats], in others barb'rously bear none") and cried for change. Mercury smiled cynically, but Jove swore, "he'd rid the bawling hive of fraud".

He does so and "honesty fills all their hearts". This generates a negative spiral that in the fable spreads through every profession and causes a general economic collapse, which leads many bees to leave the hive.

Now mind the glorious hive, and see
How honesty and trade agree . . .
For 'twas not only that they went,
By whom vast sums were yearly spent;
But multitudes that liv'd on them,
Were daily forc'd to do the same.
. . . All arts and crafts neglected lie;
Content, the bane of industry,
Makes 'em admire their homely store,
And neither seek nor covet more.

A moral closes the fable.

Then leave complaints: fools only strive
To make a great an honest hive.
T' enjoy the world's conveniences,
Be fam'd in war, yet live in ease,
Without great vices, is a vain
Eutopia seated in the brain.
Fraud, luxury, and pride must live,
While we the benefits receive . . .
So vice is beneficial found,
When it's by justice lopp'd and bound;
Nay, where the people would be great,
As necessary to the state,
As hunger is to make 'em eat.
Bare virtue can't make nations live
In splendor; they, that would revive
A golden age, must be as free,
For acorns as for honesty.

1 The text was taken from the 1806 edition, made public by Project Gutenberg (eBook #57260). https://www.gutenberg.org/ebooks/57260

3.2 The development of classical economics in the first half of the 19th century

Adam Smith's vision was shared and refined by the classical economists of the 19th century, although they were not such fiery defenders of laissez-faire as they are often painted. In general, they weren't unconditionally or dogmatically against public action, but rather, they were opposed to public action that didn't contribute to increasing the common good. And the margin for such action is limited in that they believed that the pursuit of self-interest, properly channelled through the markets, usually produces better results than any government policy could obtain.

In chronological order, Smith, generally considered to be the first representative of the classical school, was followed by three important figures in the history of economic thought: French economist Jean-Baptiste Say and English economists Thomas Robert Malthus and David Ricardo. They all worked around the turn of the 19th century and its first decades, when the effects of the Industrial Revolution were already much more evident than they were in Smith's epoch. In reality, none of these three constructed a complete theory about what the state's role in the economy should be. Their position on this aspect, however, can be inferred from some of their postulates. In particular, for Say, the production of goods generates enough revenue to create a demand capable of buying the goods offered (termed *Say's law*). This indirectly means that the level of market activity is optimal and that no (government) measures are necessary to increase or decrease it. Malthus, on the other hand, disagreed that this was the case, which implies that crises would be inherent in a market system.

Another important point is that Ricardo incorporated the ideas developed by his contemporary Jeremy Bentham, who, without expressly dealing with economics, provided economists with a theoretical tool that from that point on would be employed to evaluate the results of every economic action: the concept of utility. In his utilitarian ethics, Bentham proclaimed that every individual is the best judge of their own happiness and that the collective interest is formed by the sum of individual interests, or "utilities", of the members of that collective.

In the middle of the 19th century, the concepts that had already been settled began to be qualified. The first to do so was John Stuart Mill, whose "harm principle" states that the actions of individuals should be limited when they undermine the interests of others, which in modern terminology would be described as negative externalities. As in many other cases, this idea is far more complex than how it is often presented: situations in which public intervention could be admissible include those in which individuals are not capable of judging the result of their own actions (e.g. regarding education). Despite this, Mill shares the misgivings of his classical predecessors regarding state intervention (a clear rule governs not interfering, but no rule governs intervening), although this mistrust stems more from his lack of faith in the competence of rulers than on any solid theoretical principles. The second author who investigated the cases in which the laissez-faire principle may not maximize the general welfare was Henry Sidgwick, who increased this catalogue even further. Examples include the overexploitation of natural resources; instances in which businesses don't offer a sufficient number of goods or services, because they wouldn't be able to recover their investment; and cases where information on the effects of a certain product or action is insufficient. However, Sidgwick did not believe that these cases directly required the state to correct them. His response to the issue takes the rules of utilitarianism to their extremes, and the result is far more pragmatic than Mill's: the cost of the possible action (which includes aspects which had already concerned many of his predecessors, such as corruption or the possibility that certain groups are unintentionally favoured) should also be evaluated and then compared with the possible benefit.

3.3 The final third of the 19th century

In the final decades of the 19th century, with the Second Industrial Revolution already underway, the first great crisis of modern capitalism emerged: the long period of deflation that occurred between approximately 1870 and 1895. The fall in prices occurred as production in increasingly connected international markets grew, and it was partly caused by that growth.

At that time, marginalism had become the dominant school of economic thought. The marginalists introduced a more formal economic language, and they assumed that agents always act rationally on behalf of their individual economic interests; in other words, they rejected that autonomous social subjects could help explain economic phenomena. Some of the events that occurred around them didn't fit their restricted models, and therefore, they didn't deeply examine the causes of the crisis (this is the first episode where *economic science* is detached from *economic reality*). They argued that their objective was to establish a logical and neu-tral system (free of values) rather than to answer *political questions*. Although they didn't always explicitly state this conclusion, they believed that the market was not responsible for the problems of their time; rather, impediments to its functioning properly ruptured the equilibrium and caused all economic dysfunction.

However, the solution to the crisis did not involve *more market* but instead involved *more state*. A shift towards protectionism and imperialism occurred (in the struggle for what were thought to be finite resources), which increased the range of state economic activities, although only slightly if compared to what would occur in the second half of the 20th century. Although differences among the rich coun-tries of the era existed (the poor countries were not involved in this story), gener-ally speaking, in addition to organizing and controlling the economy, in this period the state increased its decision-making role and also started becoming a supplier. Indeed, as well as protecting property and ensuring that contracts were fulfilled, as they traditionally had done, states began to regulate a growing number of areas of activity; they created public companies to develop and exploit railroads, mines, electricity networks and communications services (telegraph and telephone); and they established the first truly social policies (worker compensation for accidents, pensions, healthcare and education).

Particularly important is that they began to develop what in this book have been referred to as policies to promote economic activity, the idea for which had emerged earlier in some countries that had been latecomers to the Industrial Revo-lution. Actually, although the chapters in history books on 19th-century econom-ics are usually filled with authors of the then booming Great Britain, the prevailing ideas in other places were not exactly the same, and it was not uncommon to look to the state in the hope that it would be capable of coordinating the process of industrialization. One of the pioneers on the list of less popular thinkers is

German economist Georg Friedrich List, who before the midpoint of the century had already suggested that free trade, and market mechanisms in general, would not provide his country with the impetus needed to match Great Britain on a technological level. On the contrary, the market would undermine Germany's efforts because of the accumulative effects of what today we call static and dynamic economies of scale. Therefore, an active state policy that emphasized the acquisition of technology (through professional training programmes and also by *importing* British operators) and that protected emerging national industries from foreign competition was needed. When Imperial Germany emerged in 1871, a quarter century after List's death, it put his ideas into practice. The Meiji Restoration in Japan in 1868 is another magnificent example of the new policies supporting technology and education, in this case without applying, at least initially, protectionist measures.

The incipient social policies referred to earlier were adopted more out of fear of civil unrest than out of conviction (labour movements had been gaining strength since the middle of the century), and of course, they did not alleviate the hardships endured by most of society. The prevalent at the time stream of economic thought defended the status quo. James Mill, the father of John Stuart, wrote, "The free enterprise system has its hardships, but it is the price we pay for progress and the general good". Herbert Spencer's social Darwinism offered ideological support to inaction in the face of general poverty; he saw the social scale as a process of natural selection, and he opposed the state's providing any kind of protection (unsurprisingly, one of Spencer's books was titled *The Man versus the State*). His book was well received in the United States, which explains some of the prevailing ideas in that country in the following century, specifically the conviction that the welfare state is detrimental to individual work ethic. Many of the opinions of other economists in this era were less radical but ultimately similar in their conclusions. One example is Vilfredo Pareto, who, apart from being remembered for establishing the rule for choosing the most efficient between two situations, studied the distribution of income in various countries and attributed the widespread inequity to the distribution of talent within the social order; in other words, both the rich and the poor deserved the lives they had for their different contributions to the marginal product. In general, the determination to convert economics into a *neutral science* eliminated the need to make value judgements regarding equity and stripped it of any moral considerations.

The condescending acceptance of inequalities was not, however, a unanimous position. The contributions of many who questioned the direction that industrial capitalism had taken, in particular the French "social utopians", have been overshadowed by the emergence of the imposing figure of Karl Marx. For Marx, the crises were not merely incidental deviations from the almost axiomatic equilibrium proposed by the economists of his time but rather the dominant form of movement that shaped the development of capitalist society. The dynamics of the system could be understood only by examining the evolution of relations between social classes and how they were expressed in the market, in the form of a highly disparate distribution of income. In *The Communist Manifesto*, Marx and Engels reserved an active role for the state once the proletariat had triumphed over political power: beyond carrying out structural reforms (e.g. the expropriation of lands, the abolition of child labour or the imposition of a progressive income tax), the state should own key resources (e.g. railways or communications networks), factories, unproductive land (so that it could be used in agriculture) and a monopolistic national credit bank; it would also provide free education. However, it would gradually cede these functions as social classes disappeared. The state would do this or, at least, as stated in the *Manifesto*, "it will lose its political character", although what economic roles, if any, it would then maintain was not defined.

READING 6.4 THE EFFECTS OF INDUSTRIALIZATION: THE EVOLUTION OF CARBON DIOXIDE EMISSIONS

By using information from the data archive left behind by the CDIAC (Carbon Dioxide Information Analysis Center)[1], a now-defunct organization that had provided the US government with global warming data and analysis for over 30 years, the website Our World in Data created a graphic, presented here as Figure 6.4,[2] which presents the evolution of the annual carbon dioxide emissions by regions, measured in billions of tonnes. The figure shows how the global total of emissions per year has grown from negligible amounts to 2 billion tonnes in 1900, 6 billion in 1950, almost 20 billion in 1980, almost 25 billion in 2000 and more than 36 billion in 2015. In the final year of the series (2015), China emitted 10 billion of the total 36 billion tonnes (in 2015, a single country polluted as much as every country on the planet did back in

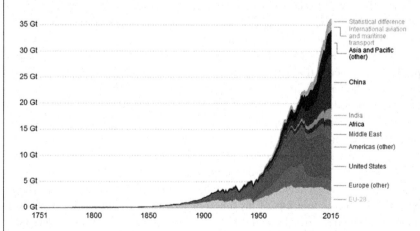

FIGURE 6.4 Historical evolution of carbon dioxide emissions (1750–2015)

1970), while around 5 billion tonnes was the number of emissions from the rest of Asia and the Pacific, from the United States, and from all the European countries combined (within or outside of the European Union).

Figure 6.4 shows that so far in the 21st century, the two regions (countries in this case) whose emissions have increased the most are China, which has nearly tripled its carbon dioxide output, and India, whose emissions have increased by a factor of 2.5. The European Union is the only region that has managed to moderate its emissions since the start of the century.

1 http://cdiac.ess-dive.lbl.gov/ This webpage is in the process of moving to http://ess-dive.lbl.gov/.
2 https://ourworldindata.org/co2-and-other-greenhouse-gas-emissions#the-long-run-history-cumulative-co2.

4 The 20th century

4.1 From the turn of the century to World War II

On the verge of the turn of the century, other economists from the Cambridge school (as Sidgwick had been) continued applying marginalist tools until the basic elements of what is generally known as neoclassical thought were established. The best exponent of this school was Alfred Marshall, who in 1890 published *Principles of Economics*, which was the dominant economics manual for decades. The economists of this school also applied their approach to the problem of the limits of the market. Marshall, through the calculation of consumer surplus, identified situations in which public activity could improve the general welfare. However, more relevant to the topic at hand is the work of his disciple and successor Arthur Cecil Pigou, who by comparing the social and private marginal net products shaped what today we refer to as the theory of externalities. His book *The Economics of Welfare*, published in 1920, became the support or target of criticism for all later contributions to the debate. Although both subscribed to the classical school and therefore trusted in the *inevitable* equilibrium generated by the market, Marshall reserved a larger role for the state (he believed that it should replace the market in areas of social relevance—for example, by directly supplying certain public goods) than Pigou (who believed that it should merely complement the market or correct it, as more of an intermediary than as a direct actor). All this was theoretical, as in practical terms, both authors, particularly Marshall, did not openly argue for public action (intervention), given their arguments on limitations and inefficiencies in political processes.

Another notable contribution by Pigou, more important for its implications than for the significance of the argument itself, was the idea that the marginal utility of money diminishes as the quantity possessed increases. Therefore, as long as the level of production remains the same, the overall welfare could increase by transferring resources of the rich to the poor; that is, it opened the theoretical door to redistribution. This was a novel conception; before, it was thought that the utility of every individual would be equally altered by a monetary loss or gain, regardless of the absolute value from which they start, which meant that redistribution did not make economic sense.

Pigou's most important book was published shortly after World War I ended, which obviously also had an economic impact. The global economy had grown at the start of the century. The process of industrialization had taken off in various countries with the help of new technological advances that had extraordinarily improved communication and transportation. One of the consequences was the emergence of what could be called, given the volume of exchanges at that time, mass markets. The war, however, interrupted the growth tendencies. When it was over, the obstacles to global trade returned, and the war reparations imposed on Germany collapsed its economy and hobbled the development of the entire continent in the following years. The United States replaced Great Britain as the premier world power. And, more germane to our story, states had assumed greater control over their economies during the conflict, and some of the measures they had adopted, such as implementing direct taxes or issuing bonds, were maintained after the war.

Also, after Russia's October Revolution, in 1917, an alternative model to organize economic activity existed. In reality, it wasn't a single model: it evolved in accordance with circumstances. Shortly after the revolution, "war communism" expropriated the main means of production, eliminated the market and monetary circulation and paid its workers in kind. But, after a heavy crisis, they soon returned to a large extent to the market with the New Economic Policy, establishing the freedom for interior trade, allowing small family businesses to exist and replacing the requisitions on peasants for taxation paid in kind. Later, at the end of the 1920s, agricultural land was consolidated into collective farms, and an accelerated industrialization policy that prioritized production goods and armaments over consumer goods was followed; all this was articulated through five-year plans that would continue to be published over the following decades.

The socialist economy was observed *from the other world* with apprehension but also, at least in some academic circles, with curiosity. That other world, the capitalist, had acquired financial overtones after the world economy recovered in the second half of the 1920s. The London and, especially, New York stock exchanges maintained their positions as *capital exporters*, capturing funds for the exploitation of imperial domains and to invest in transport and infrastructure. But more importantly, businesses and consumers, in particular in the United States, had easy access to credit, credit that was sometimes used for speculative investments. This fact explains the tremendous economic and social impact of the New York Stock Market Crash in October of 1929. Commonly thought to be the starting point of the Great Depression, *Black Thursday* significantly changed the relationship between the state and market from the perspective of economic history and the history of economic thought.

After the Wall Street Crash of 1929, the gap between economic theory and reality became more evident than ever. The theories had no place for painfully obvious realities such as chronic unemployment, economic cycles, stockpiling gold for speculation or the spread of market structures that were neither monopoly nor perfect competition. The use of the word *economics* in Marshall's celebrated work signalled the end of the term *political economy* that had been employed until then. The change sought to symbolize its solidity as a science. However, as the rigour of the mathematic construction of the neoclassical approach increased, so too did its inability to explain the events that were occurring. Some distinguished economists continued to maintain the idea that all these phenomena were something like temporary alterations in the model that always tended towards equilibrium. For example, Joseph Schumpeter, who today is highly regarded for other reasons, believed not only that recovery would be spontaneous but also that it could only be effective if it were spontaneous.

Then again, the views of economic thinkers on the *new realities* were not uniform, and some were concerned with them or carried out heterodox analyses. However, as often occurs in history, a celebrated individual (or contribution) eclipses the work of all those who came before, even if those previous contributions were decisive in shaping their ideas. In this case, the individual was John Maynard Keynes and the work *The General Theory of Employment, Interest and Money*, published in 1936.

Keynes did not explicitly renounce the marginalist tradition (in fact, he also came from Cambridge), but he did construct a theory that considered economic activity from a global perspective, mostly abandoning methodological individualism. Keynes believed that when prices or (especially) wages do not automatically or rapidly adjust (are "sticky"), the markets are generally unable to generate efficient results; in other terms, an equilibrium can coexist with unemployment. In this case, Say's law does not apply, and a lack of demand *could be* the case. Then, the government can and should encourage demand by bending the precept of a balanced budget.

The balanced budget precept had been taken as a given before the Great Depression, although deviations from budget orthodoxy were considered inevitable in times of war. Similarly, actions taken in the monetary markets had been directed at maintaining the convertibility of the currency in gold at a fixed price (the gold standard), without considering the effect that these actions could have on other variables, such as unemployment; to that point, money had been considered a basic, but neutral, element that simply facilitated exchanges. Thus, the idea of using a fiscal or monetary policy to achieve greater economic output and employment stability is also, to a large degree, a result of the Great Depression.

The implementation of Keynesian-style policies is commonly associated with the New Deal put in place by the United States in 1933. Between 1933 and 1936, the banking system was restructured and regulated, subsidies to reduce agricultural production were introduced and money was invested in public works. Before 1933, the United States had followed the (neo)classical formula of not doing anything.

However, other countries had already taken measures similar to the New Deal. A few years earlier, under the influence of economists such as Knut Wicksell, Sweden had allowed the state budget to be deliberately imbalanced to contribute to sustaining demand and employment. Adolf Hitler himself had undertaken a great public works programme when he reached power in 1933 (investing in civil works before armament) so that in 1936, unemployment, which had been a key factor in his rise to power, had practically disappeared. Despite the previous fact, fascism did not have a clear economic vision: it offered ideological justifications to implement a mixture of technocracy, autarky and corporatism; public property wasn't an aspiration, even though they nationalized industries to meet greater objectives.

READING 6.5   UNDERSTANDING THE CONTEXT OF ECONOMIC IDEAS: THE EVOLUTION OF POVERTY SINCE THE START OF THE 19TH CENTURY

The independent Swedish foundation Gapminder has used data from the United Nations and the Clio Infra website to elaborate historical estimates (from 1800 to 2015) of the number of people who, in a specific year and in the entire world, had a certain income. Its website allows these data to be presented graphically.[1] The monetary values are adjusted for purchasing power parity of the US dollar in 2011. That is why the extreme poverty line, which had been set at USD1.25 a day in 2005, was increased to USD1.85 a day.[2]

The difficulties involved in making this calculation are evident. Moreover, defining what should be considered extreme poverty in different historical periods is a highly questionable undertaking, since the socioeconomic conditions at any other time in the past were far from what were considered normal living standards when objective criteria to define poverty were set. Bear these caveats in mind when looking at Figure 6.5, which is based on data from Gapminder on eight periods of time and which offers an interesting perspective on the evolution of global poverty (in size and in dollar per day income) in four of the five continents (Oceania is not included).

The figure shows that in 1800 only 15% of the world population lived above what today we consider the threshold of extreme poverty. Industrialization in the 19th century did not lead to tangible improvements in quality of life until the beginning of the 20th century, when a large part of the European and American populations escaped extreme poverty. The situation further improved on both of these continents in 1930 and was even better by 1960 when both Europe and America had generally left severe hardships behind; nevertheless, the impact of the advance in these regions on the reduction of global poverty was small, because of overall demographic

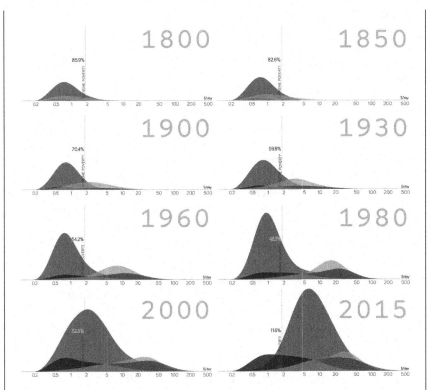

FIGURE 6.5   Evolution of the number of people around the world who receive a certain annual income (1800–2015)

growth, particularly in Asia. In 1980, half of the world population still lived in extreme poverty, although Africa had improved its situation at the time compared to the situation in 1960. From this point, in the 1980s, Asia's economy began to take off in such spectacular fashion that in just 20 years more than half of its population had passed to the right of the extreme poverty line and in another 15 nearly the entire continent had done so. In contrast, the situation in Africa was worse in 2000 than in 1980 and has not improved significantly in 2015. In Europe and America, although their curves had been moving to the right gradually and without interruption for 200 years, this tendency has been stopped in the 21st century (it has arguably been reversed in the case of America). Finally, we highlight that because of Asia's weight in the global population, the percentage of extremely poor people in the world has shifted from almost half in 1980 (48.3%) to 32.3% in 2000 to only 11.6% in 2015.

1 https://www.gapminder.org/tools/#$chart-type=mountain.
2 Which is not erroneous since at the end of 2015 the World Bank increased the extreme poverty threshold to USD1.90 a day.

4.2 From the end of World War II to the oil crisis

The state's active role in the economy was consolidated after World War II. In the developed *capitalist world*, where unemployment remained low and inflation was controlled, Keynesian approaches were followed, and redistribution by the state was increased to levels that had never been seen before. Fiscal pressure mounted. In 1966, James Tobin said that "increased taxation is the price of growth". In fact, a progressive taxation model with a stable tax base was believed to be capable of financing ambitious and costly policies, such as those related to expanding the welfare state, without creating disincentives to economic activity. This was especially true after 1960, when public spending grew extraordinarily without a war or depression to justify the increase. International relations had been established through the Bretton Woods agreement, signed in July 1944 and based on the principles of international financial stability and trade liberalization.

Meanwhile in the centralized, planned economies of the *socialist world*, the state distributed the goods produced on the basis of supposedly egalitarian criteria. Of course, the economic models applied throughout this block were not monolithic or invariable. That said, in the three decades following the end of the war, these countries made barely any movement at all towards creating a market economy; this finally began to occur, cautiously and almost experimentally, just before or during the 1980s.

In the field of economic thought, in the middle of the century, Paul Samuelson popularized what was termed the *neoclassical synthesis*, which in reality merely sanctioned the model that was already being applied in many countries. The basic idea was that in the long term, markets work correctly, but in the short term, the state must correct problems that arise, and for this purpose, fiscal policies would be more effective than monetary policies. The market failure theory is therefore essential to supporting public activity. The construction of this theory during this period progressed in the hands of economists such as Meade, Scitovsky and Buchanan, who, building on the work of Pigou, not only expanded and further shaped the theory of externalities but also progressed in the mathematic proof of the benefits of public intervention (therefore necessary) in these situations, and also thanks to others who advanced in the classification of public goods, most notably the works of Samuelson on "collective consumption goods" and Buchanan on impure public goods.

At the same time that those efforts were being carried on, other economists were already challenging their conclusions: the critical work of Ronald Coase was a milestone in this sense. Although Coase's arguments had been formulated in earlier papers, he structured them in the article "The Problem of Social Cost", published in 1960. He believed that when an activity is restricted for presenting negative externalities, this restriction generates costs that are not considered when calculating common and private welfare. Which of the two "damages" is allowed is a question of allocated rights that a priori do not necessarily lead to an efficient result. Ideally, rather than public intervention, negotiation (the market) would lead to the optimal (efficient) outcome, as long as the rights were well-defined and no transaction costs needed to be factored in. When this is not the case, other options are available, such as regulation. However, regulation also comes with associated costs that might exceed the costs that it is trying to avoid, which would leave doing nothing as the only solution. This is why having an appropriate institutional structure is important.

This last conclusion is the reason why Coase is sometimes included in the school of institutional economics, but arguably, his work instead helped consolidate some of the postulates that this school advocated. For *true* institutionalists, who followed the ideas introduced at the start of the century by Thorstein Veblen, there are no "economic laws", but rather economic events are phenomena contingent on historical, social and institutional factors. Insofar as that framework precedes (and conditions) the market, nothing is wrong, in principle, with the state's taking action to reach social and political objectives.

The study of social factors is also a basic aspect in the development of another theory parallel to that of market failure, also in the second half of the century: the theory that deals with government failure. The precedents to the so-called public choice theory can be traced back to the work of Knut Wicksell and the Italian school of scienza delle finanze, which had included the public decision-making process in theoretical analyses (therefore, turning it into another factor that contributes to determining what should be the nature and scope of state functions), and to the subsequent work of Kenneth Arrow. Building on this foundation, economists from the University of Virginia shaped a theory that was based on the maxim that individuals make choices guided by the same rationale, whether acting as public officials or on their own behalf: they always tend to maximize their own interest.

4.3 The final quarter of the 20th century

In 1973, political circumstances (the Yom Kippur War), rather than economic, led to a dramatic rise in the price of oil, which remained high throughout the decade and spiked again in 1979 (this time because of the Iran–Iraq War). The 1973 Oil Crisis has been identified as an event that altered the economic narrative in almost every country in the world. The truth is that signs of trouble within the system that arose in the postwar era had already been evident. This was especially true in the United States, where inflation had begun to accelerate at the end of the 1960s while the deficit in its balance of payments, multiplied by disproportionate spending on the (seemingly endless) Vietnam War, increased. These war expenditures were used as an argument to unilaterally end the international convertibility of USD to gold in 1971 (one of the Bretton Woods agreements).

Keynesian theory had emerged at a time in which high unemployment existed alongside falling prices, and it seemed to work during the years of growth and stability, but it didn't appear to function when inflation was not subdued. Therefore, other currents of economic thought offered alternatives. Modern monetarism, mainly associated with the work of Milton Friedman, who had reformulated Irving Fisher's quantity theory of money from the beginning of the century, persuasively argued that high rates of inflation were caused by the rapid growth rate of the money supply. The state's only task with regard to adjustment policies should be, therefore, to control the amount of money in circulation, set at the level "required by the economy"; in general, the state's role should be confined to lowering taxes and privatizing. The adverb *persuasively* was used intentionally, because for a few years, monetarism became the new paradigm accepted (and adopted) by many governments in response to the global crisis. Nevertheless, it was not the only option, at least initially: some European countries and Japan opted for regulating prices and salaries, which left the economy even more in the hands of the state. In any case, these were short-term episodes with little continuity. By the time inflation was tamed, after a long period in which the term *stagflation* was coined (stagnation and inflation), we were already at the start of the 1980s, and the global panorama was not exactly optimistic in terms of economic activity. The medicine had not been easy to swallow.

In this context (specifically in 1981), François Mitterrand's France tried to implement the most radically antimarket policy adopted in by developed country over the past 50 years (including nationalizing a large part of the banking sector and various industrial groups, raising taxes, enlarging the public sector and increasing social spending). The imbalances generated, coupled with internal (capital flight) and external (pressure on the currency, with three devaluations of the franc) backlash, forced these measures to be completely abandoned barely three years later.

In the middle of the 1980s, the tides changed in the global economy, and a period of growth followed, which, after an interruption when stock markets around the world crashed on *Black Monday* in 1987, continued during the final years of the century. This period had no single *economic prescription* to which successes could be attributed or on which failures could be blamed. That said, the role of the state generally continued to diminish, with the exception of a reinforced (and increasingly complex) regulatory function, although with paradoxically growing public expenditures. Indeed, the savings derived from renouncing certain functions did not make up for the increases in certain basic areas of the budget, such as servicing debt or paying for healthcare and pensions; ever since, in the richest countries, controlling spending on these last two items has been hindered by the rising demand caused by changing demographics. The most notable function that was renounced was public provision in many areas of activity. Privatization was frequently accompanied by sectorial regulation, which is why the reinforcement of regulatory function was emphasized earlier. Three clarifications should be made regarding this regulation. First, its principal aim was, and is still today, to ensure competition—or, in other words, regulation is understood as a transition phase in which the conditions for unfettered markets are created. Second, in some key sectors, especially the financial sector, the opposite was done: controls and requirements were dismantled. Third, many of the regulatory bodies that were created were not exactly public entities but rather (supposedly) independent ones.

All this happened while monetarism was being replaced as the dominant ideology by new schools of thought that incorporated the rational expectations theory.

The *new* classical economics posits that government actions would be anticipated by the agents that they are directed at and therefore would be ineffective. Following this reasoning, the state should abstain from guiding the economy because any "intervention" is inefficient, and therefore, public spending, which is excessive in almost every area, should be reduced. Breaking down barriers to competition is always the best policy. Meanwhile, Keynesian policy didn't disappear entirely (in theory or in political practice): for the *new* Keynesians, public action could improve the distribution of resources, but the emphasis is placed on actions affecting the supply side and not so much the demand, contrarily to what traditional Keynesians had favoured. This is compatible with a *regulatory state*, although in this case, the objective is more to regulate competition rather than to regulate *for* competition. The ideas of the Austrian school also regained popularity in academic circles during this period. This school is usually thought to have originated in the final quarter of the 19th century, and it has been active ever since. It proposes that spontaneous order generates a more efficient allocation of resources than any other design could achieve. Indeed, the concept of social justice for the Austrians is muddled because only the actions of individuals can be just or unjust, never the effects generated by impersonal mechanisms such as the market. Therefore, public action is unjustified. Moreover, it would be harmful, as any hindrance to individual actions ruins the fundamental values of merit and freedom.

Returning to the historical narrative, we should mention other crises that occurred in the final quarter of the 20th century whose impact was felt mainly on the national or regional level. Most notable among them, for reasons we shall now see, were the Latin American debt crisis of 1982 and the 1997 Asian financial crisis. The first is important because it brought the same *market confidence prescriptions* being applied in the richest countries to other geographic areas, with certain nuances. Indeed, when offering aid to resolve unsustainable debt situations, the World Bank and the International Monetary Fund suggested, or directly imposed, a package of reforms known as the *Washington Consensus*: tax reform, cuts in public deficit, the liberalization of trade and foreign investment and *structural adjustments*, such as introducing competition and privatizing state enterprises. The 1997 crisis is also notable because it directly affected some (at the time) recently industrialized Asian countries that had opted for a development model that clearly emphasized public action, an approach quite different from the one followed under the Washington Consensus. A few years earlier, these countries had achieved surprising growth rates and a presence in the world economy thanks to a guided industrial and trade reform process, offering financial incentives and tax exemptions to businesses and following unorthodox policies to finance public expenditures.

All the same, the most important event of the end of the century in terms of the state/market relationship was indisputably the *fall of the Berlin Wall* in November 1989. It was largely provoked by the Soviet Bloc's state of near economic collapse at the start of the decade (despite the USSR's attempt a few years earlier to reform its economy through *perestroika*, which literally means "restructuring" in Russian, a process that later accelerated the collapse in some ways). In just a couple years, all the Eastern European countries and the USSR itself were in the process of joining the market economy. It was not easy; the transition in the following years was so difficult that in some cases the per capita income fell drastically (up to 50%) while the population lost all the social benefits once provided by the centralized economic system. In other planned economies (China and Vietnam are good examples), the transition to capitalism has taken place without (at least nominally) renouncing communist political principles. Although no definition for the resulting model has been found, the truth is that the state continues to firmly steer national economic activity while their companies conquer new markets.

5 The economy at the start of the 21st century

5.1 The first two decades

At the turn of the century, two events occurred that are extraordinarily representative of the economic tendencies that mark the new century. The first was the burst of the *dot-com bubble* which began in March 2000. Not only did it affect the stock markets, but it also caused many technology companies to shut down and put a damper on the "irrational exuberance" surrounding the digital economy. The second was not an economic event, but it had an enormous economic impact: the terrorist attacks of 11 September 2001, the most iconic among a series of attacks that have been carried out around the world. Both events preceded one of the most serious economic crises of modern times, in some ways comparable to the 1929 collapse: the financial crisis caused by *subprime mortgages* and *toxic* financial assets that were hidden and packaged within complex, but sold as safe, investment products. Although the first signs that *something was wrong* emerged as early as 2007, the key date was 15 September 2008, when Lehman Brothers declared bankruptcy; this investment bank was the fourth largest in the United States and, oddly enough, had survived the 1929 crash. Like many other financial crises, it became a crisis of the *real economy*. The initial stage was the most dramatic; in fact, 2009 is the first time since the series began in 1961 that the World Bank registered a drop in the world GDP (mostly because of the fall in "high-income countries"; the crisis affected the rich above all). Its impact, however, was lasting and was felt in some countries until 2013.

The first crisis, the dot-com bubble, shines a light on an increasingly evident economic paradigm shift that began decades ago: the transition from an industrial economy to a knowledge economy that emphasized services. Regarding the relationship between state and market, we highlight that the promise of greater efficiency from the markets has not been realized. Some had predicted that a global network would create a single market that would come close to perfect competition, in which suppliers and demanders could find each other directly and in which information could easily be obtained for a negligible price. However, over time, it has become evident that many of the online interactions with the greatest economic weight are mediated by platforms that sometimes enjoy a near-monopoly situation. Moreover, the globalization of markets has not led to a global improvement in labour, environmental or consumer protection standards; on the contrary, in many cases, the protection of rights is progressively weakening, even suffering a race to the bottom, especially those concerning the working conditions of new economy jobs. Finally, various threats to governments and individuals have emerged. To name the two most obvious ones, governments are extremely concerned that the link between taxation and the place of the transaction may disappear, and individuals are seeing how their privacy is increasingly at risk. All these circumstances reinforce the idea that in the future state action in the economy will continue to be based on the same reasons that support it today.

READING 6.6   EVEN MORE ON BUBBLES: THE CATOPTROMANCERS' BUBBLE

Catoptromancy, the art of divination by using a mirror, was popular as far back as ancient Greece and ancient Rome. The Latin word for mirror is *speculum*, and to speculate is also relative to (or reflected in) a mirror. So all speculators use a bit of catoptromancy; in fact, if we meet one of them, calling them "catoptromancer" can be an elegant way to refer to them disdainfully without making them angry (because they will basically have no idea what we are saying).

But if looking for real catoptromancers, refer to the actors who played a leading role in the dot-com bubble that burst in the historic year 2000. Those catoptromancers looked into the future by using their mirrors and they were absolutely right in the majority of their predictions. But, but, but, it is said there's always a but, what they forgot was that they were using the mirror to look at the future. The mistake they made was thinking that what they were seeing in the mirror was the same as what we, mere mortals, see: a reflection of reality. It wasn't. What they divined wasn't *their present*, it was *our present*: mail carriers who have never delivered a love letter (what is that?) but rather packages, packages and more packages; big sales days on which a single Internet portal sells products worth more than a medium-size economy; and smartphones that connect us to life like umbilical cords. However, back then, at the end of the 20th century, brainy academics were still writing articles dissecting all the reasons why electronic commerce still hadn't taken off: the broadband wasn't actually broad but just slightly less narrow, which, by the way, could only be said by the few people who had it; trusting a store that you couldn't physically visit was far from common; the payment methods and the logistics and distribution had a long way to go for the system to truly work.

But academics shouldn't be taken too seriously, no matter what they say, because they are always prophets of doom and wet blankets. So they were ignored: even though that new tech startup with the crazy but genius idea was haemorrhaging money because of the mounting costs of organizing the entire framework needed to do business without yet having a single client, in just a few months it would start to earn millions. Moreover, it was just the right time to be on the wining horse, as the winner today would have a world monopoly tomorrow. This was also believed by the dot-coms who spent their time devouring other companies, whether actual rivals, potential rivals, snake oil salespeople or simply pals passing by with a website under their arm—of course, at any price.

In March 2000, the Nasdaq Composite stock market index, which listed many Internet-based companies, peaked in value at 5,000 points. But interest rates were rising, and financing these companies became increasingly more expensive. What's more, somebody realized that (surprise!) real or virtual, a company's accounts are ruled by the same criteria, and unreasonable business models do not magically become reasonable if they are uploaded onto the Internet. So some of the players cashed in their chips, and as has happened so many times with the dominos of history, everything else came crashing down. In less than a week, the index fell 9%, and that was just the beginning. In contrast to what had happened on other occasions, the crash lasted longer over time. It didn't bottom out until October 2002, when the Nasdaq landed at barely 20% of its peak value.

And even so, the mirror didn't lie. It's not just that some of these crazy ideas (did somebody actually foresee our grandmothers' being on our *WhatsApp* lists?) earn loads of money, but rather that the planet doesn't have enough cargo vehicles to carry all the money they make. And today there are indeed global monopolies that aspire to be cosmic monopolies. Except for a small hiccup during the 2008 crisis, the Nasdaq started growing and growing again. In March 2015, it recovered the value that it had when everything came crashing down. But 15 years had gone by, and a lot of water had gone under the bridge over those 15 years. When the mirror reflected the treasure chest, the catoptromancers, in their frenzy, unfortunately didn't see the tag: "open in 15 years".

The dot-com crash was more symbolic than real. It was symbolic for what it revealed about the then nebulous new economy and for having occurred at the turn of the century. It barely affected, however, the real economy. In the news, you could read sentences like "in two years, the market lost five billion dollars". That a market can lose anything more than the confidence that it can inspire in those who participate in it, though, is doubtful. Even more doubtful is that an increase in the value of an asset, if it doesn't materialize in that moment, will make somebody richer, just like that a later downward market correction will make anybody poorer is equally doubtful. They are only expectations (oh, the expectations!) with greater or lesser probabilities of coming

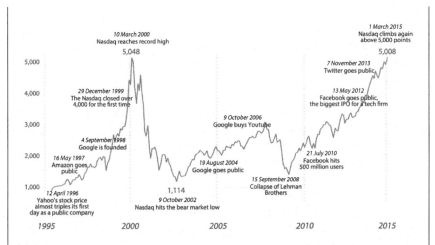

FIGURE 6.6 Evolution of the Nasdaq technology index, in basis points (1995–2015)

true. In the end, what counts is the soap, not the bubbles. It is written "if it doesn't materialize in that moment", because those pals that passed through selling tricycles with no wheels at the price of a sports car are smiling from their golden retirement while still making daily toasts to those extemporaneous catoptromancers.

The 11 September 2001 attack reveals that ethnic, cultural and religious factors can lead to conflicts which impact the global economy. In an interconnected world with fewer borders, the importance of such factors should seem to decrease, and income level (as well as the social and labour conditions associated with that income) should be what mainly marks the differences between groups. In such a scenario, public action would be expected to control aspects of the market that contribute to instability and increase social polarization. However, this is not the case. Who are bringing together people discontent with the most pernicious effects of globalization and the new economy are often movements developed around the creation of an identity (nationalists or radicals, either religious or political); these movements also defend having a more active state, but a state exhibiting different traits: concerned with combatting *the interests of the others* and prioritizing the activities of *its own*.

Finally, the 2008 crisis speaks to us of the recurrence of crises and the apparent inability of economics (as a discipline) and the economy (as a social activity) to predict them, much less prevent them. Little significant progress has been made in economic thinking over the past few years, despite the evidence that the supposed rationality and perfect adjustment of the markets had come crashing down (once again). The crisis led to the revival of work by people like Hyman Minsky, who in the 1970s and 1980s explained that at the origin of the (systemic) financial crises lies the growing complacency towards risk assumed by financial agents during boom periods, and given passing fame to others such as Thomas Piketty, who focused on the concentration of wealth and income inequality. But neither the political debate nor the internal criticisms of many economists have seemed to manage to open new lines of reasoning, just as occurred after the 1929 crisis. Although progress continues in the formalization of (not necessarily rational) behaviour and simulation models, the main schools of thought continue to make the same recommendations as they did in the past, and no novel proposals have been placed on the table.

As has been the case throughout history, the formulas applied by governments were not uniform all over the world or, necessarily, consistent over time. The majority of countries initially adopted strategies *to get out of the crisis* that combined expansionist fiscal and monetary measures to stimulate the economy, although the latter was emphasized; the monetary measures sought to provide enough liquidity to allow money to start flowing again and to rebuild confidence, even if that meant bailing out (or temporarily or permanently nationalizing) financial entities. However, the fiscal measures were quickly taken away to return to what is often referred to as the neoliberal agenda. Although defining *liberalism* in terms of economic thought is not an easy task (many schools would accept the liberal tag, although none of them carries the name liberal), in broad strokes, liberal policies trusted in the efficiency of the markets and sought to minimize the nonessential role of the state, restricting (*imposing discipline on*) its capacity to spend. In this context, public austerity and structural reforms were still the most common schemes. Furthermore, the relationship with the market was based not exactly on confidence but rather on subordination, given that the best policy seemed to be to do whatever improved credibility in the eyes of *the markets*, which, for example, implied maintaining pre-established rules and renouncing discretional policies. If the pandemic crisis referred to in the next section does not change the policies that had been in place until then, states seem to react instead of anticipate, to follow instead of lead.

The obvious problem is that they attacked only the *symptoms*, if even that, but not the root causes of the 2008 crisis. If the crisis had been caused by a set of bad decisions and carelessness by those who should have been watchful, the problem would not be as serious. But that is not the case. The crisis emerged from the architecture of the financialized global economy. Curiously (or understandably if we accept the thesis that regulatory capacity is, if not in the hands of, at least subordinated to economic power), in just a few years, the global financial markets had recovered their strength and returned to the path of rampant profits, operating at an even greater level of complexity, if possible, which allow them to circumvent the regulations that may have been promoted as a response to their excesses. If we couple this with a geopolitical situation that continues to be complicated, the conclusion is that the same risk factors are as present today as they were in the years before the *subprime mortgage* issue came to light.

Nicolas Sarkozy's statement, made when the crisis broke out, regarding the need to "re-found capitalism on the basis of ethics" was reduced to a mere afterthought. Of course, ten years later, capitalism had not been re-founded; it hadn't even been given a makeover. The reactionary countermovement that 75 years ago Karl Polanyi's double movement theory predicted would be generated to protect the social fabric from the destructive impact of market pressures did not gain the necessary impetus to unfold. Whether, with the permission of the pandemics, the 21st century holds other opportunities remains to be seen, and the social cost of taking advantage of them or of letting them pass by likewise remains to be seen.

5.2 A new turning point? The post-COVID-19 economy

As stated in the previous section, in 2009 world GDP fell for the first time in the historical series that began 60 years ago. It was an almost symbolic fall of only one-tenth of a point. The next time this happens will be in 2020. In the final days of 2020, the International Monetary Fund estimated that in that year the world's GDP as a whole would lose 4.4%. If we take into account that since 2012, world growth had remained around 3% (2.8% in 2019), we are talking about a fall of more than seven points, a real cataclysm. There is no doubt, then, that the economic crisis associated with the measures taken to try to halt the spread of the disease known as COVID-19 will be a landmark in macroeconomic data series. What cannot be said with certainty is whether it will also open up a new stage in the historical narrative of the economy or even lead to a change of direction in the relationship between public and private, between state and market.

Let's start the first question: if this book were rewritten ten years later, would the COVID crisis simply be a parenthesis in the narrative, or would it actually mark a turning point? The answer will be given by the socioeconomic situation that will exist once the pandemic is brought under control and the time that will elapse before that happens. With some optimism, some spoke of a V-shaped recovery. But it was not a good prognosis, as countries does not seem to be going to resume their pre-pandemic growth paths at the same speed as their macroeconomic figures collapsed. Even once the disease has subsided, neither consumer confidence nor activity in many productive sectors will immediately return to February 2020 levels. Even more importantly, there will be no return, as in some board games, to square one, but we will return to a different square one. The *new normal* will not be identical to the old one, as some changes that seemed circumstantial (in people's habits and in companies' processes) will become permanent. Just one of these changes, the step forward in the digitalization of the economy (with the advance of electronic commerce and teleworking as the most noteworthy phenomena), may already be sufficient to force the productive fabric to be recomposed.

Focusing on what interests this book, namely how the pandemic crisis will affect the role of the state in the economy, two levels must be distinguished: the positive and the ideological. On the factual side, the starting point is an absolutely relevant one: with a presence such as states have never had before, they have attempted, at least in the first phase, to hold on to an economy that was faltering. This commitment arose in large part from the fact that the states themselves were responsible for the slowdown (even paralysis in some sectors) of activity, as they took unprecedented actions to restrict economic endeavour with temporary closures and lockdowns. The continuation of this story will be marked by the counterpart of these support actions, which is, as Reading 6.7 shows, a rampant public debt. It is a debt that is supervening and not linked to structural problems, but it is still a mountain of debt that casts a shadow on the ability of governments to manoeuvre in the future. At the time of writing, unknowns which could make the future even more uncertain persisted. The first and fundamental one was the health crisis itself, which remained at an alarming level. Even with the vaccine just around the corner, the return to the old normality did not seem to be a matter of days, or even weeks, and Figure 6.5 eloquently shows how each additional quarter in an exceptional situation was worsening public finances. The second is linked to what was described in the previous paragraph. On the adjustment path to refloat economies, and even once refloated, public actions will be needed not only to help but also to adapt and to boost, and the cost of those actions would be difficult to fit into restrictive budgets aimed at reducing debt levels. The third question is how the markets will react in this context, particularly if some governments opt for orthodox policies in which debt reduction is the first objective. By the end of 2020, many countries were accessing the liquidity that they needed at a reasonable rate of interest, but they certainly had no guarantee that one, two or five years later, the situation would remain the same. As has occurred on so many other occasions, not everyone will notice pandemics or personal tragedies if an easy profit can be made.

As for the need to rethink the role of the public sector, what we have experienced since the pandemic was declared offers an excellent opportunity. The controversy about the appropriateness of lockdowns and closures has brought to the fore the debate about the limits of the economy as a social activity, an activity that is fundamental for society but that is intertwined with it. It also allows us to reflect on the need for the state as a coordinating body to set general guidelines in a scenario where individual behaviour can damage (via negative externalities) others. Or it allows us to reflect on the need for a protective state that ensures minimum thresholds for the disadvantaged and losers, categories which, incidentally, have been shown to be open to many who would never have imagined to fall there, and this regardless of merit or effort. Or it allows us to reflect on the importance of having quality public services and the condition attached to obtaining resources to make them work, which in turn brings us to the issue of the correspondence between demand and contribution (i.e. paying taxes). And all this happens in an increasingly interconnected world, where problems on a planetary scale are multiplying and becoming more pressing but where global agreements are still difficult to achieve and in some cases do not go beyond empty words.

Times of crisis should be times to learn, to learn so as not to repeat mistakes or to correct deficiencies that have become apparent. If the pandemic serves this purpose to some extent, at least one positive aspect can be found, although, of course, nothing will compensate the pain that so many families will have suffered.

READING 6.7   SAFETY NETS PREVENT FALLS BUT HAVE A COST

Reading 1.1 painted a fairly eloquent picture of the reduction in global economic activity justified by the need to curb the spread of the COVID-19 pandemic. The simplest economic logic indicates that a reduction in activity means a reduction in income and consequently a reduction in wages or staff members. And if the adverse situation is prolonged over time, the same logic dictates that partial closures will become total and temporary ones definitive.

In this scenario, a majority of states began to grant aid and subsidies almost immediately. The aim was, first, to try to alleviate the plight of those who were left without income and, second, to help companies in some sectors to remain in a dormant state while waiting for the conditions to be met in which they could start operating again. The same group from Oxford University, whose data were used for Figure 1.1, also compiled data on the financial support offered by states to individuals (not to companies) in an attempt to alleviate the ensuing social emergency.[1] More precisely, the heading "income support" used in Figure 6.7 "captures if the government is covering the salaries or providing direct cash payments, universal basic income, or similar, of people who lose their jobs or cannot work". The figure shows the situation at two different points in time: first, on 1 May 2020 and, second, seven months later, on 1 December 2020. As in Figure 1.1, here again note that the map can give a overstated image in that "this income support may not apply to workers in all sectors and may vary at the sub-national level".

The two parts of Figure 6.7 are almost identical, despite the seven months that had elapsed between the two snapshots. This shows that the subsidies and the aid given to companies, which the figure does not show, were in force (they were still in force at the time of writing this Reading) for a long period. Even if the states had some provision for emergencies in their budgets for 2020, in no case could such enormous expenditure be foreseen. The almost immediate impact of such programmes is shown in Figure 6.8, assembled

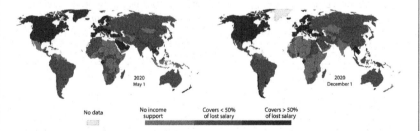

FIGURE 6.7   Income support granted during the COVID-19 pandemic: situation on 1 May 2020 and 1 December 2020

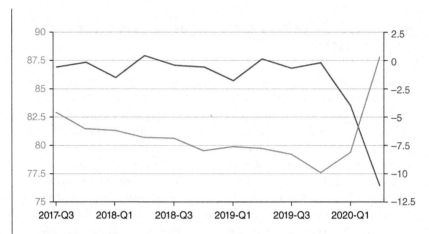

FIGURE 6.8 Public deficit (upper line) and public debt (lower line), measured as a percentage of GDP, in the European Union (27) taken as a whole—development from the third quarter of 2017 to the second quarter of 2020

with data taken from Eurostat,[2] which shows the evolution of the public deficit and public debt in the three years before the last data available at the time of the consultation, which corresponds to the second quarter of 2020 (although these data were not yet official at that time).

By the end of the second quarter of 2020, the public deficit, which had closed 2019 at almost zero (the value at which it had fluctuated in previous quarters), had advanced to 11%. Similarly, public debt had broken its downward line to rise from 77.6% to 87.8% in just six months. It would almost certainly close 2020 above 100%. The data are from the European Union, but we are confident in venturing that the situation was similar in many other regions.

1 Hale, T., Angrist, N., Cameron-Blake, E., Hallas, L., Kira, B., Majumdar, S., Petherick, A., Phillips, T., Tatlow, H., & Webster, S. (2020). *Oxford COVID-19 Government Response Tracker*. Blavatnik School of Government—Oxford University. https://www.bsg. ox.ac.uk/research/research-projects/coronavirus-government-response-tracker.

2 Eurostat. *General government deficit (−) and surplus (+)—Quarterly data* (online data code TEINA205; https://ec.europa.eu/eurostat/databrowser/view/teina205/ default/line?lang=en), and *General government gross debt—Quarterly data* (online data code TEINA230; https://ec.europa.eu/eurostat/databrowser/view/teina230/ default/line?lang=en).

Summary

This chapter presented a historical overview of *what has been* the real activity of states and of the theories that have arisen about *what it should have been*.

Often personalized by sovereigns or warlords, states have always organized economic activity as a fundamental part of social life, in which they have exercised varying degrees of control. Although different eras and regions have many nuances, over time the objective of this control has changed from merely serving the interest of the lord to serving those of the nation as a whole, and later, it became concerned with the interests of each member of society. In fact, the modern history of the relationship between the state and the market doesn't really start until the end of the 19th century, when some countries began using models of public action that had never before been undertaken, including the first steps towards the creation of social policies. The apogee of these policies (the *welfare state*) and in general the prevalence of the *public sphere* in the economy, interpreted in the current sense, occurred during the period between the end of World War II and the crises of the 1970s. The prolonged effect of these crises and later the collapse of the socialist economies marked the transition years into the new century. The start of the 21st century is characterized by the restrictions faced by states to carry out truly independent economic policies. Although it is unlikely that this will change in the short term, the crisis caused by the COVID-19 pandemic may somehow modify the scenario.

Regarding economic theory, as the basis of their ideological position, every economist has had to think about the results generated by free markets and about what the role of the public sector should be. The work of Adam Smith and his "invisible hand" marks a turning point (and not a starting point) in the construction of a system capable of evaluating the efficiency of the market. After Smith, all the major currents of economic thinking have taken a position on the debate regarding whether public *intervention* is necessary to increase social welfare. Some have done so in a formal and reflective manner; others have not, but even so, their position can be indirectly inferred by interpreting their basic concepts. The gradual construction of the theory of externalities (later broadened into the market failure theory) and the public choice theory are notable milestones in this history.

Overview

In short, this chapter will help you do the following:

- Understand the historical evolution of the functions that states have given themselves in the economy.
- Comprehend the positions adopted by the different schools of economic thought regarding the efficiency of the markets and whether public action in the economy needs to be taken.

Self-assessment questions

The self-assessment questions are meant to evaluate how well you have understood the information presented in this chapter.

1   That the first representation of state interest is the accumulation of precious metals is a basic idea of whom?

   a   Marginalists.
   b   Physiocrats.

    c   Mercantilists.

    d   Technocrats.

2   Which of the following statements most closely corresponds to the thinking of Adam Smith?

    a   The action of states is always more beneficial for society than individual action.

    b   Any individual action is always more beneficial for society that the action of the state.

    c   The most beneficial situation for society is derived from the sum of all individual actions.

    d   The pursuit of self-interest is generally harmful for social good.

3   The most common reaction to the long deflationary period that occurred approximately between 1870 and 1895 was to employ policies based on which of the following?

    a   Protectionism and imperialism.

    b   Liberalism and open markets.

    c   Totalitarianism.

    d   Marxism.

4   Who shaped the theory of externalities in their book *The Economics of Welfare*?

    a   Paul Samuelson.

    b   John Stuart Mill.

    c   Vilfredo Pareto.

    d   Arthur Cecil Pigou.

5   As a general rule, during the years following World War II in the *capitalist world*, what occurred?

    a   The redistribution function of the state grew vastly.

    b   Fiscal pressure decreased.

    c   Monetary approaches were followed.

    d   All the above.

Questions for reflection

The answers to the following questions are not in the text; they require you to search for additional information or to apply to real cases what you have learned in this chapter.

1   What event of the 20th century do you consider most illuminating about the relationship between the public sphere and the private sphere? That is, which event has taught a lesson that we should take into consideration in the 21st century?

2   The socialist economies collapsed at the end of the 1980s. Investigate the causes that led to this situation. From among the most commonly cited reasons, conduct your analysis on which were the most important.

3   The final question is always the *million-dollar question* (if you are sure you are right, run to claim the position of minister of the economy): when applying economic policies, the historical moment and the specific circumstances must always be taken into consideration; therefore, in light of what you have learned from this book about what is theoretically possible and the actions that have been taken over history, what do you think are the correct policies (the ones that would provide the best results) given the current historical moment and our present circumstances?

INDEX